Suffering as Identity
The Jewish Paradigm

Esther Benbassa

Translated by G. M. Goshgarian

VERSO

London • New York

Ouvrage publié avec le concours du Ministère français chargé de la culture—
Centre national du livre
This work was published with the help of the French Ministry of Culture—
Centre national du livre

First English edition published by Verso 2010
Copyright © Verso 2010
Translation © G. M. Goshgarian
First published as *La Souffrance comme identité*
Copyright © Fayard 2007

The moral rights of the author have been asserted

1 3 5 7 9 10 8 6 4 2

Verso
UK: 6 Meard Street, London W1F 0EG
US: 20 Jay Street, Suite 1010, Brooklyn, NY 11201
www.versobooks.com

Verso is the imprint of New Left Books

ISBN-13: 978-1-84467-403-9 (hbk)
ISBN-13: 978-1-84467-404-6 (pbk)

British Library Cataloguing in Publication Data
A catalogue record for this book is available from the British Library

Library of Congress Cataloging-in-Publication Data
A catalog record for this book is available from the Library of Congress

Typeset by MJ Gavan, Truro, Cornwall
Printed in the US by Worldcolor / Fairfield

In memory of Pierre Vidal-Naquet, who condemned
me to a career as a responsible historian

Contents

Acknowledgements

It is never easy to write a book about suffering, and it is harder still to write one about identity. I spent five years on the task.

My long apprenticeship to suffering, in the course of a life that has been agreeable, all in all, albeit repeatedly interrupted by exile and not altogether free of snares, has taught me that, as Ibsen puts it, 'sorrow makes us wicked and hateful'.[1] My high esteem for the great playwright notwithstanding, I would put the matter less categorically: as I see it, sorrow *can* make us wicked and hateful. In trying to avoid this trap, I realized that, in any case, nothing can be worse than staging sorrow or suffering. It is dignity that inclines us toward what is less bad; it is rationally grounded hope that makes us better. All those whom I have loved and continue to love have encouraged me to think so. And they know it. They are also the ones who have taught me to detest hatred and intolerance. Suffering is of course a terrible injustice, but it can be overcome.

It is customary to begin books with acknowledgements. Sometimes they are also a joyous cry from the heart. In thanking, first of all, Jean-Christophe Attias, I thank not only my spouse, but also a friend who is always at my side; his cheerful wisdom has always been of great help, and was more so during this adventure than any other. He offered me support with a smile, sometimes filling the many gaps in my knowledge of theology with gentle mockery and taking a mischievous pleasure in noting just how ignorant certain ardent partisans of the present were in this domain. In my own case, it must be said, the malady had reached a fairly advanced stage, since I have very little religion indeed. Like a good student, which in fact I never was, I learned, day after day, to read the Scriptures. Even if they inform only a small part of this book, I can only hope that that small part never goes too wide of the mark.

The research that culminated in the present book was carried out in the library of the Jewish Theological Seminary in New York and also in Columbia University Library, which is full to bursting with innumerable treasures. I began to write this book in the ten months I spent at the Netherlands Institute for Advanced Study in Wassenaar, in a scholarly and very congenial

---

1   Henrik Ibsen, *The Collected Works of Henrik Ibsen*, vol. 11, *Little Eyolf*, translated by William Archer, New York: Charles Scribner, 1910, 89.

atmosphere, thanks to Helma Lutz, Barbara Waldis and Ezra Suleiman, who have become my friends. Between my visits to museums and art galleries, I found the time to think about suffering while contemplating the bare trees in the park during Holland's long rainy months. The rector of the NIAS, Wim Blockmans, and the entire NIAS staff did their best to make my life easier. And what shall I say of my friends Else Smalbraak, Dolores Perquin, and Yves de Roo, with whom I continue to conduct conversations and trade laughs, with the help of the European express train Thalys?

Finally, I would like to express my deep appreciation to Sebastian Budgen and all others at Verso, thanks to whom this book may now also find readers in the English-speaking world.

Paris, June 2009

Introduction

Suffering isn't 'trendy'. And yet …

In our comfortable Western societies, we are, as it were, called on to chase after success, happiness, the secrets of good health, and eternal youth, against a backdrop of the still inexpressible aspiration to immortality. Our belief in the uninterrupted march of progress has afforded us a glimpse of a future without suffering.

Until very recently, however, the monotheistic *homo religiosus* suffered for God and through God. He believed in the redemptive function of suffering. Indeed, religions have traditionally concerned themselves with human suffering, seeking either to provide an explanation for it so as to make suffering bearable here on Earth, or to demonstrate that the means and methods available to mere mortals were incapable of tackling it. Even individual suffering took its place in a collective framework. The suffering visited on the group for its past or present sins, in turn, guaranteed its continuity. Suffering re-established, in and of itself, the genealogical order, without bringing on a rupture even when, as occasionally happened, it seemed inexplicable and pointless because it was inflicted on innocent believers. What is more, the suffering of the present would serve as a model for later generations wishing to strengthen their faith and keep their belief in God intact.

The story of suffering used to be inseparable from that of hope—in this world or the next. In our increasingly secularized world, in contrast, suffering symbolizes injustice and is not the prelude to hope. Indeed, what kind of hope could possibly be involved? The demands certain groups make based on their suffering elicit repentance from others—a social repentance that compensates for lost innocence by conferring, in the present, rights upon people (or their descendants) on whom we unjustly inflicted suffering in the past. The various instances of past suffering accordingly enter into competition for the attention of the public and the powers-that-be. The more obscene suffering seems, the better its claim to compensation of the kind supposed to make it disappear. Suffering and repentance beget each other endlessly, until, finally, they produce new forms of suffering in their turn, while making it impossible to make plans for the future. Suffering creates victims; victimhood is then transformed into a moral posture.

Memories of suffering make up for our alienation from religion, our solitude, and the disappearance of expressions of group solidarity. They spawn
identities based on victimhood, another mode of being and existing that has
the power to bind us to an imaginary community made up of sufferers, present
or past. This puts us in the domain of the redemptive value of suffering rather
than in that of suffering as such. The twentieth century, a century of suffering
and victims, returns to haunt us and weigh down on our present, dragging in
its wake the echoes of a still more distant past. There emerges a kind of memory
of suffering that detaches itself from history in order to impose itself as our
present and, sometimes, our future as well. In the process, it confers meaning
on the disenchantment which we advertise with the same determination with
which we advertise happiness: happiness as an ideal rather than a plausible
reality.

Can we, however, escape history? We need history, yet content ourselves
with memory, a selective memory revisited from the standpoint of this
suffering, which we mobilize to lend meaning to that which we wish to become.
Is our contemporaries' suffering or, rather, the suffering to which they lay
claim, nothing but moral capital? Is its sole horizon a rhetoric that ultimately
runs the risk of becoming sterile repetition, destined as it is to serve group
interests based on memory while legitimating political projects motivated by
compassion? In France in 2006, it proved easy to make the day of 10 May one of
commemoration of slavery; the condition of Blacks was not improved for all
that. Publicly acknowledging the evils of slavery constitutes an act of justice
towards the descendants of slaves whose memory has been insulted, but does it
suffice to fight the forms of discrimination that they suffer daily? It would be
easy to multiply examples. Might it not be that suffering and the responses to
it serve as the only ethics we can muster for the purpose of regulating our
societies, abused and disabused by a surfeit of everything? If so, ours is an ethics
of suffering, others' suffering, with which we superficially identify without
really wishing to make the experience of the victims our own.

Emotion takes priority over understanding the suffering that countless
images and commentaries in the media show us day after day, effectively anaes-
thetizing us and numbing us to pain.[1] We are so utterly overwhelmed by
emotion that the victim of suffering is ultimately banished from our intellectual horizon, leaving us face-to-face with our own narcissism. Suffering is
produced as a spectacle, dispensing us of the need to feel the kind of empathy

---

1   Carolyn Dean, *The Fragility of Empathy after the Holocaust*, Ithaca, New York:
Cornell University Press, 2004, 1–42.

that reminds us of our responsibilities. Thus it borders on a form of liberating voyeurism. We are made sensitive to a brand of suffering that is abstract, instrumentalized, and shaped by the media, rather than tangible. To be sure, the different kinds of suffering do not all have the same power to arouse our compassion; those that do are the ones with which we can most directly identify. In the case of the December 2004 tsunami, the sizeable number of European victims on holiday in the areas ravaged by the disaster helped generate an unprecedented upsurge of Western compassion.

The image of victimhood is familiar to us, yet we usually hold it at arm's length so as to avoid breaking the rules that define our individualism. Conversely, that image becomes, at certain moments, the cement for certain kinds of 'humanitarian' solidarity, forged ad hoc to help victims who once again give us, for a few weeks, the sense that we are experiencing a unity that is supposed to have existed and been lost. The victims' ordeal and the assistance we provide them binds us together and temporarily sows the illusion that our combined forces are a match for suffering. Our ideal of happiness and prosperity is reinforced in the process. Thus campaigns based on compassion promote, in their turn, a universalism of suffering.

But what if our need for identity turned out to be more powerful than our need for God? It may be that the individual, that lonely king, compensates for his existential solitude with a quest for identity that would bind him to a community welded together by shared suffering, often experienced by proxy and sustained by historical facts that can ground this memory or story of suffering. The slavery endured by one's ancestors, the colonization to which one's parents or grandparents were subjected, the genocides and the endlessly revived memories of them all serve in their own way, to cement identities and forge clearly distinct groups in this age of globalization and the weakening of national identities. Shall we call this shared suffering 'unifying suffering' or 'identificatory suffering'? The break between the way suffering was managed yesterday and the way we manage it today might well lie here, in the new functions that we assign it. In contrast, the mobilization of compassion as a mode of political regulation becomes a necessity that goes hand-in-hand with the rights based on suffering, which are now in the process of replacing civil rights.[2]

In the case of both 'humanitarian' communities instituted spontaneously and abstractly for brief moments of solidarity, and imagined communities based on the idea of shared suffering and created in order to endure and to

---

2 Didier Fassin, 'La souffrance du monde. Considérations anthropologiques sur les politiques contemporaines de la compassion', *L'Évolution psychiatrique*, 67:4, 2002, 687.

generate identity, suffering precedes the group. In a religious universe, by contrast, it welded groups together in the face of external attack and the many temptations to abandon the group for a less perilous existence.

Suffering of the latter kind was at the foundations of Judaism, which concluded an alliance with God by consenting to a sacrifice: Abraham proved willing to sacrifice his son Isaac in an act of obedience to God. Thus a father suffered unjustly in order to submit to God, who, however, told him, at the last moment: 'Lay not thine hand upon the lad, neither do thou any thing unto him: for now I know that thou fearest God, seeing thou has not withheld thy son, thine only son from me.'[3] There is no higher expression of love for God than the act of sacrifice.[4] Abraham's abnegation and devotion earned him the right to be called a God-fearing man. Indeed, acceptance of suffering here leads on to the enduring existence of the Jewish people and its election by God.[5]

Over the centuries, from generation to generation, such suffering was ritualized with the help of prayers recited at precise times of the year in different places by distinct Jewish populations. Each of these groups was endowed with its own memory of tragic events, all of which were linked to archetypal acts of destruction, among them the destruction of the First Temple in 586 BC or the Second Temple in AD 70. Their prayers integrated these events in order to invest them with significance and provide assurances of better days ahead. It was this messianic expectation which established, alongside suffering, its redemptive pendant: hope.

Suffering in Judaism and the long-term treatment of it; the evolution it has undergone in the context of a secularizing modernity; the turn that the memory of the Second World War genocide has taken over the years, until it has become nothing less than the religion of people who have less and less religion – a Judaism 'of the Holocaust and Redemption', with the state of Israel standing in for redemption[6] – such are the themes discussed in the following pages. Over and above the Jewish case, the present study can (perhaps) also provide certain keys to understanding diverse contemporary positions on suffering, positions that are at once complex, multiple, and universal; the memory of the genocide has become their paradigm. Thus the present work is not a book on the Holocaust, nor simply a book on Judaism; it is, rather,

---

3   Gn 22:12. Except where noted, all biblical quotations come from *The Bible: Authorized King James Version*, Oxford: Oxford University Press, 1998.

4   In Hebrew the story is the *Akedah*, literally, 'bond', since the sacrificial victim had to be 'bound' or 'tied' to the altar.

5   Gn 22:16–18.

6   Jacob Neusner, *Stranger at Home: 'The Holocaust', Zionism and American Judaism*, Chicago: University of Chicago Press, 1981, 79–90.

a historical meditation on the universality of suffering. To read suffering is also to read contemporary trajectories of memory and identity, which are as necessary or inevitable as they are invasive. Suffering erected into a form of identity is the mirror of our present and in equal measure, perhaps, the adumbration of the future that we will soon construct for ourselves, in which victims cling defensively to their obligation to remember while forever dreaming of an impossible forgetting. The alternative, perhaps, is a future that has at last become 'forgetful', one that will entrust to history—I do not say 'to the historians'—the legacy of our suffering pasts.

CHAPTER ONE

Suffering, Death, and Ritual

Not to mourn at all is impossible … To mourn overmuch is also impossible.[1]

A FEW PIOUS REASONS TO SUFFER

How can we possibly understand the eminent place that suffering holds today in Jewish ethics in general – or, rather, its resurgence there in new forms – without considering the biblical and Midrashic[2] interpretations, and the entire corpus of commentaries in which man is fundamentally a suffering being?

The order created by God is supposed to have been good.[3] Evil and suffering, which culminate in death, are the consequence of the actions of man (Adam), who is supposed to have turned from God. It would follow that suffering and death came about as the result of choices made by human beings who realized possibilities inherent in creation. Suffering is, in general, approached as a fact of life. Moreover, the problem in Scripture does not consist in determining why suffering exists, but in learning the reasons for the unfair way in which it is distributed. Why is it that the evil prosper while the just suffer?[4] For someone with traditional beliefs, this question is inseparable from faith.

Let us consider, for example, the individual suffering of the poor man, which finds full expression in the Psalms. The poor man is a victim of social injustice, but also of evil men and those who, because they are lacking in good-will, do not help him even when they are in a position to do so. The needy or distressed man of the Psalms is also a just man,[5] whose suffering derives from his desire to do what is good in God's eyes while avoiding evil. His virtue becomes the reason for his suffering. The moral crux lies here; it drives Job to

---

1   *BT, Baba Batra* 60b.

2   The Hebrew word *midrash* (plural *midrashim*) signifies the classic rabbinical commentary on the Scriptures as developed, for the most part, in the Holy Land. The major collections of *midrashim*, witnesses to the ancient traditions, were composed from the fifth to the twelfth centuries in various places in the Jewish Diaspora. The Jerusalem Talmud and the Babylonian Talmud also contain important Midrashic developments.

3   Gn 1:31.

4   John Bowker, *Problems of Suffering in Religions of the World*, Cambridge: Cambridge University Press, 1970, 7–9.

5   Hebrew *tsadik*.

distraction. 'Yet man is born unto trouble, as the sparks fly upward'.[6] Job's friends vainly seek an explanation for his undeserved suffering, trying to bring to light sins of which he is unaware in order to restore the equation of suffering with punishment.

Job's complaint has basically to do, not with his suffering in the proper sense, but with his inability to grasp the meaning of it. The book named after him opens with his lament about his unjust fate; one might suppose that he is seeking an explanation for his apparently unwarranted suffering.[7] Early in the book, Job pleads that he is innocent and calls on God himself to render justice and pronounce a judgement.[8] Is the suffering of innocents compatible with a world created by God? Job, a virtuous man, does not seem to deserve his fate. He will eventually come to understand the divine nature of his suffering, which is based on a mystery in which the religious essence of the world finds expression. In fact, Job's problem is less the rational or irrational nature of the suffering inflicted on him than man's relationship to God. Much of the Bible addresses evil and suffering, but it is in the Book of Job that the discussion of these questions is of fundamental importance. At the end of the book, Job realizes that man's relationship to God is not limited to a mechanical causal relation between good and its reward, sin and punishment, but far more complex. He accepts his suffering, which is thus not transformed into an argument against belief in God. The book comes to the conclusion that suffering is not necessarily an indication of sin. This represents a major break in religious thinking.[9]

Christian commentators suggest that the solution to the problems raised in the text of Job lies in Jesus's mediation between heaven and earth. God sends his son Jesus to share the world's suffering and, through him, atones for his creatures' sins and reveals himself to them. The Book of Job would thus find its continuation in the New Testament. In Islam, a number of messengers play an intermediary role comparable to Jesus's, if in different ways. Moreover, there are certainly Jewish prophets who find themselves in a similar position: Moses's most closely resembles Muhammad's. Yet the fact remains that in Judaism the relationship between God and the world remains, overall, far more distant than in the two other monotheistic religions.

---

6   Jb 5:7.
7   Oliver Leaman, *Evil and Suffering in Jewish Philosophy*, 2nd edn, Cambridge: Cambridge University Press, 1997, 2–49.
8   Jb 13:18; 23:3–5.
9   Jb 42:7.

God's acts in this world appear as a riddle beyond man's comprehension; if God does not answer Job's questions, it is in part because God himself is the answer.[10] Job's suffering is sometimes interpreted as a metaphor for, and anticipation of, the trials and tribulations of the Jewish people. But Job symbolizes, first and foremost, the man who suffers unjustly in this world. The author (there may have been more than one) of the Book of Job was inspired to write it in order to express his theological views on the problem of human suffering and tragedy. He sought to resolve the contradiction between the existence of a just, moral God and the suffering of good men.[11]

While the unjust distribution of suffering remained an insuperable problem, it was at the very least necessary to find more positive grounds for it. Hence very early on it was identified as a test of faith. In Proverbs, this idea appears in the form of an injunction: 'My son, despise not the chastening of the Lord; neither be weary of his correction: / For whom the Lord loveth he correcteth; even as a father the son in whom he delighteth.'[12] Certain texts go so far as to evoke the ennobling virtues of suffering. The classic response, however, is always that suffering is a punishment for sin.[13] This is the thesis that the authors of Deuteronomy uphold when they evoke the nation's tribulations, including exile—a thesis that applies to individuals as well.

This position is, nonetheless, not affirmed with the same constancy everywhere. In the Bible, the case of Jeremiah offers a good illustration. Deeply attached to God, Jeremiah knows that he must prophesy. He is persecuted for the message he transmits, and this message is scorned; God, however, does not come to his rescue.[14] The prophet then raises the question of the way suffering is distributed, but clings firmly to his conviction that everything is in God's hands,[15] notwithstanding the folly and evil of the people who surround him.[16] He exclaims: 'Righteous art thou, O Lord, when I plead with thee: yet let me talk with thee of thy judgments: Wherefore doth the way of the wicked prosper? Wherefore are all they happy that deal very treacherously?'[17] But Jeremiah is also the prophet of hope. God declares to him that the Babylonian exile will

---

10 Yeshaiah Leibowitz, 'L'épreuve et la crainte de Dieu dans le livre de Job', trans. Judith Kogel, *Les Cahiers du judaïsme*, 16, 2004, 27.
11 Reuven Hammer, 'Two Approaches to the Problem of Suffering', *Judaism*, 35:3, 1986, 301–3.
12 Pr 3:11–12.
13 Pr 10:27.
14 Jr 20:7–9.
15 Jr 18:1–6.
16 Bowker, *Problems of Suffering*, 12–7.
17 Jr 12:1.

come to an end and that he will one day send his captive people back to the country that he gave to its ancestors.[18]

In itself, suffering remains an indecipherable riddle. Man must submit to God: 'Naked came I out of my mother's womb, and naked shall I return thither: the Lord gave, and the Lord hath taken away; blessed be the name of the Lord.'[19] Like Abraham, Job submits to an inscrutable divine will. The nation faces up to its suffering the same way – by submitting and waiting, while maintaining faith in God. Thus the world finds itself at all times before God's tribunal and can at all times be redeemed by him. From this standpoint, it can be said that Judaism is the vehicle of a tragic vision of history.[20] Yet that vision does not rule out happy promises. Moreover, other biblical episodes, such as the story of Ruth, offer a comforting, humane response to suffering.

Ruth, the heroine of the book of the same name, is the archetype of the woman who consoles those who suffer. The story evokes human feelings, the aid and support with which one human being can provide another in times of distress. With her husband and two sons, Noemi leaves a Bethlehem struck by famine and goes to live in the plains of Moab. One of her boys marries Ruth the Moabite. When Noemi's husband and sons die, she leaves her adopted country with her two now widowed daughters-in-law. On the way home, she urges each of them to return to her mother and authorizes both to remarry. Ruth chooses not to return and accompanies Noemi to Bethlehem, refusing to leave the disconsolate old woman alone. Ruth marries the old man Booz, preferring him to younger suitors. Albeit a non-Jew, she enters the house of Israel upon marrying and gives birth to a lineage.

The acts that Ruth performs for her mother-in-law are acts of love and goodness free of ulterior motives (such as a desire for recompense). She is under no legal obligation to perform them. They are acts of *hesed* – grace or generosity. This term was later assimilated, in rabbinical Hebrew, to the concept of *gemilut hasadim*, which summons members of the community to show simple human generosity: to comfort the grieving, visit the sick, provide poor young women with dowries, or bury the dead. The book of Ruth anticipates this rabbinical development, exhorting everyone to perform such acts. Thus God has not ceased to perform acts of grace and real generosity, he has simply confided their execution to human beings such as Ruth or Booz, who

---

18   Jr 30:3.
19   Jb 1:21.
20   Frederick Plotkin, *Judaism and Tragic Theology*, New York: Schocken Books, 1973.

carry them out in his stead. These acts are of such great value that they bring the highest possible reward. Thus Ruth and Booz deserve to become the ancestors of King David himself, from whose line the Messiah will come.

In Judaism, the book of Ruth is read on *Shavuot*, an annual harvest feast that also commemorates the gift of the Torah to the people of Israel. Ruth transmits an ethics that encourages people to assume their responsibilities toward those in distress in a simple way: to take part in the divine work of consolation and assistance without asking unnecessary questions about the origin of the evil afflicting those they succour.[21] Suffering here is an opportunity; it impels the Other to demonstrate magnanimity and compassion, behave ethically, and adopt a properly messianic perspective of salvation and hope.

As for the poor man of Psalms, he too resolves to do good, in the awareness that the path taken by those who persecute him is the path of evil, despite their success in life: 'Blessed is the man that walketh not in the counsel of the ungodly, nor standeth in the way of sinners, nor sitteth in the seat of the scornful. But his delight is in the law of the Lord; and in his law doth he meditate day and night ... For the Lord knoweth the way of the righteous: but the way of the ungodly shall perish.'[22] The just man knows that he is oppressed, yet does not consider God to be the adversary responsible for his torments. Evil stems from man, not God. The just are advised to ignore the wicked and concentrate on the essential aspects of their relationship to God.[23] They wage God's battle against evil, and the will of God will triumph. In the Psalms, God is repeatedly implored and entreated to step in and establish the way of truth. The virtuous man disregards his own misfortune in order to engage in a divine struggle against evil, with the prospect of future victory. In prayer, he feels that God is at his side; he is touched by divine love and certain of his salvation.[24] With this confidence that God is just and will save the tormented just man, hope clearly asserts itself once again.[25]

Suffering of this sort is not its own horizon, as it often is for our contemporaries, many of whom, moreover, generally experience it vicariously. Their suffering is first and foremost that of relatives, ancestors, or a lineage that is sometimes quite remote. In appropriating it for themselves, they create history.

---

21 Hammer, 'Two Approaches to the Problem of Suffering', 304–8.
22 Ps 1:1–2, 6. *Complete Parallel Bible*, p. 1132 (King James Edition).
23 Nb 16:26; Ps 101:2–4, 6, 8.
24 Ps 62.
25 Eliezer Schweid, *The Jewish Experience of Time: Philosophical Dimensions of the Jewish Holy Days*, trans. Amnon Hadary, Northvale NJ: Jason Aronson, 2000, 230–44.

In the scriptural texts and the commentaries on them, in contrast, suffering possesses its own 'history', sustained by founding myths, such as that of the Covenant or the exodus from Egypt, which can always be reactivated as a means of interpreting new calamities inflicted on the nation or the individual. To be sure, these responses did not prevent the Jewish people from entertaining doubts about its future, nor did they prevent some Jews from despairing to the point of abandoning Judaism and seeking a better life elsewhere.[26] The texts at our disposal are even rigid prototypes, conceived by those who proved capable of facing up to the challenge of despair and erected into stock responses for future generations. While they do not provide direct information about the intensity of the misfortune endured by those who lived in the past, they do, at least, as if in anticipation, confer meaning on the suffering of those who will undergo similar ordeals in the future.

The biblical responses to the destruction of the First Temple in 586 BC, a consequence of the annihilation of the Kingdom of Judah, are not merely theological, they are also political. With the disappearance of sacrificial religion and the loss of national unity that resulted from this destruction, the Jewish people was obliged to reconceive its relationship with God. The biblical authors, grasping the enormity of the disaster and the tribulations it brought with it, feared, at the same time, its corrosive effects on the collective identity of the Hebrew people and its vision of the world. Their responses are formulated in national terms and seek to ensure that their distraught nation would have a future. A strong sense of community prevented disintegration of the kind that is always possible after such a calamity. At another level, the Temple symbolized the direct relationship between God and his people: the fact that it had been reduced to ruins could thus be understood as a sign that their bond had been shattered and that God was now absent from this place. It could even perpetuate the rupture in its turn, should the Jewish people not find other means of maintaining contact with its God in exile – as it did in its synagogues, little versions of the Temple, or by praying, studying the Torah, and fulfilling the commandments.

In fact, the biblical responses to catastrophe are many and varied, ranging from the sober Deuteronomist's to the visionary Ezekiel's: there exists more than one way of accounting for suffering. Protest against divine justice is integrated into the response of faith. The pathetic cries of Lamentations, Jeremiah's

---

26 Yosef Hayim Yerushalmi, 'Un champ à Anathoth: vers une histoire de l'espoir juif', in Jean Halpérin and Georges Lévitte, eds, *Mémoire et histoire. Colloque des intellectuels juifs*, Paris: Denoël, 1986, 94.

laments, or the dialogues in Job legitimate the expression of anger against a
God who listens to his people. His justice is not projected onto a world to come;
rather, the divine plan intervenes in this world – not least in apocalyptic literature, in which the prospect that the divine kingdom will be brought down to
earth relieves present suffering. The poets establish a liturgical framework
for Lamentations in order to ritualize tragedy and make suffering bearable,
whereas the prophetic authors try to chart a post-catastrophic future. The
myth of the Covenant, by including Israel's destinies in God's universal plan
and assigning a meaning to the idea that God dwells among men as well as
to human expiation in the ordeal of the desert, allows the biblical authors to
construct a model which makes it easier to confront the experience of exile.

Misfortune, as a result, ceases to be absurd. Lamentations, Job and
Deutero-Isaiah treat the problem of unjust suffering by way of individuals
identified with the nation. The privileged relationship between God and Israel
implicates the nation as a whole in past sins, present punishment, and future
redemption.[27] Destruction is perceived as a period of chastisement in the
history of this relationship, not as an absolute end. Regarded as punishment,
destruction itself stands as an expression of God's continued interest in Israel,
inasmuch as the suffering that it causes ensures that Israel will, by expiating the
sins which brought it on, enable God's penitent people to survive in the context
of a restored relationship with him. An approach of this kind, be it noted in
passing, is altogether foreign to current secular mentalities. This makes it easier
to imagine the despairing solitude of many Holocaust survivors, deprived of
the consolation, however fragile, of faith.

Deutero-Isaiah appeared in Babylon 50 years after the exile. He takes up
the old theme of the exodus from Egypt as a means of evoking the promised
departure from Babylon, a second Exodus that will provide the nations of the
world with fresh proof of the supremacy of the Eternal.[28] God presents himself
directly and immediately as the one who comforts Israel for the suffering that
he himself has inflicted on it. Exile is interpreted as a punishment that allows
Israel to expiate its sins. The success of the Babylonian armies thus ceases to be
a sign of God's impotence. Quite the contrary: it becomes an instrument for the
realization of his plan. If God used Nebuchadnezzar against Israel as a chastening rod, he uses Cyrus, the Persian King, as an agent of redemption and
restoration. Deutero-Isaiah's prophecy recreates the conditions required to

---

27 Robert Cohn, 'Biblical Responses to Catastrophe', *Judaism* 35:3, 1986, 263–76.
28 Is 40:3–5; 49:7.

make what God says plausible in the face of the overwhelming distress of the people in exile. God's return and the new consecration of his bond with Israel become the equivalent of a new Covenant. This restoration invests history with meaning, since it is now no longer a series of prosperous periods alternating with ones of sudden decline, of shifts from one regime to another, but, rather, reflects the continuity of the relations binding man, nation, and God.

Independence and prosperity were signs that the people of Israel had observed the divine commandments. The opposite resulted from sinful revolt against the Law. Judaism's contribution to a human response to suffering lies here as well: suffering now takes on redemptive virtue, bearing within itself the beginnings of a better future for the group and the individual alike. This aspect of suffering would subsequently acquire central significance in Christianity with the emphasis put on Jesus's crucifixion. Of course, Christianity would reject the earlier vision of suffering as punishment, which, however, would never cease to prevail at the level of popular belief: here, the question of what one had done to merit one's suffering was always pertinent.

At the heart of the ordeal in ancient Judaism there thus resided the certainty of the promise. The Bible offered a bulwark against despair. But this confidence did not breed utopianism or a questioning of the dominant, tragic conception of human and national vicissitudes, punctuated by destruction, calamities, and suffering. Such a conception is not altogether unrelated to one that continues to preoccupy contemporary Jews, including the most secularized. Desolation and expectant waiting are, in the long run, intertwined. At the same time, there emerges an eschatological, apocalyptic justification of suffering, sustained by belief in an afterlife. The promise of recompense in the world to come for the torments endured in this one, reinforced by the confident belief that God will intervene in history at the end of it, could only give the suffering new courage.

Thus the latter half of the book of Daniel, an apocalyptic work *par excellence*, was written by pietistic circles in Palestine between 167 and 164 BC, in the last years of the reign of Antiochus IV Epiphanes and prior to the rededication of the Second Temple after the Maccabees's victories. To root out Jewish religion and make Jerusalem a Greek city, Antiochus had abolished sacrifices and religious holidays and outlawed circumcision, the observance of the Sabbath, and the rules of *kashrut*.[29] In the book of Daniel, the contemporary crisis is not directly described, it is projected four centuries into the past, the period of the

---

29   The corpus of Jewish religious rules governing the preparation and consumption of food.

Babylonian exile. In recompense for his loyalty to Judaism, Daniel, one of the exiles, is bestowed prophetic visions about future historical events.

The future is presented as a series of struggles and a succession of earthly kingdoms. When the end comes, all kings will perish and the turbulence of history will cease to carry on. At that point, those who kept faith with God will be resurrected and enjoy eternal life; those who faltered will become objects of contempt and horror.[30] The pious are accordingly enjoined to endure persecution in silence while maintaining faith in their own goodness, and to await the end.[31] This acceptance of suffering by no means excluded lament and protest. Indeed, so that annihilating the enemy would not become an end in itself, the rabbis toned down the possible subversive implications, since such a perspective entailed the risk that the present would be made to seem insignificant, leading the devout to neglect their duties in this world. A belief in resurrection and life after death completely transformed man's relation to suffering by making it bearable. However, such a belief clashed with the role of the practising believer, who could help to ensure the survival of Judaism only by staying alive and acting in the present. The Roman conquest of Jerusalem in AD 70, at the end of the first major Jewish revolt, gave this apocalyptic doctrine new relevance. Indeed, this conquest, which coincided with the destruction of the Second Temple, was considered a prelude to redemption and, thus, the arrival of the Messiah. The city and its sanctuary, the implication was, were destroyed in order to hasten his coming.[32]

The destruction of the Temple paved the way for the uncontested domination of the Pharisean school of thought, the basis for what is known as rabbinical Judaism.[33] The rabbis' responses to suffering did not radically differ from the Bible's, but rather, redefined and extended them. Moreover, the classical theme of suffering as chastisement for sin recurred frequently. Thus Rabbi Ammi says: 'There is no death without sin, and there is no suffering without iniquity'.[34] This teaching from the Babylonian Talmud was nevertheless followed by others contradicting it, proof that the compilers of this work did not regard it as absolute truth.[35] A man's suffering did not imply that the

---

30   Dn 12: 3, 2.
31   Alan Mintz, *Hurban: Responses to Catastrophe in Hebrew Literature*, Syracuse: Syracuse University Press, 1996, 3, 19, 42–7.
32   II Ba 20:2.
33   Rabbinical Judaism is the current, descended of Phariseeism, which came into being at the end of the Ancient period, after AD 70. The thought of this current crystallized in the major, classic Mishnic and Talmudic corpuses of the period.
34   *BT, Shabat*, 55a.
35   Bowker, *Problems of Suffering*, pp. 19–32.

man himself, his body or soul, were bad or sullied, nor that God had rejected him. Here we rather far from the Christian doctrines on the fundamentally negative nature of the body or the effectiveness of suffering as penitence.

Physical suffering might be desirable or acceptable when it affected the individual, but it was neither good nor efficacious in itself. Mortification of the flesh was not an end prized for its own sake. The Talmud by no means recommends renouncing the pleasures of the flesh, such as food, drink, or sex. True grandeur, to be sure, resides in suffering. Yet suffering does not absolve the individual of his responsibilities to himself or others, and it in no sense separates him from the community, physically or emotionally. This confers universal value on suffering, already observable in several biblical episodes. In Judaism, with a few rare exceptions, those who suffer do not constitute sects of the suffering comparable to medieval Christian self-flagellators, whose movement of voluntary poverty found a means of identification with Christ in penitence and expiation.

The man who suffers escapes from this prison-house by opening himself to the suffering of the Other. This principle of availability, indispensable to the suffering and the oppressed, was perpetuated by the tradition even after it began to decline, and continued to influence generations of secularized Jews in the modern period. For a long time this principle motivated Jews to join various struggles to change society and identify with peoples and groups targeted with discrimination or violence. Thanks to their historical experience of suffering, many Jews gravitated almost naturally to the side of those who continued to suffer setbacks, in solidarity with their struggle for a better future. This makes it easier to understand the commitment of Jews to socialism, anarchism, Bolshevism, the fight for Black civil rights, and numerous other struggles to improve the lot of men and women.[36]

The tradition strove hard to ensure that a positive value would be set on suffering. The suffering that God inflicted on men in this world out of love was intended, according to tradition, to secure greater rewards for man in the world to come.[37] It was through suffering that human beings gained eternal life.[38] The real benefits of suffering accrued to those capable of drawing the right lessons from it. Thus the amount of pain one endured mattered less than the way one perceived it. Furthermore, the suffering of the just could relieve the

---

36   See Michael Löwy, *Redemption and Utopia: Jewish Libertarian Thought in Central Europe*, Stanford, CA: Stanford University Press, 1992.

37   In Hebrew that suffering is *yisurei ahavah*, literally, 'torments of love'.

38   Genesis *Raba*, 9, 8 (on Gn 1:31).

distress of later generations. What counted was not one's own suffering, but the reaction of the people for whose sake one suffered.[39]

In rabbinical Judaism, indeed, suffering is regarded as positive. It is one of the four blessings that God wished to bestow on the world because it represents one of the paths leading to him. According to Rabbi Simeon bar Yohai, a second-century sage, God bestowed three precious gifts on Israel, all amid suffering: the Torah, the land of Israel, and the next world.[40] Several passages in the Midrash encourage acceptance of suffering as a means of progress and self-improvement. Indeed, suffering appears there as inseparable from human nature, as both a driving force behind man's development and a form of atonement.[41]

The New Testament extended the Jewish interpretation of suffering, while accentuating it differently. The Epistle of James reflects the Jewish influence on nascent Christianity. It is here that trials and tribulations are said to be good discipline: those who endure them are promised 'the crown of life'.[42] Theodicy was of particular importance for Christians. How could the principle of God's justice and rectitude be upheld in the face of the existence of evil and suffering? Yet if suffering is problematic for Christianity as well, it is above all because it runs counter to the affirmation that God is love.

In Islam, suffering has to do primarily with the principle of God's omnipotence. It is treated as a penalty for sin in the Koran too, necessary because it forms part of the Almighty's plan and reveals man's true nature.[43] It is a direct emanation of divine justice. In practice, this amounts to an affirmation that suffering is best approached as an expression of God's will. For many Muslims, it is an inherent part of life; it can be accepted in this world because equilibrium will be restored in the next. According to certain later traditions, good men suffer more because they are the closest to God and the ones he loves best.[44]

It will thus be readily seen that while each of the three major monotheistic religions offers their responses to suffering, present a particular approach to the problem, and vary in space and time, there is nevertheless a real convergence between all three. Thus suffering can be justified as punishment, a test of faith, discipline, or a sign of God's proximity.

---

39   Matthew Schwartz, 'The Meaning of Suffering: A Talmudic Response to Theodicy', *Judaism* 32:4, 1983, 444–51.

40   *BT, Berakhot* 5a; *Tanhumah, Shemot* 1.

41   See, for example, *Midrash Tehilim*, on Ps 94:12.

42   James 1:2–4, 12.

43   Koran 4:78–79; 11:9–11; 41:49–51.

44   Bowker, *Problems of Suffering*, 33–4, 51, 79, 102, 106–27.

THE PROPER USES OF FREELY CHOSEN DEATH

In Judaism and, for that matter, other religious traditions as well, suffering is not merely an evil to be endured. One may also freely choose to suffer, as the martyr does.

The term used in Hebrew to designate martyrdom means, literally, 'sanctification of the Name' (the Name of God).[45] 'Sanctifying the [divine] Name' consists firstly in proclaiming it holy in prayer,[46] but also in manifesting holiness before both one's fellow believers and also non-Jews, through strict respect of the commandments and exemplary moral conduct. Every violation of this basic principle counts, conversely, as 'profanation of the Name' of God.[47] The ultimate form of sanctification is martyrdom. The obligation to sanctify the Name of God is mentioned for the first time in Leviticus.[48] The most appropriate way of accomplishing this duty would be developed in the Talmud and, still later, in commentaries directly bound up with the historical experiences of the day.

According to rabbinical Law, every Jew is duty-bound to die rather than let himself be forced to violate certain commandments, notably the prohibitions on murder, incest, and idolatry.[49] This principle conflicts with another, no less fundamental, of 'respect for human life',[50] according to which a Jew may or even must violate commandments if that is the only way he can save his life. The attitude that the believer is encouraged to adopt depends on circumstance. If the violation of the commandments occurred publicly – in the presence of at least ten males of Jewish faith – death is in principle always preferable, whatever the commandment involved. On the other hand, only *living* Jews are in a position to serve their God; thus it is not recommended that they risk their lives simply in order to respect the divine prescriptions. However, in periods of religious persecution – for example, when the persecutors' avowed objective is to bring the religion of Israel to ruin – one is under no moral or theological obligation to save one's life at the expense of denying one's religion.[51] Martyrs are witnesses to God's sovereignty.[52] Their suffering and death manifest the tragic, yet also redemptive nature of history.

---

45   *Kiddush ha-shem.*
46   Is 6, 3.
47   In Hebrew, *hilul ha-shem.*
48   Lv 18:3–5; 22:31–2.
49   *BT, Shabat,* 74a.
50   In Hebrew, *pikuah nefesh.*
51   Moses Maimonides, *Mishneh Torah, Yessodei ha-Torah,* 5, 2.
52   See, for example, Is 43:11–12: 'I, even I, am the Lord; and beside me there is no saviour. I have declared, and have saved, and I have shewed, when there was no strange god among you: therefore ye are my witnesses, saith the Lord, that I am God.'

The Judaism faithful to the Law first adopted an explicitly positive conception of martyrdom during its confrontation with Hellenism and, more specifically, in the face of persecution by the Seleucid king Antiochus IV Epiphanes in the second century BC. The structure, form, and religious inspiration of this conception were elaborated in Jewish and Christian literature from 2 Maccabees and 4 Maccabees to the New Testament, which provided the historical and narrative basis for subsequent treatments of it. The stories in Maccabees were theologically linked to, and enriched by, the motif of the sacrifice of Isaac and the book of Job in particular. As crisis succeeded crisis, the model of martyrdom changed over time. The glorified actions of the martyrs sustained, after their deaths, the faith of the communities for which they had made the supreme sacrifice. Cast in more contemporary form, this model remains relevant, continuing to play a role in the sanctification of secular 'heroes'.

The books of the Maccabees, excluded from the canon of the Jewish Bible, relate the story of the Maccabees's resistance to the Hellinization imposed by Antiochus IV Epiphanes in the first half of the second century BC. Nothing proves that these texts are contemporaneous with the events they recount. The similarities between the acts of resistance mentioned in 2 and 4 Maccabees and those of later Christian martyrs bear witness to the emergence of a new Jewish tradition and its influence on early Christianity. In 2 Maccabees, the aged Eleazer refuses to eat pork, preferring to die rather than violate the commandment. Thus he provides future generations with an example of virtue. Another episode in the same book involves a mother and her seven children who go to their deaths rather than submit to the king's demands.

Indications are that the episodes centred on Eleazer and the martyred mother were written in the latter half of the first century of our era; this would make them contemporaneous with the first New Testament writings. It has therefore been suggested that they predate the notion of martyrdom later developed by the Christians, the more so as the first appearance of the word 'martyrdom' itself as a designation for death at the hands of secular-minded enemies is to be found in the story of Polycarp, who associates the word with the act in Asia Minor around the year 150.[53] In the Gospels and Acts of the Apostles, in particular, the Greek term *martus* (from which 'martyr' was later derived) occurs in the sense of 'witness'; it is used for witnesses to the passion and resurrection of Jesus, who was himself the witness to the glory of God.

---

53   Apostolic father, bishop of Smyrna, where he died a martyr's death.

There is nothing surprising about the fact that one religion should have borrowed these literary and legendary themes or theological beliefs from another. The political and spiritual structure of the Roman Empire made such borrowings possible; Judaism and Christianity took at least two centuries to consummate their divorce.

In any event, had it not been for the Roman tradition exalting suicide, the theme of martyrdom would not have been as extensively developed as it was in first-century and second-century Judaism and Christianity: the Greek and Jewish traditions did not encourage martyrdom, even if the Jewish idea of the martyr–prophet holds an important place in Jewish sources. Martyrs would have remained simple witnesses, without attaining the glory they ultimately did; indeed, in the Christian world, it was only with Augustine, in the fourth century, that the Church took a firm stand against suicide. 'For he who kills himself kills no other than a man,' Augustine says in *The City of God*.[54] The notion of martyrdom as witness would reappear later in the Muslim tradition; the Greek word for 'witness' would be translated into Arabic as *shahid*. This was the name given to the Muslim martyrs who fell in combat against the infidels and could expect a reward for their commendable deeds in the world to come. In Arabic, however, the word *shahid* is derived from a passive grammatical form meaning 'witnessed'. This has led to debate over whether the martyr himself 'bears witness' or whether someone else must do so for him. In the latter perspective, God or the angels bear witness to the martyr's death.

During Hadrian's second-century religious persecutions, the conventional doctrine of punishment and reward underwent an acute crisis in the Jewish world. The result was a revision of the rabbinical doctrine of theodicy. What now required explanation was neither the torment inflicted by a higher power, nor the misfortune that befell the good man, but, rather, the fact that even obedience to the commandments led to suffering and death.

According to late Midrashic sources, Rome under Hadrian had subjected ten eminent personalities of ancient Judaism, including Rabbi Akiba, to a death of this kind.[55] When Akiba's disciples learned of his martyrdom, they donned a sackcloth and rented their garments in recognition of their mourning; they considered the execution of the rabbi to be symbolic. Akiba taught that loving

---

54   Glen Bowersock, *Martyrdom and Rome*, Cambridge: Cambridge University Press, 2002; Augustine, *The City of God*, cited in Bowersock, 74; H. A. Fischel, 'Martyr and Prophet', *Jewish Quarterly Review*, 37:3, 1947, part I, 280; Daniel Boyarin, *Dying for God: Martyrdom and the Making of Christianity and Judaism*, Stanford CA: Stanford University Press, 1999.

55   *Asarah harugei malkhut*, literally, 'the ten victims of the kingdom'.

acceptance of suffering was the supreme goal of God's servants, who would fulfil the commandments even if it cost them their lives. It was in the context of martyrdom that Akiba understood the commandment 'you shall love the Eternal your God with all your soul', which he interpreted to mean 'even if he takes your soul'.[56] His death recalls Socrates', despite the differences in the way the two men were executed.[57] The Greek doctrine of virtue had permeated both the Christian and Jewish ideals of the period. It was no accident that Judaism and Christianity were termed martyrs' religions, imbued as they were with such Stoicism.

Martyrdom was draped in the colours of a popular ideal; it gave expression to the Jewish and Christian believers' ardent desire for sacrifice. The course of events was to consecrate the model of the martyr–prophet that crystallized after the Maccabean period. To be sure, the prominence in the Midrash of the figure of the prophet suffering for his faith and persecuted by his own people seems to have served mainly as a self-accusation with didactic purposes. However, in the Tannaitic period, in the first two centuries of our era, it was the image of the martyr–prophet suffering under the yoke of a foreign tyrant which dominated. The prophet tested by God, like Abraham and Isaac, was likewise a common motif. The Midrash also quite frequently refers to the stories of the biblical martyr–prophets, such as Jeremiah, Uriyahu, or Daniel and his companions.[58]

Every prophet suffered or died and every martyr thus found himself endowed with prophetic powers; prophets and martyrs alike were elevated to the rank of angelic figures. Christianity adopted this Jewish model: the ideal of Christian martyrdom expressed the aspiration to be an *imitatio Christi*. Popular piety, investing martyrs with the characteristics of divine figures, heroes, or angels, influenced both religions. The Greco-Roman tradition was also influential, setting the style of Jewish and Christian martyrology. Martyrology sought not only to strengthen the believer's faith, but also to win new converts to Judaism and Christianity. The episode of the Ten Martyrs took its inspiration from older legends about martyrs.[59] Such stories of martyrdom appeared more frequently in periods of tension among both Jews and

---

56   *BT, Berakhot*, 61b.

57   Ephraïm Urbach, *Les Sages d'Israël. Conceptions et croyances des maîtres du Talmud*, trans. Marie-José Jolivet, Paris: Cerf, 1996, 459–60.

58   H. A. Fischel, 'Martyr and Prophet', 267–72.

59   H. A. Fischel, 'Martyr and Prophet', *Jewish Quarterly Review*, 37:4, part II, 377–85.

Christians, who bore the brunt of Roman persecution in the early Christian period. The two traditions developed in closely related contexts.

The martyrs' edifying example ensured the cohesion of the group in the face of external attacks. Suffering now wore its best finery: 'Suffering is precious', Akiba declared.[60] At the same time, the faithful were urged not to rebel against suffering, on the grounds that there was no man who had never sinned. The connection between the individual's tribulations and those of his community became still more conspicuous. The individual's suffering was now said to lead him toward the hereafter, while that of the community was transformed into a sign: 'The Holy One, blessed be He, brings suffering upon the righteous in this world, in order that they may inherit the future world'.[61] Individual and community fused, suffering in the knowledge that a better world awaited them. Down to the eve of the First Crusade of 1096, martyrdom was associated with the benefits that it procured for the nation. Even after the period of persecution came to an end, Akiba's heroic example, which summoned the faithful to die for the sanctification of the divine name, continued to inspire future generations. The martyr's spectacular death ensured the group's continuity. The day of Akiba's death coincided with the day a scholar who was to perpetuate his memory and continue his work was born: Rabbi Juda, the son of Simeon the Prince. When Hadrian's successor curtailed persecution and the Jews returned to their schools, their studies, and the practice of their religion, a now mature Rabbi Juda extended the work of Akiba's disciples. It was Juda, late in the second century, who published the Mishna, the basic code of rabbinical law that was to become the heart of the Talmud. The Talmud would be studied by Jews in exile throughout the world for centuries.

After the destruction of the Temple in AD 70, the sages began to evoke the suffering of God himself in the Midrash: they imagined him weeping inconsolably and appealing to patriarchs, matriarchs, and prophets for help. Over five centuries we find both sages who sought out suffering and multiplied fasts so that it could not be said that they received their reward in this world without waiting for the next, and others who, in contrast, stood opposed to mortification and self-inflicted ordeals.[62] Attitudes thus varied widely, with some sages

---

60   BT, Sanhedrin 101a.
61   BT, Kidushin 40b.
62   Urbach, Les Sages d'Israël, 460–72; Louis Finkelstein, 'The Ten Martyrs', in Israel Davidson, ed., Essays and Studies in Memory of Linda R. Miller, New York: JTS, 1938, 29–55; David Roskies, The Literature of Destruction. Jewish Responses to Catastrophe, Philadelphia: Jewish Publication Society, 1988, 49–50.

attaching a positive value to suffering as such and others refusing to suffer. We should no doubt interpret the latter stance as evidence of a desire to temper the zeal likely to come over certain people in periods favourable to such excesses. One scholar has gone so far as to write that 'martyrdom as it was invented and martyrdom as it is now understood is as powerful a force in the Church that created it as it is in Islam, though obviously in a different way'.[63] It must be said that today, in Judaism, the attractive power of martyrdom has been largely neutralized.

SUFFERING TAMED

In traditional Judaism, ancient catastrophes are commemorated on fixed dates in the liturgical calendar; these days are marked by mourning rituals and acts of penitence.[64] Catastrophes, each one unique, do not materialize *ex nihilo*. They are embedded in an established order which may not provide an explanation, but does invest them with meaning. That meaning may be impenetrable but it takes its place in a comprehensible frame of reference that has the power to mitigate the experience of suffering thanks to the hope of restoration. By the same token, the ferment of subversion inherent in suffering is overcome by this ritualization, which, by encompassing a series of catastrophes, opens up a space of hope: because all the calamities of the past are commemorated simultaneously, their memory weighs less heavily the rest of the time. In a sense, the obligation to perform the ritual dispenses with the obligation for the faithful to remember. It is, in and of itself, an injunction incorporated into the religious person's calendar. It is inseparable from the study of the Torah required of every Jew, especially after the destruction of the Second Temple: in a way, study of the Torah replaced the sacrificial cult that it was no longer possible to practise. This very peculiar way of dealing with the memory of misfortune contrasts sharply with our contemporary, secular attitude. In ritualized commemoration, individual suffering is at one with the group's. In the cyclical apprehension of existence in this world, life returns once the moment of mourning has passed. After desolation comes the time of consolation.

In Numbers, we read: 'And all the congregation lifted up their voice, and cried; and the people wept that night.'[65] According to the Midrash, the night in question occurred on *Tish'ah be-Av*, the ninth day of the Hebrew month of *Av*

---

63   Bowersock, *Martyrdom and Rome*, 20.
64   Roskies, *The Literature of Destruction*, 4.
65   Nb 14:1. *Complete Parallel Bible*, 307, (King James Edition).

(July–August). This event is interpreted as follows: seeing his people weep without reason, God is supposed to have said: 'I will set [this night] aside for a weeping throughout the generations to come'.[66] God ensures that the creature who suffers is not alone. There is no rupture and no history, but an intergenerational chain reinforced by a controlled mythology and explanations that are intended to make suffering acceptable, even when it escapes human understanding. The interpretations of this annual day of mourning differ, but it is always a day on which Jews, wherever they may be found, weep together, regardless of frontiers. Jewish tradition encourages the faithful to experience and conceive of *Tish'ah be-Av* as a day of ritualized suffering and to ask not *why* but *how* suffering occurs.

This day marks the four great tragedies: the destruction of the First and Second Temples; the defeat of the last major Jewish revolt, which was led by Bar Kochba in 132–135 and is supposed to have come to an end on the 9th of the month of Av in 135, when Bethar, the rebels' last stronghold seven miles from Jerusalem, fell to the Romans; and, finally, the 'ploughing under' of the soil of Jerusalem after the revolt was put down, an allusion to the fact that, in 136, Hadrian built a pagan sanctuary on the site of the destroyed Temple, renaming Jerusalem 'Aelia Capitolina' and banning all Jews from it.

The subsequent expulsions of the Jews from England in 1290, France in 1394, and Spain in 1492 were also associated with this emblematic date. Thus history found itself absorbed by a conception of events as repetitive, leaving God as the supreme authority and depriving man of any possibility of intervening in them, except by way of obedience to the commandments. Only under these conditions does it become possible to avoid all ruptures that might be detrimental to the faith of the group, thereby ensuring its future. Memory itself is atomized by the superposition of events. In the long run, mourning and the commemoration of mourning take precedence over events themselves.

The mourning of 9 *Av* is prepared during a three-week period that begins on 17 *Tamuz*: these are days of distress that make up the darkest period in the Jewish year. Restrictions become more severe the week before the fatal date, during which Jews may not marry, cut their hair, shave, eat meat, drink wine, travel for pleasure, wear new clothes, dance, or listen to music. By 9 *Av*, they are ready for the experience of ritualized suffering.

On that day, the faithful go to the synagogue barefoot or with shoes that contain no leather. There, they sit on the floor to pray, wearing neither phylacteries nor prayer shawls during the morning service; this is, moreover, the only

---

66   *BT, Taanit* 29a.

day of the year when the Torah is not read. A twenty-five-hour fast is observed, preceded by a symbolic mourning meal of bread and a hard-boiled egg. The day is celebrated in the same way as one of individual mourning, as if the individual were in mourning because a member of his immediate family had died. This link between public and private mourning has its source in the prophet Ezekiel's grief at his wife's death, which eventually came to symbolize the suffering that the destruction of the Temple caused the Jews. The mourning rituals observed by the prophet prefigure the suffering of the Jewish people; in their turn, the rabbis utilize them to commemorate all the suffering that has befallen the Jewish people. Suffering offers lessons about suffering. 'Thus Ezekiel is unto you a sign: according to all that he hath done shall ye do: and when this cometh, ye shall know that I am the Lord God.'[67]

In order to learn about the Other's suffering, one must observe it. The sages believed that it was easier to learn from and about others' suffering if one suffered oneself. Hence the Jewish people has to suffer on 9 Av if it wants to learn something on that day, when weeping is a duty. The people suffers as Ezekiel suffered, and, like him, it has confidence in God. In the oppressive atmosphere of this day of mourning, the biblical Book of Lamentations is read in the synagogue; tradition attributes it to the prophet Jeremiah, who witnessed the destruction of the First Temple. The Hebrew title of the book is a question, *eikhah* – how? – that recurs several times in the text itself. Also read are elegies (*Kinot*) that express the yearning of the people of Israel for its land and which exhort those in mourning to direct their gaze toward the future: toward the hour when the Messiah will arrive to bring their exile and the associated suffering with it to an end, and toward the place, the land of Israel, where their so ardently desired redemption will come about. Indeed, according to rabbinical tradition, 9 Av, the day the Temple was destroyed, is also the day on which the Messiah will be born. Thus the day itself contains a promise.[68]

This day of mourning does not bring the Jewish year to a close. The following month is given over to the penitential prayers (*Selihot*) that precede the New Year's celebrations, and then to the Great Pardon (*Kippur*), during which the faithful manifest their repentance, atone for their sins, and ask for divine pardon. The memory of the Ten Martyrs, the heroic rabbis we have already mentioned, is evoked on the morning of the day of the Great Pardon, among the most solemn moments in the Jewish calendar, on which *Eikh ezkerah* (*I remember these men*), one of the most moving poems in the Jewish

---

67   Ez 24:24.
68   *TJ, Berakhot*, 2:4.

liturgy, is recited. The hope for better days once again becomes of central importance.[69] The expiatory period culminates in a pilgrimage festival (*Sukot*) commemorating the Jews' wanderings in the desert, in which God appears as an active agent in history; the festival helps to reinforce community bonds around happy moments this time.

The feast of *Purim*, celebrated on 14 *Adar* (February–March), is, typically, a feast of exile that commemorates deliverance more than anything else. It is associated with the memory of catastrophe, but also the providential nature of avoiding catastrophe. Preceded by a period of fasting, *Purim* evokes the miraculous salvation of the Jews (whether a real historical event is involved is a subject of controversy), secured by Esther and her cousin Mordechai at a time when Haman, a minister of the Persian King Ahasuerus and the archetypal persecutor of the Jews, had hatched a plot to wipe them out. *Purim* shows how it proved possible to reverse a disastrous destiny. This holiday is an occasion for rejoicing and also for a carnival; those celebrating it are encouraged to drink wine. What makes it paradigmatic is the fact that different communities eventually began celebrating local *Purims* at other times of the year to commemorate the natural disasters and persecutions from which they had 'miraculously' escaped at various points in their history. These local *Purims* had their own 'scrolls' (*Megilah*), that is, books recounting the episode they commemorated, just as the biblical *Purim* has its 'scroll' in the Book of Esther, which is ritually read. *Purim*, a 'minor' feast not established by the Pentateuch, refers to an event late in biblical history. But while God may be responsible for the 'miracle', his name is never mentioned in the Book of Esther. Rather, human beings are put centre-stage as the actors of a history which, to be sure, they do not control but can influence. One here takes a certain distance from the dialogue between God and man in order to approach its apparent historicity as a story of suffering.

In any event, calamities were explained and commemorated in line with schemas which, albeit focused on suffering, opened onto the prospect of a happy end brought on by divine intervention. The models of suffering defined in the scriptural and canonical texts ultimately created their own memory, by virtue of a constant reactivation that respected pre-established, immutable norms. In the Middle Ages, the anguishing vicissitudes that the Jews went

---

69   Theodore Weinberger, '*Tish'ah B'av* and the Interpretation of Suffering', in Dan Cohn-Sherbok, ed., *Theodicy*, Lewiston NY: Edwin Mellen Press, 51–63; Todd Linafelt, *Surviving Lamentations: Catastrophe, Lament, and Protest in the Afterlife of a Biblical Book*, Chicago: University of Chicago Press, 2000, 119–31; Roskies, *The Literature of Destruction*, 5; Schweid, *The Jewish Experience of Time*, 238–43.

through because of the deterioration of their situation in Europe led to an interweaving of suffering with history. Models from the past in the biblical canon continued to endow meaning on this chain of ordeals, experienced in different contexts. Some of them gained the status of typical historical configurations of suffering, engendering new schemas that were fitted into the old ones. This may be observed in the Jewish martyrologist of the First Crusade (1096), which, in its turn, served as an edifying example during later episodes of persecution that themselves gave rise to chronicles, immortalized in their turn. Thus elegies and hymns recounting the tragic events of the day were added, from time to time, to the already existing ones which, inspired by the Book of Lamentations, had been composed to commemorate the destruction of Jerusalem and the Temple.

This accumulation was reassuring, since the present took its place in the framework of the past on a path blazed by earlier generations: sin, punishment, restoration of Israel's glory and dignity. In Lamentations, the faithful believer exclaims: 'Turn thou us unto thee, O Lord, and we shall be turned; renew our days as of old.'[70] This expectation preserves the coherence of the group in the most trying moments. At the same time, the believer can learn to bear his suffering by taking his inspiration from past examples which, anchored in his present cultural practice, open onto a messianic horizon. In time, the liturgization of punctual events depersonalizes and universalizes them, without draining them of their emotional charge. It recalls the ordeals endured in from generation to generation, in a period when history, in the sense we give the word, did not yet exist. It becomes the memory of these events. At a time when the printing press did not yet exist and the written word remained the prerogative of cultivated social strata, liturgy and memory joined hands to create this story of suffering and to perpetuate it. Although posterity has preserved the names of some of the authors of these chronicles and liturgical poems, the memory produced by the liturgy was foremost a collective one: it thus resembled the way one then went about being a Jew, following a mode of existence based on the community, not the individual. The exhortation to remember was fundamentally collective.

Today, the duty to remember primarily forges individual identities. This individual relationship to suffering is not altogether new. It goes back to the nineteenth century, when Jews left their communities, confronted a non-Jewish society with its own set of values, and attempted to meet its challenges.

---

70   Lm 5:21.

Traditional memories of suffering could not be revived here as they had been in the past; nor were they capable of generating faith and social cohesion, because the 'codes' of the religious universe in which they had their roots no longer held any appeal for contemporary Jews. Only the visible part of this universe held people's attention: suffering itself. The task now was to write its history.

CHAPTER TWO

Manufacturing a Suffering History

The people of Israel, professing pure monotheism, became the suffering people in history ... suffering has become its vital source ...[1]

The memory of the First Crusade (1096) haunted the imagination of medieval Jews and would later haunt those Jews of the nineteenth and twentieth centuries, not without reason. The memory crystallized the traditional schemas used to justify suffering and became, in its turn, a model for explaining later persecutions. This model, which inspired a certain historicization of suffering, was handed down to us as a legacy and was reactivated in the nineteenth century by Jews who had left the ghettos behind and were fearful of losing what little of their Judaism they had left. The major disasters of ancient times represented by the destruction of the two Temples probably struck these Jews as much more remote from their culture than the Crusades, which had emerged in the very heart of the Christian world in which they continued to reside. This relative proximity offered them resources which were better adapted to their own questions and could help shore up their crumbling identity. The break with the Christian world inaugurated by this and the Crusades was transformed, for these Jews, into a sort of historical backdrop, reminding them, even as they were being integrated into European society, that such breaks could recur at any time. Thus the Crusades marked the beginning of a new stage after that of the ancient biblical and post-biblical narratives. One after the other, they provided raw material for the Jewish historical imagination, which chose to centre itself on suffering.

The biblical myths, for their part, assimilated the history written down by the flesh-and-blood people who describe the events of the Crusades in their chronicles. Even if these chronicles do not yet comprise historiography as we conceive it, they generate history, one of suffering. Often, they are the only available historical source on the persecutions the Jews endured and thus have the status of historical documentation. Together with the elegies and penitential prayers recited on symbolic dates of the Jewish calendar, they paint a

---

1   Hermann Cohen, *Religion of Reason. Out of the Sources of Judaism*, trans. Simon Kaplan, New York: Frederick Ungar, 1972, 234.

didactic panorama of suffering. The Crusades, too, contributed to the elaboration of a liturgy of catastrophe (*gezerah*) they were integrated into already existing schemas and soon were being evoked in contemporary synagogal worship services. Thus the penitential prayer *Et ha-kol kol Yaakov nohem* ('[Listen to] Jacob's voice, his moaning voice') by Kalonymos ben Juda of Mainz, who witnessed the events he describes of the self-immolation of Jews from the Rhineland during the First Crusade. Kalonymos was also the author of an elegy, *Mi yiten roshi mayim* ('May my head turn into a fountain!'),[2] on the massacres perpetrated in the big towns of Speyer, Mainz, and Worms; he does not spare us any details. Other penitential prayers by well-known poets are also based on the trials and tribulations of the day. Later, when the Talmud was burned in Paris in June 1242 or 1244 on orders from the king, Rabbi Meir of Rothenburg wrote an elegy that quickly became one of the dirges chanted on 9 *Av*. These penitential prayers welded together, in a single set of texts, the sacrifice of Isaac, the Martyr of the Ten, and the torments to which men, women, and children were subjected during the Crusades. This poetry is transhistorical. By combining the most recent calamities with their archetypal models, it presents the Jewish people as a single organism. This discourse of suffering is also transformed into a didactic tool: it carries present generations back to the suffering of past generations and establishes a tie between them, thereby strengthening Judaism, which might otherwise falter in the face of new ordeals.[3]

Alongside these works we may range the 'memory books' common in the medieval period, especially in the Ashkenazi world; they preserved, besides the names of rabbis and famous community leaders, lists of persecutions and accounts of the martyrdom which people endured during them. These lists were read aloud in the synagogues at ceremonies commemorating the anniversaries of people's deaths. Often, these memory books evoke the past of the communities that produced them. Others are broader in scope. Thus the Nuremberg memory book recounts the persecutions and martyrology of German and French Jews between the 1096 Crusade and the Black Death of 1349.

Fast days could also be established by Jewish communities to memorialize local persecutions. Such commemorations were accompanied by the recitation of penitential prayers recalling ordeals undergone over a long period of time. The slanderous accusation that the Jews had committed a ritual murder in

---

2   After Jr 9:1.
3   Leo Trepp, 'Toward a "*Slihah*" on the Holocaust', *Judaism*, 3, 1986, 344–50.

Blois, the point of departure for an affair that culminated in the execution of 38 Jews who chose to die rather than be baptized, was commemorated in this way. The Blois martyrdom of 26 May 1171 so profoundly affected the Jews that, in addition to the narratives and penitential prayers composed to commemorate it, Rabbi Jacob Tam, a well-known religious authority of the period, also made 26 May a day of fasting for the communities of France, England, and the Rhineland.[4]

Thus there sprang up a discourse of suffering reflecting the dramatic events that the Jews lived through from, in particular, the Middle Ages on. Handed down through the generations, this discourse would later serve written history as its living memory and even become confused with history as such. The Jews' socio-political condition in exile had something to do with this confusion. It was responsible for the fact they did not have court chroniclers or professional chroniclers and could not constitute archives; what the communities had in the way of written documents was as a rule lost or destroyed whenever massacres occurred.[5] Moreover, the rhetoric of suffering reflected the convictions of both the Christian and Jewish populations. Day-to-day suffering, the consequence of famines, the havoc wrought by epidemics, and conditions of life in general, intersected with spiritual suffering and was made bearable by it.

The chronicles produced from the time of the Crusades on are written representations of suffering. The twelfth-century tribulations of the Jews under the Almohades, the expulsion from Spain in 1492, the massacres perpetrated by the Cossacks in Poland and Ukraine in 1648, successive expulsions from various places in Europe, accusations of ritual murder, and a variety of other acts of persecution found chroniclers in their turn. Even today, whenever Jewish history is mentioned, it is this memory of suffering that is cited first; having become the common denominator of a people in dispersion, it creates an identity for secularized Jews and, at the same time, cohesion in exile. Of course, such utilization of the memory of suffering often stands in the way of a proper understanding of history, which makes it harder to maintain the appropriate distance between history and emotion, history and memory. Often, all that Jews – but also, following their lead, non-Jews – retain of Jewish history is this discourse on suffering, because the real or imagined

---

4   Yosef Hayim Yerushalmi, *Zakhor: Jewish History and Jewish Memory*, Seattle: University of Washington Press, 1996, 64–6.

5   Elias Tcherikower, 'Jewish Martyrology and Jewish Historiography', *Yivo Annual of Jewish Social Science*, 1, 1946, 9–23.

memory of suffering has long served in history's stead, and continues to do so today.

How, then, was this memory with medieval roots constructed? Since the genocide, it has haunted us more than ever, tending to dictate an interpretation of the past as nothing but suffering, while closing off the present and future from the kind of hope that was once nourished by faith: a hope that is fragile, yet was, only yesterday, omnipresent in Jewish life.

LIFE IN THE SHADOW OF MARTYRDOM

For those who saw every historical period as a new link in an interminable chain of suffering, the Crusades had the status of the first link.[6] From this point of view, the 1096 events and those that followed constituted the eternal foundation of the story of suffering. Their impact was unforgettable, both because they taught the Jews that one learns amid affliction, and also because they prepared them to accomplish their supreme duty, the sanctification of the Name of God.[7]

Throughout spring 1096, bands of Crusaders heading eastward left Western Europe. The devastating attacks that they carried out on their way decimated a number of big Jewish communities in Germany. Given the scope of the attacks to which Jews were subjected and the martyrology to which they gave rise – the basis for a new type of Jewish hero, the martyr who chooses death in order to avoid apostasy – the 1096 events have been described in detail. These descriptions focus on the most outrageous of the acts committed.[8] Martyrdom, consequently, became an emblem of the Ashkenazi world. Both before and after 1096, the torments that Mainz and other Rhineland communities inflicted on themselves remain acts without equivalent elsewhere.

Yet biblical law condemned homicide, and the sages of the Talmud, faithful to the Pentateuch's affirmation of the fundamental value of life, had put suicide among those acts falling under this prohibition. That the Judeans heroically committed suicide when Masada fell to the Romans in 73 or 74 (as is attested by recent archaeological discoveries) suggests the opposite, it is true. The Rhineland Jews, however, knew nothing of these suicides, because knowledge of the Matzada episode was available only in Greek: *Wars of the Jews*, by

---

6 Tcherikower, 'Jewish Martyrology', 14.

7 David Myers, '"*Mehabevin et ha-tsarot*": Crusade Memories and Modern Jewish Martyrologies', *Jewish History*, 13:2, 1999, 59.

8 Robert Chazan, 'The First Crusade as Reflected in the Earliest Hebrew Narrative', *Viator*, 29, 1998, 25.

the Roman historian and Jewish military leader Flavius Josephus, was not read by Jews in the original version until the sixteenth century. Josephus's account was partially known from the tenth century on, thanks to a Hebrew translation–adaptation, the *Sefer Yosipon*. In this version, however, the besieged Jews do not commit suicide but fight until the last man falls. Another collective suicide took place in Jotapata in 70, after the failure of the Judean revolt against the Romans (Josephus escaped it by a ruse, surrendering to the Roman Emperor Vespasian and gaining a reputation as a traitor). This suicide however is presented in the *Sefer Yosipon* as contrary to the teachings of Judaism.

The ideology of the Zealots of Matzada was, it should be added, at least partially based on that of the priests of the Temple of Jerusalem. Several ancient Jewish sources report episodes in which priests killed themselves when the Sanctuary was destroyed.[9] Josephus goes so far as to treat this suicide as a priestly obligation, but attributes the idea to Vespasian himself rather than a Jewish authority. It does not follow that priestly circles did not cherish an ideal of freely chosen death, one capable of sustaining an ideology of resistance to Rome. That said, we have to distinguish between martyrdom as voluntary acceptance of death and as suicide or homicide. While dying in the Name of God is, in certain circumstances, a commandment, rabbinical literature hardly encourages or calls for suicide, let alone ritual homicide.

Thus, when the martyrs of Mainz engaged in this ritual, they were not honouring an ancient ideal that had fallen into disuse. Their act was spontaneous. It is, moreover, reasonable to assume that there was a relation between the call to die for one's faith, an ideal of voluntary suffering that proceeded from the *imitatio Christi* and had roots in the early Church, and the new configuration of Jewish martyrdom in the period of the Crusades, which put freely chosen suffering and death back on the agenda. The Hebrew chronicles of the First Crusade associate martyrdom with a heavenly reward and, for the first time, offer a clear picture of the world awaiting martyrs. Yet the Talmud and Midrash repeatedly signal their reticence to posit a relationship between martyrdom and reward. Thus the choice made by the Rhineland martyrs inaugurates a new attitude in Jewish history. It establishes, in the Ashkenazi imagination, a kind of ideal norm for the response to catastrophe, one that would persist for the next 800 years, even when these suicides found no imitators in actual practice.[10]

---

9 *TB Taanit* 29a, *Avot de-Rabbi Natan* B, 7.

10 David Goodblatt, 'Suicide in the Sanctuary: Traditions on Priestly Martyrdom', *Journal of Jewish Studies*, 46:1–2, 1995, 10–29; A. Mintz, *Hurban*, pp. 88–89; Shmuel

The chronicles produced after the events are the source for the little we know about these tragic episodes. Only five have come down to us; others may have been lost. On the First Crusade, we have, for Mainz, the chronicles of Eliezer bar Nathan and Salomon bar Samson, as well as that of the chronicler known as the Anonymous of Mainz; all are presumed to date from the twelfth century. We also have at our disposal, for the Second Crusade the chronicle of Ephraim, the son of Jacob of Bonn, and, for the period just before the Third, that of Juda of Worms. These accounts were known in manuscript form in the Middle Ages and utilized by later Jewish chroniclers.[11] They are not eyewitness accounts and their logic is that of survivors, not martyrs. It is assumed that they were written on the basis of material provided by Jewish observers in the besieged cities, and on reports depicting the barbarity of the attackers, probably circulating in the form of community letters. They reflect the difficult situation of Ashkenazi Judaism between the two Crusades as well as fears of new unrest. Although they stand in the tradition of the discourse on the sacrifices of martyrs, they nevertheless tend to rationalize the choice of those who renounced their religion to save their life.

Like their Christian contemporaries, the Jewish chroniclers approach the 1096 conflict as if it were a holy war. While the Crusaders were fighting to capture the earthly Jerusalem, the Jews of the Rhine valley were creating, with their acts of sacrifice for the sanctification of the Name of God, a spiritual Jerusalem in the midst of their communities. Mainz is in effect compared to the Holy City, while the fall of Mainz is likened to the destruction of the Second Temple. As for the martyrdom of the Mainz Jews and, albeit it to a lesser extent, other communities as well, it is taken to correspond to reconstruction of the Sanctuary. It is not impossible that the sacralization of Mainz was the inspiration for the martyrs who, identifying with the priests of the Temple, chose to die. Indeed, they did not stop there: they also killed the other members of their family, like the Zealots at Matzada.

The Jews described in these chronicles practised Judaism scrupulously. They did not differ greatly from the Christian monks and nuns who cherished such opportunities as they were given to sacrifice themselves, or from the Crusaders who believed that dying in battle against the Infidels would gain them immediate entry to heaven. The Anonymous of Mainz shows that martyrdom was also the ideal of the Crusaders who expected that their

---

Shepkaru, 'From after Death to Afterlife: Martyrdom and its Recompense', *AJS Review*, 24:1, 1999, 42.

11   Tcherikower, 'Jewish Martyrology', 14.

enterprise would bring them spiritual rewards. Martyrdom was at the heart of the appeal to which they responded: it ensured them a reward in the heavenly Jerusalem. The ideal that inclined the Jews toward martyrdom when they were attacked by the Crusaders was thus quite similar to the one that inspired their foes, whose objective was to subjugate or destroy the Infidels. The Jews had to choose between conversion or death. The context in which the confrontation unfolded was plainly, for all concerned, that of a holy war. Moreover, just as women held a prominent place in the Christian martyrology of the day, so the Jewish chroniclers too underscore the role women played during these persecutions. In the authors' imagination, men and women alike were cast in the role of the male priests of the Temple. Their accounts repeatedly evoke the doubts of the survivors, whose weakness does not compare with the martyrs' heroism. Without a doubt, these chronicles point to what the Jews had in common with their Christian contemporaries.[12]

The accent in them lies, first of all, on the armed resistance put up by the Jews, who opt for suicide only after going down in defeat. It is courage in the positive sense that impels them to kill themselves with their own hands; they act out of devotion to their faith, not in despair. Fathers slay their wives and children, then sacrifice themselves rather than be baptized. The sacrifices described here are modelled on Isaac's sacrifice at Mount Moriah, both the paradigm for, and leitmotif of, these chronicles.[13] For the survivors, this web of allusions not only forges a link in the chain binding them to the founding Covenant of Judaism, but also confers meaning on their suffering of the moment. They have suffered and continue to suffer because they are Jews.

Moreover, the elegies and penitential prayers that supplement the stories of persecution during the Crusades do not mention sin as a cause of the tragedy. The martyrs are supposed to have died pure and to have offered their children spontaneously. That the Jews of Mainz turned their arms on their enemies is not mentioned – they are described as having freely accepted death without resisting, as Isaac did.[14] This writing of suffering is legitimate and helps to bring the community together. It would fulfil a similar function among Protestants at the beginning of the wars of religion. Martyrdom provided the

---

12   Jeremy Cohen, 'The Hebrew Crusade Chronicles in their Christian Cultural Context', in Alfred Haverkamp, ed., *Juden und Christen zur Zeit der Kreuzzüge*, Sigmaringen: Jan Thorbecke Verlag, 1999, 17–34; Ivan Marcus, 'From Politics to Martyrdom. Shifting Paradigms in the Hebrew Narratives of 1096 Crusade Riots', *Prooftexts*, 2:1, 1982, 40–52; Chazan, 'The First Crusade', 35–8.

13   Yerushalmi, *Zakhor*, 53.

14   Trepp, 'Toward a "*Slihah*" ', 346.

new Reformed Church with a frame of reference, legitimating it through sacrificial suffering.[15]

Fear of damnation and the conviction that true devotion is rewarded with eternal bliss explain these acts of sacrifice. How else was it possible to justify the calamities that befell these pious, irreproachable Jews, whose sufferings could not be construed as simple chastisement? If left unexplained, such suffering would seem intolerable and could lead to an undermining or violation of religious precept that might culminate in abjuration in extreme cases. The question as to how God could allow such atrocities to happen haunted the mind of the period. The traditional discourse about sin followed by chastisement is not entirely absent from the writings of these chroniclers, which do indeed tend to inculcate later generations with that concern, but they provide an explanation different from the one usually proffered by those attempting to understand the meaning of catastrophe. Ultimately, it is Abraham's sacrifice which reveals the solution to the mystery. Those who voluntarily sacrifice themselves prove even more audacious than the founders of Judaism, because they go even further than Abraham. The answer lies here. Far from abandoning his people, God has once again put it to the test, as he tested the patriarch. As for his people, it has once again fulfilled his hopes and expectations. The consolation lies here. The chroniclers, as survivors, assuaged pain and doubt by trying out a response to the weighty questions posed by the First Crusade. In so doing, they salvaged elements out of which Jewish lives that had been smashed might be rebuilt.[16]

At another level, paradise offered a great deal more pleasure and serenity than did the tormented earthly existence of medieval Jews; the martyrs who dwelt in paradise enjoyed both the divine feast and eternal Sabbath rest. The chronicles teem with such idealized images of the theocentric world to come, images that must have been quite attractive for those who wished to make a voluntary sacrifice of their lives. Sacrifice was the path leading to God and brought the greatest possible benefit for the martyr, who was rewarded for his absolute selflessness. The new situation prevailing in the Latin West, together with veneration for martyrdom and the felicitous rewards it brought, combined to flesh out the notion of paradise for both Christians and Ashkenazi Jews. Messianic expectations entered into the atmosphere of the period, and the Jews were in all probability affected by the exalted mood then prevailing.

---

15   On the Protestants, see David El Kenz, 'L'homme de douleur protestant, au temps des guerres de religion', *Médievales*, 27, 1994, 59–66.

16   Robert Chazan, 'The Hebrew First Crusade Chronicles', *Revue des études juives*, 133:1–2, 1974, 235–54.

Such expectations became more acute among Jews after the Crusades, with the appearance of calculations announcing the end of the world in 1102.[17]

The notion of martyrdom that emerged in the late twentieth century in extremist Muslim Palestinian organizations such as Hamas, and also in Hezbollah and loose groupings such as Al-Qaida—a notion for which the idea of a reward in a mythologized paradise is an integral part—is not altogether unlike the one that prevailed in the Middle Ages, in a Western environment this time. In the Palestinians' case, the bliss that is the expected reward for sacrifice serves to palliate the despair spawned by the situation on the ground. However, while the pairing of martyrdom and reward operates in particular historical situations that are often situations of despair, the mechanism established in the Middle Ages, at least as far as the Jews were concerned, was distinguished by the fact that the exalted sacrifice was first of all that of the person of the martyr and his immediate entourage. Modern martyrs, for their part, kill others as well as themselves in the name of their faith. Without indulging in simplistic comparisons, the other point to underscore here is that the Middle Ages witnessed the appearance of female martyrs, in the ranks of both the Crusaders and the Jews who fell victim to their attacks. The same may be observed among contemporary Muslim martyrs. These few reminders should suffice to refute the idea, often heard today, that certain contemporary phenomena are utterly unprecedented or else typically Muslim. Flight to a more merciful afterworld remains a temptation in extreme situations, whenever the strength of a faith is still capable of sustaining that hope.

The coupling of martyrdom and recompense continued to mark the writings of French and German Jews after the First Crusade. The popularity of martyrological images soared after 1096, becoming a major feature of Ashkenazi literature and faith. Even today, Ashkenazi notions of heavenly reward come to mind whenever martyrdom is evoked.[18]

A poetry of martyrdom developed hand-in-hand with the chronicles. Beginning in the latter half of the twelfth century, this poetry gave formal expression to the ideal of Jewish resistance to persecution and the blandishments of conversion. It also reflected community values and an ideal of social order inspired by contemporary non-Jewish models. This demonstrates yet again that, despite an often sharply hostile environment, Jews did not live in isolation

---

17 Haym Soloveitchik, 'Halakhah, Hermeneutics, and Martyrdom in Medieval Ashkenaz', part 2, *The Jewish Quarterly Review*, 94:2, 2004, 285.

18 Shepkaru, 'From after Death', 43–4.

from their Christian neighbours. What is more, notwithstanding the ideal of martyrdom that this poetry held up, it by no means justifies the affirmation that Jewish life of the day was limited to suffering and persecution. While some Jews were indeed persecuted, or converted to Christianity under duress, others were the architects of a Jewish cultural renaissance in harmony with developments in the institutional, intellectual, and social context of the Christian Europe of which Jews formed a part.

Jewish martyrological literature was a response to contemporary ideas, attitudes, beliefs, and modes of representation. Historians have a tendency to read martyrological prose and, to a lesser extent, poetry as if they were archival documents, forgetting that even the realism that sometimes marks them is one stylistic form among others. Again, the large part that this literature gives to married and pregnant female martyrs bears witness to the existence of a feminine ideal that contrasts with the Christians' holy virgins and female martyrs. The artistic effects that poets and prose writers deployed did not mean that they were inventing the events whose dramatic aspects they depicted. These writers simply highlighted certain aspects rather than others in order to transmit the message they wished to communicate. Martyrological poetry not only exalted the memory of the dead; it also provided models for the collective identity of the living. The idealized figure of the martyr possessed virtues that gave the Jews a reason to live as Jews in spite of the surrounding pressure, even at the moment when dying as a Jew was the sole remaining option. Martyrdom was thus a destiny of last resort.[19]

In their turn, the German–Jewish Pietists (*Hasidei Ashkenaz*) of the twelfth and thirteenth centuries were perfect incarnations of a life lived in the shadow of martyrdom and of a popular education the ultimate objective of which was the sanctification of the Name of God, the supreme trial that it is sometimes given to man to attain. Sanctification of the Name of God is the absolute negation of the sublunary world, of material reality in its totality, and of the human in man – of all his feelings and desires. It incites us to renounce all the temptations of this world in order to devote ourselves unreservedly to the truth of the next, and to God, who created man so that he might put him to the test. The experience of the sanctification of the Name of God led thinkers to an awareness of the fact that it is not the hour of martyrdom alone which constitutes a test, but every moment of life, since each instant provides the occasion for martyrdom on a small scale. The death of the martyr is merely the highest form

---

19 On martyrological poetry, see esp. Susan Einbinder, *Beautiful Death: Jewish Poetry and Martyrdom in Medieval France*, Princeton: Princeton University Press, 2002.

of a negation experienced and acquired day-by-day in resistance to the desire for food, pleasure, and the exploitation of nature for the purpose of procuring comfort for human beings. Thus sin is linked to pleasure and the religious life to suffering. The repentant man's suffering is accordingly proportionate to the pleasure he has taken in sin. To suffer like a martyr is thus equivalent to, in God's view, martyrdom itself. This is an aspiration common to profoundly religious people, whether Jews or Christians, Catholics or Protestants. The German–Jewish Pietists, like, for that matter, other Pietists as well, were always cognizant that to die for God was easier than to live for him. They too were far from realizing martyrdom in the literal sense. 'Spiritual martyrdom', the recurrent sacrifice of one's basic instincts for the love of God, held a much bigger place in Jewish thought than martyrdom in the correct sense of the word.

The reference to martyrology nonetheless enduringly shaped the realities and cultural, social, and anthropological conceptions of Ashkenazi Judaism in the Middle Ages. The behaviour of the Rhineland communities during the persecutions that accompanied the Crusades was laid down as an obligatory cultural norm. It would long remain engraved in people's memories as an archetype of suffering, providing the raw material of a story of suffering periodically revived by other events; these events were read, every time, along the lines furnished by past experiences, coming together as a whole wherein suffering took primacy over history.

It is not impossible that the ideal of voluntary martyrdom crystallized in the mid-thirteenth century in response to the aggressive conversion campaign launched by the Church and the French and English thrones, as well as the degradation of the condition of European Jewry in Northern and Western Europe.[20] The persecutions associated with the Crusades of 1147 and 1187 and the anti-Jewish riots brought on by the Black Death of 1348–9, which the Jews were accused of causing, were perceived as occasions to bear witness to the unity of the Name of God in martyrdom. Even if nothing comparable to the episodes of 1096 occurred, the symbol continued to serve as an intellectual yardstick.

Both scholarly and popular literature seized on the subject. At the popular level, the martyrs of antiquity and those of more recent periods spawned a profusion of marvellous tales and legends that left a profound mark on

---

20 Yossef Dan, 'Issues Regarding the Sanctification of God's Name in the Pietistic Movement of Ashkenaz', in *Holy War and Martyrology in the History of Israel and the History of the Nations*, Jerusalem: Israeli Historical Society, 1968, 128–9 (in Hebrew); Soloveitchik, '*Halakhah*, Hermeneutics', part 1, 101; part 2, 292–7.

Ashkenazi culture.[21] These narratives, in their turn, helped to sustain the memory of suffering.

Although the chronicles of the Crusades did not circulate for long in manuscript form and never became part of the liturgy, the events they described were incorporated into the liturgical calendar in another way. A new prayer, *Av ha-rahamim* ('Father of mercy'), was composed in memory of the martyrs. It was initially recited in the communities of southern Germany on the Sabbath before the Feast of the Weeks, on the anniversary of the First Crusade, and also on 9 *Av*. In the Ashkenazi rite, it became an integral part of the Saturday morning service. The prayer focuses on the merits of martyrs who have died to sanctify the Name of God. It cites various verses of Scripture, drawn, notably, from Deuteronomy and the Psalms; on the same occasion, God is asked to remember the martyrs, to avenge them and preserve their posterity. This liturgization of martyrdom, which forges a tie between the biblical past and the present, between yesterday's catastrophes and today's, opens onto a future, even as it transmits, from generation to generation, a story of suffering which, paradoxically, prevents suffering from overwhelming the group. Thus framed and ritualized, this domesticated suffering forestalls the kind of subversion that suffering, if left uncontrolled, might incite, with results that would go beyond the limits of religion.

With the generations that came after the Crusades, the ceremony of remembrance of the dead began to be celebrated not only for the martyrs, but also for all those who had died a natural death unrelated to the persecutions. It was, moreover, the duty of the son of a man or woman who had died to recite an Aramean doxology, the *Kaddish* in order to save his parent's soul from torment in the next world. The *Kaddish* alludes to resurrection, not to death or mourning. Even in such moments of grief, the future is not in mourning; only the present. From the fifteenth century on, this prayer began to be recited on the anniversary of the death of the deceased person (*Yortsayt*), so that he might attain immortality and peace. It was, again, the Ashkenazi tradition which produced a commemorative liturgy, the *Yizkor*,[22] recited four times a year after the reading of the Torah: during the morning service on the last day of the pilgrimage festivals (Easter, the Feast of Weeks, and the Feast of Tabernacles), and on the Day of the Great Pardon. It is marked essentially by the recitation of

---

21   Mintz, *Hurban*, 100.

22   *Yizkor*, literally, 'May [God] remember', is the first word of the prayer recited on this occasion.

the prayer *El male rahamim*.[23] *Yizkor* expresses the fervent hope that the souls of the dead will enjoy eternal life in the presence of God. It eventually became one of the most popular prayers among Ashkenazim. On the days of *Yizkor*, synagogues tend to be very well attended by both men and women.

The Sephardim of Italy and the East have an equivalent prayer, the *Hashkavah* (prayer for the repose of the dead). Every male Jew called to the Torah recites it in memory of the deceased members of his family. This prayer, which opens with the recitation of verses from the Psalms and Proverbs, ends with words of consolation: 'May he (or she) and all the children of Israel who are sleeping peacefully in the dust be included in his indulgence and pardon. May that be his will, and we shall say amen.' The Sephardim sought to bring solace to the living with this prayer, recited on holidays, Saturdays, Mondays and Thursdays, and also at the graves of the deceased. Here, too, we have an intimacy with death and grief framed by a ritual that helps the living from feeling overwhelmed. This was obviously only possible in a space delimited by a system of hierarchized beliefs (even if those beliefs changed over time) that no longer exists for most of our contemporaries, Jewish or not, who now have to make their way in a disenchanted, very individualistic world.

Despite the secularization and acculturation of the modern world, the mourning rites and rites of the *Kaddish* are the only ones to have constantly followed the Jews in their wanderings; they remain fairly tenacious even today. It is easy to imagine how the cult of the martyrs and the practices connected with death in general served to reinforce the story of suffering over the centuries and to preserve the always fragile unity of the community in diaspora. For centuries, this story (*histoire*) of suffering stood in for History (*Histoire*) in the proper sense of the term. It was far more compelling than History for a religious group whose vision of the world was closed to any form of historicism. Thus the history of the Jewish people was long limited to a religious narrative of persecutions and martyrdom. The oral and written discourse of suffering played the role of a historical narrative.[24]

In this connection, it is highly instructive to observe how the cult of the dead that resurfaced with the establishment (two decades after the event) of the obligation to commemorate the genocide has revived ancient customs, even among secularized Jewish communities. The commemorative service for the repose of the dead now includes prayers for the six million Jews murdered during the Second World War, as well as for those who have laid down their

---

23 Literally, 'God full of mercy'.
24 On historical–religious narrative, see Tcherikower, 'Jewish Martyrology'.

lives for the state of Israel. The current practice of reading out the names of genocide victims recalls the reading, on Saturdays and during special commemorative services, of the names of those martyred during the Crusades, which were recorded in the 'memory books' of many Germanic and Eastern European communities. Let us also note the special days of commemoration in memory of Holocaust victims in which non-religious Jews find it easier to participate: for example, *Yom Ha-Shoah*, the day of remembrance of the genocide, which is celebrated in Israel and the Diaspora in accordance with a ritual reminiscent of the traditional practices associated with the cult of the dead. Some communities also celebrate a special service in memory of the martyrs of the 1943 Warsaw ghetto uprising against the Nazis. In Israel, *Yom Ha-Zikaron*, the day of remembrance, is dedicated to the memory of those who have fallen in defence of the state.

These cults of the dead, which took their inception in the world of the Ashkenazim, were, with variants, eventually generalized to the whole of the Jewish world. Nevertheless, when the Ashkenazim made the sanctification of the Name of God into a question of life and death and Jews began to exalt and commemorate the apotheosis of self-sacrifice with poems, prayers, and memorial rites, a model for the response to persecution was established. It had little tolerance for apostasy, in contrast to developments in the Sephardic world, in which conversion was often presented as a viable option.[25] This difference in attitude would, over time, shape two distinct responses to suffering. The rhetoric of suffering, extremely rich among the Ashkenazim in this period, in a context of European intolerance and intensive 're-Christianization', comprised not only an expression of suffering, but also a kind of remedy for it. At the same time, it promised to weld together a Jewry that was threatening to disintegrate in the face of an increasingly radical Christianity.

The fact remains that martyrs, given the immensity of their act, thanks to which they attain sainthood, defy ordinary religious norms, those that recommend studying the Torah and fulfilling the commandments above all else. There is transgression even in the martyrs' desire to identify with the priests in the Temple by making a sacrifice of their lives and those of their loved ones, or by constructing, by means of martyrdom, the Temple of Jerusalem anew in Mainz. Yet a comparable transgression of institutional religion surfaced in the behaviour of the ordinary people who joined the Crusades. Their acts, too, went beyond what was actually authorized and recommended. Indeed, during the anti-Jewish persecutions that accompanied the Crusades,

---

25   Roskies, *The Literature of Destruction*, 89.

the Church did not fail to intervene in order to contain the explosion of popular hatred in the name of humane values and, above all, for the sake of preserving law and order. In the case of the Jews, the liturgization of martyrdom also made it possible to control the transgressions that might have been brought on by the transformation of martyrdom into a religious symbol.

While the Jewish martyr dispenses with intermediaries when he gives his life to God, the remembrance of the act of martyrdom is mediated by prayer, offered up on precise dates in the restricted space represented by the place of worship and in the presence of the community of the faithful. Thanks to this process, martyrdom ceases to be an individual case of transgression committed in the name of faith; it is a mediating instance between the community and God. It thereby strengthens the sense of belonging to this community. The symbolic value of the act of martyrdom tempers it, curbing the martyrological frenzy that might otherwise be sparked by this individualized religiosity, in which the martyr communicates directly with the King of heaven, making short shrift of classical mediations.

The discourse on suffering was the driving force behind this symboliza-tion. Staging suffering, discourse helped to transcend it. Ultimately, it became not just an expression of suffering, but also a remedy for it. It consoled people more than it made them suffer.[26] And it was amplified over the centuries in which the Jews were beset by misfortune upon misfortune. But this by no means signifies that Jewish life in the Middle Ages was nothing but a series of persecutions. That is far from the truth.

THE HISTORY OF THE JEWS: A HISTORY OF UNRELIEVED
MISFORTUNE?

Even if the Jews suffered from prohibitions and contempt, they formed rela-tively privileged minorities in the places where they were tolerated. Jews were regarded as one corporation among others, whose status was established by a combination of legal decrees and customs dating from time immemorial and maintained by medieval traditionalism. The ruptures that occurred did so in very precise contexts. The Jews were in fact beholden to their de facto alliance with the existing authorities. In times of change, this inevitably left them in a vulnerable position, earmarking them as the prey of whatever forces were in the ascendant. They paid kings high taxes in exchange for protection and exercised

---

26 Piroska Zombory-Nagy, 'Les larmes du Christ dans l'exégèse médiévale', *Médiévales*, 27, 1994, 37–49.

such professions as tax collector or administrative councillor; thus they were associated with established authority. During popular uprisings, they were the rebels' natural targets. Scapegoats for accumulated resentments and frustrations, they served as a sort of safety valve in the societies of the day.

The attacks on Jews that occurred during the Crusades, or again during the 1391 riots in Seville that took on the character of pogroms, were not organized by the monarchies. Nor can we put everything down to religious fanaticism, despite the rising in tensions during the re-Christianization of Europe. Notwithstanding all that separated Jews and Christians, there existed a unity of principle which transformed all these conflicts into wars not between foreign nations but between brothers. Moreover, Church censorship rarely interfered with the autonomous development of Jewish culture. Again, the Jews were not only victims, and not every act of violence exercised against them counts as a case of persecution. In the same period, other groups suffered as much as they did. Finally, the history of the Jews was not a passive history, and the history of Jewish offensives and bravura does not start with Zionism.[27]

In antiquity, the Maccabees were not distinguished by the humaneness of their methods of warfare. The recurrent Jewish revolts against the Romans were punctuated by bloodbaths. As for the unrest in Alexandria at the beginning of the Christian era, it involved a series of conflicts between Jews and other social groups, not anti-Jewish persecution in the strict sense. Certain contemporary historians describe various bloody riots as the result of persecutions aimed specifically and directly at Jews, but this was not always the case. Similarly, in the Middle Ages the Jews may have suffered more than others because they were perceived as an affluent social stratum. They were also easier targets because, unlike other groups of merchants, as a result of their condition and also because they did not own land, their wealth primarily took the form of gold and their property was easy to transport. Disturbances and crises were the common lot of the majority in the period. Sometimes the Jews became the sole victims of this unrest by chance, not for racial or religious reasons. And while repression ultimately led to the disappearance of the Albigensians, this fate was spared the Jews, who continued to enjoy protection both because they were economically useful and because they were considered witnesses to Christ's truth. The Church did not seek their destruction. Quite the contrary: the continued existence of these faithful guardians of the Book in which the word of God had been written down was proof the Christian faith was true. Thus

---

27   David Biale, *Power and Powerlessness in Jewish History*, New York: Schocken, 1986.

economic and religious factors militated in favour of the Jews, despite the onerous prohibitions imposed on them. They were, moreover, not the only ones to be persecuted by the authorities.

The Lombards, (Italian financiers) were subjected to similar treatment. Philip the Fair, King of France and with a government needing large amounts of money, confiscated both the Jews' and the Lombards' property and forced the Knights Templar to issue him loans. He expelled the Jews in 1306, but he also expelled the Lombards in 1311 in order to acquire funds for his treasury. Allowed back into France and then re-arrested, the Lombards were subjected to the same humiliating treatment as the Jews in the French kingdom. The Jews did suffer massacre and expulsion with the Black Death of 1348–9, thanks to the popular influence of the Flagellants, a group of penitents of apocalyptic inspiration who whetted the anger of the poor against the Jews by accusing them of poisoning wells and spreading disease. They were also accused of ritual murder; but let us not forget that the Gypsies, for their part, were long accused of cannibalism.

At all events, the condition of the Jews was for a long time preferable to that of the serfs, if only because they enjoyed relative mobility from having the right to pass from one lord to another. They were not, it may be added, the only minority in the Middle Ages. In the Christian countries, Muslims, like Jews, had to wear insignia distinguishing them from the dominant majority, as did Christians in Muslim countries, who were subject to similar treatment and various restrictions. The most acute form of persecution of the Jews in Christian lands never took on systematic character. It is certain that they suffered from intermittent popular rioting; however, thanks to the 'royal alliance', and despite the fragility of that alliance, they were also protected by the secular authorities. Even the Church protected them, although it professed anti-Judaism because the Jews did not acknowledge Christ's divine nature or the fact that he was the Messiah. It extended this protection to them even while affirming that they should remain inferior, representing both punishment for their blindness and a sign of the authenticity of Christ's message.

By the same token, the oft-mentioned 'ghettos' of the Middle Ages were initially neighbourhoods in which Jews willingly lived together with small numbers of Christians. It was only much later that restrictive legislation transformed these neighbourhoods into segregated areas whose inhabitants were separated from the rest of the population. The autonomy that Jews enjoyed in these ghettos made it possible for them to survive as a 'distinct nationality'. Furthermore, it is a mistake to believe that Jews had no economic or cultural contact with Christians and lived in isolation and extreme poverty, subject to constant harassment. In the centuries preceding emancipation, the demo-graphic growth of Jewish communities exceeded that of the Christian population. Because they were not required to perform military service, a few exceptions aside, and thanks to their neutrality, they were not decimated the way the Christians were during the wars of religion that ravaged Europe up to the eighteenth century. Jews were not as poor as other groups, due to the struc-tures of mutual aid that they put in place; thus their poverty was less severe than that of the peasants. As for the Inquisition, it did not directly persecute the Jews *stricto sensu*, except in the sense that it censured Hebrew books. The Inquisition targeted crypto-Jews and Christians attracted by Judaism. The exceptions to this rule were Jews accused of attacking Christianity or proselytizing among Christians. Jews as such, even if they were considered heretics, were beyond the Inquisition's purview. Moors and Protestants were among the categories in which it took an interest, but its activities were aimed primarily at apostates and renegades.

Some contemporary historians, such as Salo W. Baron, Cecil Roth, and, to a lesser extent, Ismar Schorch, have attempted to restore a less tragic vision of the Jews' fate in the Middle Ages. In the process, they have departed from a historiographical current that, to put it summarily, was in the ascendant from the eighteenth century on, after Jews gained citizenship. This current sought to credit the age of emancipation with every positive achievement, while damning everything that preceded it. This 'lachrymose' approach to history was to prevail again after the genocide: the entire Jewish past was now cast as a vale of tears with, at the end of it, the Final Solution. The resulting story of suffering has never ceased to haunt our present. From this point, every attempt to under-stand the past was to set out from the experience of anti-Semitism and the extremes in which it culminated.[28]

Of course, in the medieval Jews' own descriptions of the violence they endured, such violence takes on inordinate proportions. These accounts should be treated with caution and understood as responses to violence

---

28   On all these interpretations of the period before emancipation, and against the lachrymose reading of history, see esp Salo Baron, 'Ghetto and Emancipation: Shall We Revise the Traditional View?', *Menorah Journal*, 14:6, 1928, 515–26; Cecil Roth, 'The Most Persecuted People?', *Menorah Journal* 20:2, 1932, 136–47; Roth, 'European Jewry in the Dark Ages: A Revised Picture', *Hebrew Union Annual*, 23, part 2, 1950–1951, pp. 151–169; Ismar Schorsch, 'The Lachrymose Conception of Jewish History', in Schorsch, ed., *From Text to Context: The Turn to History in Modern Judaism*, Hanover: Brandeis University Press/University Press of New England, 1994, 376–88. See also Esther Benbassa, *Histoire des Juifs de France*, 3rd edn, Paris: Seuil-Point Histoire, 2004, chaps. 2–3.

designed to stabilize the group. In the aggregate, their effect is to underscore the Jews' constancy in the face of their suffering at times of insecurity, when Jews needed consolation and support in order to remain Jewish in the face of intermittent waves of attacks inspired by religious fanaticism. Vulnerable to 'national' and 'religious' disintegration during the expulsions, the group had to struggle to maintain its existence and cohesion. This type of reaction allowed the Jews to resist acts of aggression as a community bound by shared interests – if not political, then, at least, religious.

The discourse of suffering that was put in place beginning with the First Crusade and developed in different registers – literary, liturgical and, later, historiographical – highlights only the violence endured by the Jews of the Middle Ages. It does not tell us what constituted the specificity of medieval Judaism and says nothing of the contributions it made to the civilization of the period. Yet the Christian world generously cited the views of Moses Maimonides and other medieval Jewish teachers and thinkers. The Spaniard Ibn Gabirol was able to produce a philosophical œuvre, Fons Vitae, which was long mistakenly believed to have been the work of a Christian or Muslim. The rhetoric and the story of suffering elaborated in it tend to reduce the Jew of the Middle Ages to an eternal victim, a passive creature subject to the caprices of the secular authorities and the will of God.

Curiously, this Jewish perception of Jews as victims has by no means disappeared, although Zionism has taken it upon itself to efface it by creating a triumphant Jew who has taken his destiny into his own hands. A new Jew was supposed to emerge: the Israeli. Even today, in a period of tension in Israel, the 'Jewish victim' overdetermines the image Israeli Jews seek to project. The dominant idea is that everyone bears a grudge against Jews, although Israel in fact risks virtually nothing from its neighbours given its military supremacy; if the summer 2006 Lebanese war somewhat altered this situation, it did not end it. The figure of the Israeli as anti-Palestinian aggressor is attenuated by that of the Jew as victim: they form an inseparable couple that not only shapes the image transmitted to the outside world, but has also become part of the self-perception of the Israelis as well as Diasporic Jews observing both the Israelis and themselves. Since the creation of the Israeli state, Israeli political discourse has itself been grounded, from one end to the other, in this relationship to self and Other that turns on the ideas of the victim and the hero.[29] The traditional story of suffering and the lachrymose history that prolongs it, written as modern historiography was emerging in the Jewish world, created

---

29   Biale, Power; Biale, Pouvoir et violence dans l'histoire juive, Paris: L'Éclat, 2005.

the conditions in which a Jewish memory of victimhood could be put on lasting foundations.

While Jews were indeed victims of the circumstances of the day in certain historical periods, they were not eternally so, as the remembrance of suffering would suggest. In general, their heroism is reduced to a religious heroism that blots out, at the imaginary level, all their attempts to defend themselves. Jewish heroes are bequeathed to posterity in the guise of victims supposed to have sacrificed their lives for their faith in order to perpetuate Judaism. The liturgization of the Jews' humiliations and martyrdom, which, ultimately, had a profound impact on the behaviour of the Ashkenazi communities, reinforced their self-perception as victims. The lack of an authentic written history played a primordial role, century after century, in memory's usurpation of the story of suffering in the Jewish imagination. For as long as elegies and penitential prayers did duty as historical sources, one can readily understand why, with the legitimacy that their religious character conferred on them, they contributed powerfully to producing a memory based on the exaltation of suffering.

The 1648–9 massacres in Poland and Ukraine that followed the Cossack rebellion led by Bogdan Chmielnicki stand as some of the best illustrations of this usurpation. Although what was involved was a political reality affecting both Polish Christians and the Jewish population, the event was transformed into a Jewish story of suffering *par excellence*.

These massacres are regarded as the greatest disaster to have befallen the Ashkenazi world prior to the modern period. They left an enduring mark on people's minds in the geographical region concerned. The transmission of the memory of this disaster to posterity proceeded in line with the model of Ashkenazi piety and religious heroism. This episode of the story of suffering is linked to that of earlier tragedies: the Jews of the present were supposed to have suffered just as the Jews of the past did. It is clearly the religious project which guides the story of suffering. Contrary to what goes on in secular history, this articulation underscores the inevitability of suffering. In this framework, the aim is less to give a rational account of the event than to exhibit a tragic destiny.

Nathan Hannover's chronicle *Yeven Metzulah* ('deep mud', sometimes translated as 'abyss of despair') published in Venice in 1653, is a key document that respects the canons of the classical chronicles of the Crusades in recounting the event,[30] which was in fact a revolt motivated by political and economic

---

30   Nathan Hannover, *Abyss of Despair: The Famous Seventeenth-Century Chronicle Depicting Jewish Life in Russia and Poland during the Chmielnicki Massacres of 1648–1649*, trans. Abraham Mesch, New Brunswick NJ: Transaction Books, 1983.

factors. Bogdan Chmielnicki, with the help of the Ukrainian peasantry, hoped to put an end to the big Polish landowners' control over Ukraine.[31] The Jews, whom the Poles had brought with them to administer their fiefs, became targets of the attacks. The Cossacks slaughtered indiscriminately as many Jews and Catholics as possible. Their goal was neither to convert the Jews to Christianity nor to convert the Catholics to Orthodoxy. Hannover and other Hebrew chroniclers nevertheless present the conversion of the Jews as the rebels' main objective. Their accounts assimilate the events they relate to a model of the past familiar to every Jew; they take the revolt as an opportunity to show how, in the face of this ordeal, the Jews remained faithful to their religion, like their ancestors, preferring to die as Jews rather than live as Christians.[32] The material from which Hannover took his inspiration in describing the situation in Tulczyn in 1648 was drawn from three contemporary Hebrew chronicles published before his own.[33] Sometimes he copies their contents; sometimes he paraphrases them; in other cases, he incorporates events that occurred elsewhere into his account of Tulczyn. Readers of these chronicles were not so interested in the historical narrative than in the story of the massacres and the accompanying martyrology. What emerges from a reading of them is a tale about the annihilation of Jews by perverse Gentiles. All Chmielnicki's Jewish victims are assimilated into the Ashkenazis' ideal of martyrdom.

In this particular case, however, there is no evidence that the Jews had to choose between conversion or death, even if some did abjure their faith in panicked belief that they could escape torture or execution. Some succeeded in fleeing to Poland, where they continued to live as Jews, while others spent the rest of their lives in the Orthodox fold. There must have been enough of these

---

31   After the eighteenth-century Mongol invasion, the Poles gained control of most Ukrainian territory, with the exception of the united principalities of Galicia–Volhynia, shared by Poland and Lithuania: the 1386 union of these two countries brought much of the future Ukraine into the Polish–Lithuanian state. Many Ukrainians, because of the difficult position of the peasantry and the persecution of the Orthodox in the Catholic Polish–Lithuanian state, went into exile in lands on the other side of the Lower Dnieper river. Here they formed the independent group of Cossacks of Zaparog who, under Bogdan Chmielnicki's lead, rose up against Poland in 1648.

32   Edward Fram, 'Creating a Tale of Martyrdom in Tulczyn, 1648', in Elisheva Carlebach, John Efron, and David Myers, eds, *Jewish History and Jewish Memory: Essays in Honor of Hayim Yerushalmi*, Hanover and London: Brandeis University Press, 1998, 89–103.

33   *Tsok ha-itim* ('The misery of the times') by Meir Ben Samuel de Szczebrzeszyn, published in Cracow in 1650; *Megilat Eifah* ('The scroll of terror') by Shabtai Ben Meir Katz, published in Amsterdam in 1651; followed by penitential prayers and elegies, *Petah Teshuvah* ('The gate of repentance') by Gabriel Shusburg, published in 1651 in Amsterdam. See Fram, 'Creating a Tale', 90.

conversions to convince the King of Poland, Jan Kazimierz, to declare in May 1649 that the converts could return to the religion of their ancestors. Yet Hannover and the other Hebrew chroniclers, like the authors of the elegies composed for the occasion, first wanted to show how faithful the Jews had been to the religion of their fathers, preferring to die rather than embrace Christianity.

As is well known, Maimonides considered it a waste of time to study history. Later, a major codifier of rabbinical law, Joseph Caro, the author of *Shulchan Aruch* ('Set table'), prohibited the reading of history not only on the Sabbath, but on weekdays as well.[34] Yosef Hayim Yerushalmi's *Zakhor* abundantly illustrates with numerous examples how little the Jewish world was interested in history, in our sense, for many centuries. The gap between historical reality and the chroniclers' narratives offers a new, interesting illustration of this. It made it possible for the discourse of suffering to maintain its grip on Jewish memory for a long time.

Hannover structured his account of collective martyrdom in Tulczyn by combining stories related by others with Jewish martyrological motifs. Few Jews in Poland and elsewhere had had an opportunity to find out what really happened, but all were familiar with the ancient, edifying example of Jews who had died rather than commit religious treason. The Jews who had been wiped out in Tulczyn, together with Jews from other Polish and Lithuanian communities, were promoted from victims to martyrs. Jewish sources claim that 100,000 people perished during the events and that 300 communities were destroyed. Once again, the victims of this catastrophe are said not to have died in vain, but, rather, to strengthen the Judaism of future generations; they had accepted death like the Jewish martyrs of times past, for the sake of their faith and in order to serve the Almighty. Here, too, it is impossible not to notice the consoling effect of this rhetoric of suffering amid total despair. By the force of their example, the martyrs made possible reconstruction after destruction and the perpetuation of Judaism in Poland and elsewhere.

Hannover's chronicle concludes by paying homage to the Jewish community of Poland, said to possess the six 'pillars' mentioned in the *Tractate of the Fathers*:[35] the Torah, worship of God, charity, justice, truth, and peace. This idealization echoes classical rabbinical literature's idealization of Jewish society before the destruction of the Temple in Jerusalem and also the eulogies of the liturgical poets, which evoke the piety and love of the Torah of the Jews from

---

34   See Tcherikower, 'Jewish Martyrology', 11.
35   *Avot*, one of the treatises in the *Mishnah*, see *Avot* 1, 2 and 18.

the Rhine valley. Thus the circle is closed and the genealogical lineage of the suffering Jews is re-established and traced all the way back to the Bible. This chronicle was extremely popular: it was translated into many different languages, and it was decreed that it should be read between 17 *Tamuz* and 9 *Av*, that is, between the anniversary of the day the first breaches were made in the walls of Jerusalem by its Babylonian and later Roman assailants, and the anniversary of the destruction of the two Temples. The liturgization of this discourse of suffering introduced order and stability into the chaos resulting from the historical situation by cancelling the disruptive force of the catastrophe and inserting it, as one more link, in the long chain of Jewish tribulations. The chronicle had its practical uses as well, since it compiled the dates of the various massacres, making it easier for the survivors to commemorate the anniversary of the death of their loved ones. Did it come into more regular use for this reason, becoming indispensable to the present generation and those that followed?[36]

Let us add that, beginning in 1650, on a decision of the Council of the Four Countries,[37] the Cossack revolt and its repercussions were marked by a day of fasting, to be observed on the twentieth day of Sivan. Penitential prayers composed to narrate the massacres were chanted on this day, together with older prayers, notably those written after the martyrdom of Blois in the twelfth century. This fast to commemorate the events of 1648 was still being observed in Eastern Europe on the eve of the Second World War.[38]

It should be noted, by way of conclusion, that the writing of suffering succeeded in, thanks to its translation into Yiddish, finding new readers among the Ashkenazim and, thus, gained a wider distribution. Chronicles such as those described above and, later, other writings of a more historical cast, originally produced in regions of Sephardic culture, made their way deep into the lands of the Ashkenazim, reinforcing the already well-established story of pain and suffering. Yiddish literature was enriched with historical elegies on the disasters and persecutions endured by Jews, but also by liturgical poetry—lamentations on the death of the martyrs—which transmitted to posterity the details of the circumstances that wrought havoc in Jewish society. This

36 On this chronicle, see Hannover, *Abyss of Despair;* Fram, 'Creating a Tale'; Tcherikower, 'Jewish Martyrology', 20; Roskies, *The Literature of Destruction,* 108–9; Mintz, *Hurban,* 102–4.

37 The Council of the Four Countries, created in the sixteenth century, was a centralized leadership body that surveyed Jewish activities in Greater and Lesser Poland, and also in the provinces of Lemberg and Volhynia.

38 Yerushalmi, *Zakhor,* 65–6.

vernacular literature of religious inspiration helped to carry the story of suffering from generation to generation. In the eighteenth century, it led the dean of Lithuanian Jewish culture, Gaon de Vilna, to declare: 'the Torah is acquired only in pain'. To be Jewish, one must suffer.[39]

HEROISM OR MESSIANISM: CHOOSING THE LESSER EVIL

Sephardic Judaism, established in the Muslim countries, also produced a liturgization of suffering. It too depicted the calamities that had befallen Jews. An elegy by Abraham Ibn Ezra, for example, which evokes the twelfth-century Almohadic persecutions, describes how the Jewish communities of Spain and the Muslim West were destroyed, and depicts the suffering that they endured. In many cases, the Jews are said to have been forced to choose between death or apostasy. *The Book of Tradition* (*Sefer Ha-Kabalah*) by the Spaniard Abraham Ibn Daoud, a historical work completed in 1161, likewise written after the event, also evokes the ordeals the Jews were subjected to under the Almohadic yoke.

In the same period, the family of the famous philosopher Maimonides left Cordoba and went to Fez, the Holy Land, and then to Egypt. Nowhere in Maimonides's writings do we find an apology for martyrdom of the sort that appeared among the Ashkenazim with the Crusades or the Cossack revolt. Martyrdom is in no sense elevated into a model of piety. Maimonides's father, Maimon ben Joseph, wrote a *Letter of Consolation* to comfort the Jews who had converted to Islam and continued to live as Muslims in public, while secretly practising Judaism.[40] In his letter he took issue with the idea of embracing martyrdom to avoid forced conversion. To be sure, in the world of the Ashkenazim no less than among the Sephardim, martyrdom as such was not encouraged, but the Ashkenazim nevertheless put a high value on it, whereas in the Sephardic world, while it could be envisaged as a solution *in extremis*, it did not have the same symbolic role.

Maimonides, does not call either the principle or the value of the sanctification of the Name of God into question. He clearly regards it as a crucially important commandment, the reward for which is considerable. In his *Letter on Persecution*, he nonetheless defends a non-heroic position with regard to the Almohades and the conversions that they tried to obtain by force. When an

---

39   Tcherikower, 'Jewish Martyrology', 23.
40   Gérard Nahon, *Métropoles et périphéries séfarades d'Occident*, Paris: Cerf, 1993, 58–70.

oppressor seeks to bring someone to abjure his faith, one owes it to oneself to examine the matter: 'If it is a time of persecution he is to surrender his life and not transgress, whether in private or in public, but if it is not, he should choose to transgress and not die if it is in private, and to die if it is in public'.[41] Maimonides, however, adds:

> But if anyone comes to ask me whether to surrender his life or acknowledge [the apostleship of Muhammad], I tell him to confess and not choose death. However, he should not continue to live in the domain of that ruler ... When our rabbis ruled that a person is to surrender himself to death and not transgress, it does not seem likely that they had in mind speech that did not involve action ... What I counsel myself, and what I should like to suggest to all my friends and everyone that consults me, is to leave these places and go to where he can practice religion and fulfil the Law without compulsion or fear. Let him leave his family and his home and all he has, because the divine Law that He bequeathed to us is more valuable than the ephemeral, worthless incidentals that the intellectuals scorn; they are transient, whereas the fear of God is eternal.[42]

Thus Maimonides draws a distinction between speech and act, between what one does in public and in private. The essential thing is to save one's life in order to fulfil the Law; from this point of view, it is preferable to contemplate exile rather than opt for self-sacrifice pure and simple. This Sephardic discourse, as articulated by the philosopher from Andalusia, comforts its readers and relieves them of their guilt. It is, first and foremost, pragmatic and encouraging. It announces that the persecutions may end. Indeed, Maimonides, in his Epistle, cites this verse from Jeremiah: 'In those days, and in that time, saith the Lord, the iniquity of Israel shall be sought for, and there shall be none; and the sins of Judah, and they shall not be found: for I will pardon them whom I reserve'.[43] By the end of the world, sin will have disappeared, even that of the converted.

Three centuries later, however, the banishment of the Jews from Spain, Sicily, and Sardinia, the forced conversion of all the Jews of Portugal, the expulsion from Navarre, Provence and the Kingdom of Naples precipitated a massive trauma, comparable, at the subjective level, to that of the

---

41 Moses Maimonides, 'The Epistle in Martyrdom', in *Epistles of Maimonides: Crisis and Leadership*, trans. Abraham Halkin, Philadelphia: Jewish Publication Society, 1993, 25.

42 Maimonides, 'The Epistle in Martyrdom', 30–1.

43 Maimonides, 'The Epistle in Martyrdom', 43; Jr 50:20.

Holocaust.[44] The Sephardic world, uprooted and shaken to its foundations, tried to formulate a response to this new challenge. It was deeply imbued with messianism.

In areas of Ashkenazi culture, the discourse on suffering was produced and the story of suffering written in order to assimilate the ordeals undergone by the Jews to models that offered support and religious 'stability' in an environment in which faith could easily waver. Hope lay in the repetition of the responses to affliction, martyrdom among them. However alien these responses may seem to us, they served to counter, at the very least, the survivors' despair. Doubtless they did not express the full intensity of all the suffering that people actually endured. But neither suffering nor despair can be measured. That, precisely, is the reason that we can never be anything more than spectators of the Other's suffering. Yet later generations lent an ear to this suffering and attempted to understand it with the instruments at their disposal.

In the Sephardic world, in a different, yet equally complex way, the messianic hope that found expression in the discourse on suffering by no means ruled out a real sense of despair. Quite the contrary: it found an ally in such despair. The deeper the despair born of exile, the better suited messianic hope was to offering the afflicted comfort. Exile was, certainly, an existential condition shared by Ashkenazim and Sephardim alike. The question remains, however, as to whether the Sephardim did not consider their departure from the Iberian peninsula to be a veritable *new* exile, whereas, for the Ashkenazim, the lands in which they lived were places of persecution that *already* corresponded to the exile evoked in biblical texts.

Traditionally, exile was presented as, above all, punishment and expiation for Israel's offences against God. The sanction consisted in a distorted relationship to the land where the people resided (deportation), to other nations (powerlessness and servitude), and to itself (dispersion). This situation, perceived as unnatural and temporary, was made bearable only by the biblical promise of a return. Redemption, defined as the restoration of the relationship between God and Israel, would come about by way of the return of the people of Israel to their land, the restoration of their political autonomy, and the 'gathering up of the exiles'.[45] After the destruction of the First Temple, the Prophets had confidently assured the exiles that their situation would not last forever.

---

44   Yosef Hayim Yerushalmi, 'Un champ à Ananoth: vers une histoire de l'espoir juif', in J. Halpérin and G. Lévitte, eds, *Mémoire et Histoire*, 97.

45   See, for example, Dt 30:3–5: 'That then the Lord thy God will turn thy captivity, and have compassion upon thee, and will return and gather thee from all the nations,

Hope in the future is omnipresent in the Bible. Isaiah and Jeremiah prophesy the arrival of a king, descended from the House of David, whose reign will be a happy one. However, in the First Temple period, Judaism was not yet a messianic religion in the proper sense, and the term *mashiah* (messiah) did not yet have the connotation that it would later acquire via its association with the end of the world. Messianism conveys an idea of restoration and, at the same time, utopia. The Book of Isaiah depicts the messianic era in double perspective, as both catastrophe and utopia. Final deliverance means the end of the exile, a gathering together of the scattered tribes in the Holy Land, and restoration of Israel's political sovereignty under the rule of a descendant of David's. But it also means the establishment of a universal peace, made possible by the nation's adhesion to the religion of the one God. Some saw the messianic era as the sudden irruption of the supernatural on the scene of history and the end of history. For others, in contrast, it does not imply a radical transformation of that sort, but is just the restoration of an ancient, idealized historical situation, the Davidian monarchy.

Messianic speculation runs like a red thread through the whole of the Middle Ages. Thus neither expulsion from Spain nor forced conversion in Portugal gave rise to an entirely new wave of messianism. Messianic and apocalyptic movements emerged in various forms among both Jews and Christians after the fall of Constantinople in 1453. From the 1460s on, messianic rumours spread throughout the ranks of the New Christians in Spain when letters circulating in Valencia predicted that the end of the world was at hand and announced that the Messiah had been born and was living on a mountaintop near Constantinople. This news sparked acts of repentance. Thus 70 families of converts left for Valona, Albania with the intention of returning to Judaism. The Ottoman Empire welcomed Jewish immigrants well before the expulsion from Spain. The contrast between a Christendom rejecting its Jews and an Ottoman Empire welcoming them with open arms lent the Empire a special aura in the view of Jews in general. Thus a woman in Valencia declared that the Turk was the Antichrist: he destroyed churches but protected Jews and their synagogues. A phenomenon of the same kind would be observed again in the

---

whither the Lord thy God hath scattered thee. If any of thine be driven out unto the outmost parts of heaven, from thence will the Lord thy God gather thee, and from thence will he fetch thee: And the Lord thy God will bring thee into the land which thy fathers possessed, and thou shalt possess it; and he will do thee good, and multiply thee above thy fathers.'

sixteenth century among New Christians in Portugal, where the Iberian tragedy gave fresh impetus to messianic movements.[46]

Despite various warnings in the Talmud condemning prognosticators and admonishing people to be patient,[47] Jewish sages were, on the one hand, regularly tempted to calculate the date of the end of the world on the basis of sophisticated, endlessly repeated exegeses of certain scriptural texts, and, on the other, to wonder whether it was not possible to find ways of hastening the end. Thus calculations that purported to determine the precise date on which the Messiah would arrive were made on the basis of the numerical value of words and passages in the Bible. They were encouraged by the fact that, in traditional Jewish literature, the advent of the messianic era, which was supposed to be heralded by the return of the prophet Elijah,[48] was associated with diverse cataclysms, wars, revolutions, and scourges. Sometimes the anticipated dates of the redemption of the world coincided with major upheavals or persecutions, such as the 1096 Crusade, the years of the Black Death in Europe preceding the expulsion of the Spanish Jews, or the massacres of Polish and Ukrainian Jews perpetrated by the Cossacks in 1648.

Regions where Ashkenazi culture prevailed were of course not unaffected by messianic expectations, but such expectations had particularly deep impacts on the chronicles, stories, and meditations that made up the Sephardic literature of suffering. The tenor and tone of Ashkenazi and Sephardic discourse about suffering were shaped by different historical experiences. The exile of the Sephardim came to resemble a peregrination. Their approach to it was informed by their memory of the happy period they had spent on the Iberian peninsula and its hours of glory under both Muslims and Christians, episodic unrest notwithstanding. In the lands in which they had newly settled, the myth of their past grandeur on the Peninsula, a harbinger of better days to come, helped them to recover from long periods of depression.

In the sixteenth century, Sephardic discourse on suffering quite naturally turned toward historical-eschatological speculation, as in Isaac Abravanel's messianic three-act play depicting God's revenge on the Christians and Muslims, the return of the ten lost tribes, and, finally, the resurrection of the dead.[49] The process of redemption was supposed to begin in 1503 or 1531,

---

46   Yosef Hayim Yerushalmi, *A Jewish Classic in the Portuguese Language*, Lisbon: Calouste Gulbenkian Foundation, 1989, 24, 29–31.

47   See, for example, *TB Sanhedrin* 97b.

48   In line with the promise made in Ml 3, 23.

49   See the texts from Abravanel's messianic trilogy in Jean-Christophe Attias, ed. and trans., *Isaac Abravanel. La Mémoire et l'espérance*, Paris: Cerf, 1992.

according to complex calculations based on an interpretation of certain biblical verses. Let us recall that Abravanel, who imagines that God was conducting history toward an absolute, cataclysmic end, was the treasurer of the kings of Spain at the time of the events that led to the expulsion, with the result that his career was unexpectedly brought to an end.

Abravanel's mission, as he defined it, was to bring 'his people [out] of the valley of Akhor in order to lead it to the door of Hope' ('the valley of Akhor' was the 'valley of misfortune'). The calamity of the moment constituted, for Abravanel, an invitation to reflect on past calamities and blaze a path toward a hopeful future. His writing accordingly took on a prophetic cast. Amid trials and tribulations, he teased out a memory of hope which he based on inter-woven interpretations of the messianic biblical texts and the historical events he was witnessing. Abravanel evoked biblical episodes that had strong symbolic value in the Jewish memory of the past, such as the Exodus from Egypt, the first, paradigmatic experience of exile; the destruction of the First Temple, which coincided with the loss of independence, and the resulting exile; and the story of Esther, a tale of persecution and rescue in exile. While he regarded the expulsion from Spain as a calamity that had befallen the Jewish people in the situation of vulnerability represented by exile, he was also capable of prophecying liberation, a prophecy authorized by the analogy between the expulsion and the exodus from Egypt. Abravanel dates the expulsion from Spain to 9 *Av*, the anniversary of the destruction of the Temples, although the last Jew actually left Spain on 31 July, that is, 7 *Av*. Here we see how he brings out a continuity that has consoling power by situating the vicissitudes of his day in the liturgical framework in which tradition had put the major catastrophes.

Spain and the expulsion are identified with the land of Israel and the destruction of the Temple, while Abravanel himself is transformed into a new Ezekiel, a prophet of exile. Thus one is, as in the story of Esther, encouraged to look for a surprise happy ending. The purpose of Abravanel's messianic trilogy is to revive the Jewish people's memory of its hope. If liberation resembles the exodus from Egypt, the messianic period will resemble that of Moses, David, and Solomon; as for the Messiah, he will combine the traits of Solomon, David, and Ezechias. In glossing Isaiah (11–12), Abravanel also paints a portrait of the Messiah and describes his reign, which he situates in an ahistorical future representing a return to the time before sin came into the world – that is, the beginning of Creation.[50] Creation follows destruction: thus light is born after

---

50 Roskies, *The Literature of Destruction*, 91, and especially Attias, *Isaac Abravanel*, Introduction (p. 33 for the citation).

darkness, in a cyclical vision that is part of a divine scenario which repeats itself while history continues to unfold in linear fashion. The Judeo-Spanish language spoken by these exiles from the Iberian Peninsula preserves, let us note in passing, a trace of this vision in the proverb '*tanto eskurese es para amaneser*': 'the night is never blacker than just before dawn'.

Given the conditions just outlined, it is not surprising that the Sephardic world was the theatre of an interminable welling up of messianic feeling in the decades following the expulsion, with the emergence of a number of redemptive figures such as David Reuveni and Salomon Molcho in the sixteenth century. Reuveni, who died in 1538, was a curious sort who claimed to represent the ten lost tribes. He arrived in Portugal in 1525, where the largest group of Marranos was to be found; these Jews, who had been converted to Christianity by force in 1497, yet continued to define themselves as members of the Jewish people and to adhere to its rites, practices, and belief systems, regarded Reuveni as a herald of the end of the world. Molcho, a Portuguese crypto-Jew whose real name was Diego Pires, succeeded in leaving Portugal, converted back to Judaism under the name of Salomon Molcho, and eventually proclaimed himself the Messiah. The Reuveni and Molcho episodes show how extensive the messianic ferment was among Portugal's crypto-Jews: it was an integral part of the spirituality of the New Christians.

This messianic activism is revelatory of the aspirations and expectations of an entire group who had undergone a traumatic change in a still recent past. The fever was at its worst in the eighteenth century, when Sabbatism developed in the Ottoman Empire, the land where the Jews expelled from Spain had settled. They too had been traumatized by an experience of exile whose painful effects had persisted, despite the high self-esteem that they had succeeded in preserving when they arrived, distinguished as they were by a stratum of creative intellectuals proud of their heritage and talents. Under the impact of exile, the past associated with the Iberian Peninsula was endlessly glorified and mythologized. Judeo-Spanish identity was now rooted in this past, a collective historical experience and a set of shared sorrows: this was the end result of the process that tore these exiles from a land that they considered to be theirs, in line with a myth that traced their presence in Spain back to the destruction of the First Temple in 586 BC. They sought to recreate this 'paradise lost' and find a meaning in their tribulations by preserving their customs and traditions in their adoptive land. While they had made sacrifices in order to remain Jews, they were also under a sacred obligation to transmit a Spanishness that was inseparable from their Jewishness.

The problem of transmission appears in all its acuity when we examine the experience of these expelled Jews over several generations. All were haunted by the question of posterity. Exile had literally destroyed family structures, separated couples, and cost many parents their children. The vicissitudes of the voyage had aggravated the situation by causing the death of loved ones—children, husbands or wives. Forced conversions, illness, kidnappings, and exhaustion had shattered the family unit. Some Jews had remained in the Peninsula, preferring to convert than leave.[51] As a result, many Iberian Jews arrived in the Empire alone, without a family to help them confront the new reality. In these late Middle Ages, when Jews were still attached to their faith and the notion of the individual did not exist in the sense in which we know it, the break-up of families meant, above all, a break in the continuity of the lineage and increased doubts over the very survival of the Jewish people.

In such a universe, the expulsion from Spain would remain, for many, an originary trauma constitutive of the Jewish experience in the East. Both exile and personal misfortune demanded explanation, and the tradition was not at a loss to provide answers to catastrophe. In the sixteenth century, rabbis such as Joseph Yaavets or Moses Almosnino interpreted the expulsion as chastisement for Israel's sins and the means that God had chosen to put it back on the straight and narrow. Although they were now in a Muslim land, these Sephardim remained deeply preoccupied with Christianity and the misfortunes that they had suffered at its hands. Christianity was the great tyrant and the main enemy. It is here, no doubt, that we must look for the source of the messianic fervour that seems to have run through the whole of the sixteenth century. An event as important as the expulsion from Spain was clearly of a nature to reawaken the exiles' messianic expectations, as is attested by the theology of authors such as Isaac Abravanel.

While it is difficult, today, to gauge the intensity of these Jews' suffering, since time has all but assigned to oblivion an event that profoundly marked whole generations (as the Second World War genocide continues to do today), we can derive some idea of their pain from the mass of sorrowful writings filled with expectation and hope for a consolation that was slow in coming. The cataclysm that had struck the Jews was associated with the extraordinary spectacle of the rise of the Ottoman Empire, a Muslim power capable of dealing Christianity one staggering blow after the next on the field of battle. To an Elijah Capsali, who observed this confrontation from Crete, or a Joseph Ha-Cohen,

---

51   Joseph Hacker, 'Superbe et désespoir: l'existence sociale et spirituelle des Juifs ibériques dans l'Empire ottoman', *Revue historique*, 578, 1991, 261–93.

writing a history of the kings of France and the Ottoman sultans in Italy, the end of the world seemed to be drawing nigh. In this context of agitated expectation, individuals such as Reuveni and Molcho could come to the fore and channel a subterranean messianic fervour of considerable intensity, hatching fantastic plans to bring about geopolitical readjustments and the conversion of the Pope. Similarly, Jacob Berav could try to revive the ordination of rabbis in the Holy Land in anticipation of the re-establishment of the Grand Sanhedrin that would announce the coming of the Messiah. All these upheavals, or projected upheavals, made up, to some degree, for God's silence in the face of unbearable suffering.

Is it an accident that as late as the seventeenth century, in Western Europe this time, in the new big Jewish metropolis of Amsterdam, home to a population of former Marranos who had returned to Judaism, Menasseh ben Israel, himself a crypto-Jew from Madera, entitled one of his works *The Hope of Israel*? In it, he describes the discovery in Latin America of the ten lost tribes: this is one of his messianic themes, inasmuch as these ten lost tribes are destined to come together in the Holy Land when the time of final deliverance arrives. Ben Israel's text, full of messianic themes bolstered by references to Jeremiah, Daniel, and Ezekiel, points to the 'times that are drawing nigh'. The text, as its title indicates, transmits a message of hope. 'The argument, which we bring from our constancy under so many evils, cannot be eluded, that therefore God reserves us for better things,' Ben Israel writes, a century and a half after the expulsion and more than half a century after the Portuguese Jews' massive conversion to Catholicism. In one and the same movement, *The Hope of Israel* attests the impact of messianism and the promise associated with it.[52]

I shall not go into the complex question of the relationship between the Kabbalah and messianism. For some, the new developments – especially the sixteenth-century Lurianic School, named after its leading thinker, Isaac Luria – resulted from an internalization of the themes of exile and suffering; they made it possible, the argument runs, to bring under a single, coherent explanatory scheme all the events that followed the expulsion, the effects of which continued to make themselves felt generation after generation. On this interpretation, the shock of the expulsion led to a renewal of Jewish mysticism and messianism, culminating in the Sabbatean explosion, which embraced not

---

52   Menasseh Ben Israel, *The Hope of Israel*, trans. Moses Wall, 1652, in Ben Israel, *The Hope of Israel: The English Translation by Moses Wall*, eds. Henry Méchouan and Gérard Nahon, Oxford: Oxford University Press, 1987, 151. See, for example, pp. 164 and 172–3.

only the Judaism of the Sephardim, but also that of seventeenth-century Eastern Europe.[53] Others put the accent on developments within the Kabbalah, downplaying the impact of the expulsion on the new esoteric tendencies.[54] The fact remains that the psychological and spiritual shock of the expulsion and the various forms of suffering that accompanied it continued to haunt the Sephardim for many generations; they were, if not the only factor, then at least one of the many factors that sustained, throughout the sixteenth and seventeenth centuries, a powerful mystic and messianic current with diverse origins.

The economic problems of the late sixteenth-century Ottoman Empire exacerbated the profound existential fragility of a stratum of learned men who had assimilated the trauma of the expulsion. The massacres perpetrated by Bogdan Chmielnicki in Poland and Ukraine, where thousands of Jews lost their lives between 1648–9, had a profound effect on the Sephardim of the Levant. With the influx of refugees into the Ottoman Empire, the horror of these massacres must have left a deep impression on a group that had itself experienced its founding tragedy. And there can be no doubt that certain forms of messianic ferment in Europe, Russia, and the Muslim countries converged to revive various eschatological expectations. All these factors conspired to create a receptivity to messianism, the full potential of which would be revealed only with the emergence of Sabbetai Zevi, born in Smyrna in 1626 and proclaimed Messiah by Nathan of Gaza in 1665.

Zevi created various new rites, publicly transgressed Jewish law, abolished fasting, declared that prohibited foods were authorized, and announced the onset of a new messianic age in which established truths would cease to apply. Messianic fervour affected not just the masses, but the rabbinical authorities as well. Endlessly embellished stories about Zevi's powers and the miracles he worked reached every corner of the Jewish world, while rabbis and 'lay people' became his followers, suspended their activities, and set about preparing for the Jewish people's return to the Holy Land, which was to bring the years of exile to an end. When this effervescence proved uncontrollable, the Ottoman authorities in 1666 gave Zevi a choice between conversion to Islam and death. He chose conversion. Here again, is a typical rejection of the heroism of martyrdom sharply at odds with the Ashkenazi model of fidelity to Judaism. As we have seen, Maimonides had already adopted this stance in his *Letter on*

---

53   Gershom Scholem, *Sabbatai Sevi: The Mystical Messiah, 1626–1676*, trans. R. J. Zwi Werblosky, Princeton NJ: Princeton University Press, 1976.
54   On this subject, see especially Moshe Idel's many works.

Persecution, written in exile to console those who had converted to Islam during the twelfth-century Almohadic persecutions.

In fact, few Jewish martyrologies are to be found in the Muslim world.[55] The different historical contexts and experiences of Jews in Christian and Muslim countries are not, by themselves, enough to explain the virtually total absence among the Sephardim of an oral or written discourse on martyrdom. To understand better this disparity in the Jewish responses to suffering, we must also take into account the diversity of the perceptions of Islam and Christianity in the Jewish world. It must, however, be added that the Sephardim also composed elegies and penitential prayers around painful episodes experienced at precise moments in history. These texts make up an integral part of their discourse on suffering, even if they do not comprise the most important strand in it. Thus there exist elegies on the 1391 persecutions, composed in the style considered appropriate for exercises of this sort. The social and economic crisis of the 1380s, the rise of the fiercely anti-Jewish polemicist Ferrant Martinez, who became archdeacon of Seville in 1390, the power vacuum caused by the death of John I, and the 1390 accession to the throne of a minor, Henry III, leading to a temporary break in the royal alliance between the king and the Jews on which the Jews' 'security' was based, were all factors contributing to the creation of a context favourable to the outbreak of serious violence. On 4 June 1391, the first massacres took place in Seville; violence then spread like wildfire throughout the Iberian Peninsula. Thousands of people were killed and hundreds of Jewish neighbourhoods were attacked and burned down. In the atmosphere of crisis and terror reigning in the period, many Jews converted, under duress or of their own free will.

Long afterwards, the Jewish communities remembered the persecutions as a stupefying experience that initiated the irreversible degradation of their situation in Christian Spain. When recounting the vicissitudes of their own times, poets referred to the anti-Jewish violence of 1391, thus creating a kind of continuity capable of accounting for the events unfolding in the present. An elegy written in 1391 served as a model for another relating the persecutions of 1412: it was enough to change the place names and historical information. Another 1391 elegy pronounces a benediction on martyrdom that takes its inspiration from the elegies and chronicles of the period of the Crusades. It was probably borrowed from the Ashkenazi legacy, along with other ideas and traditions

---

55   Yaakov Rothschild (exhibition curator), *The Sanctification of the Name of God over the Centuries. Literary Exhibition*, Jerusalem: Ministry of Education and Culture, Department of Religious Culture, National and University Library, 1968–9 (in Hebrew).

related to martyrdom: this shows that there were reciprocal influences and contacts between Ashkenazim and Sephardim, despite the specificities to which we have pointed. All these elegies were incorporated into the liturgy, appended to various prayers. They deplored the death of innocents, affirmed that God had not yet taken revenge on Israel's enemies, and invoked the souls of the dead, who remained silent. One of these elegies, inspired by Lamentations, is recited on the morning of the Sabbath preceding the fast of 9 Av[56] by the survivors, who protest their fate and weep for their people, then chant the prayer *Nishmat kol hay.*[57] Another elegy, known as the *Sabbath Shim'u,*[58] calls on the converted to renounce their sinful apostasy, so that God may show compassion and send the true Messiah. Thus these elegies review the history of the Spanish Jews' suffering, beginning with the attacks of 1391. Similarly, various liturgical poems take their inspiration from archetypal events, such as the destruction of the Temple, to evoke known misfortunes, simultaneously reaffirming faith that the future will bring salvation. This literature is saturated with spiritual anxiety: it betrays a fear of abandonment by God that reflects the increasing exclusion of the Jews in this period, the prelude to the expulsion.[59]

While there is no lack of interaction between the Sephardic and Ashkenazi discourses on suffering, and while the ultimate aim of both is to provide solace, the Sephardic elegies rarely allude to martyrdom and do not yet evince the powerful messianic expectations that would be expressed in the 'historiography' of suffering produced after the expulsion.

---

56   It is known as the *Eikhah* Sabbath because on this day the word *eikhah* ('how') is read three times, as it appears in Dt 1:12 ('So how can I cope by myself with the bitter burden that you are, and with your bickering?' [The word 'how' is dropped from the King James's Bible but retained in the *Complete Parallel Bible*, Oxford: Oxford University Press, 1996, 367]), Is 1:21 ('How the faithful city has become a whore! She that was full of justice, righteousness lodged in her – but now murderers!' [*Complete Parallel Bible*, p. 1472]) and Lm 1:1 ('How deserted she sits, the city once thronged with people!' [*Complete Parallel Bible*, p. 1793]).

57   Literally 'The soul of all that lives', in line with the first words in this prayer: 'The soul of all that lives will bless your name, O our eternal God ... we have no other saviour besides you ... who respond and perform acts of mercy in all periods of suffering and distress.'

58   The day on which Jr 2:4 is read: 'Hear ye the word of the Lord, O house of Jacob, and all the families of the house of Israel.'

59   On the elegies, see Wout van Bekkum, 'O Seville! Ah Castile! Spanish–Hebrew Dirges from the Fifteenth Century', in Nicholas de Lange, ed., *Hebrew Scholarship and the Medieval World*, Cambridge: Cambridge University Press, 2001, 156–70; Dan Pagis, 'Élégies sur les persécutions de 1391 en Espagne', *Tarbiz* 37:4, 1968, 355–73 (in Hebrew).

According to Yerushalmi, the rupture represented by the 1492 expulsion of the Jews from Spain gave rise to a form of writing that more closely resembled history in our sense of the word. 'In effect, the primary stimulus to the rise of Jewish historiography in the sixteenth century,' he writes in *Zakhor*, 'was the great catastrophe that had put an abrupt end to open Jewish life in the Iberian Peninsula at the end of the fifteenth century ... Thus, for the first time since antiquity we encounter a ramified Jewish historiographical response to a major historical event.'[60] The question, however, is whether these works in a historical register, despite the fact that they appeared well after the events they relate, were not interpreted by their readers as testimony about the suffering actually endured that would help to reinforce and perpetuate the memory of it.

With these texts we are dealing with a corpus that presents itself as the recitation of a story of suffering, in the same sense as the chronicles of the Crusades that antedated this corpus, or those of the persecutions carried out by Cossacks, which came after it. Furthermore, this corpus is rather reminiscent of elegies and penitential prayers of a more traditional cast. To be sure, the new narratives do not usually incorporate the liturgy, like the other components of the story of suffering. And, apart from certain features which make them resemble historical writing properly speaking, what interests us here is how they were perceived and utilized by Jews themselves. Might their Jewish readers not have regarded them from the standpoint of the continuity that made the Jewish people a suffering people that bore witness to its misfortunes, precisely, in this story of suffering?

The Vale of Tears, a chronicle by Joseph Ha-Cohen, is revelatory, if only by virtue of its title, of those aspects of the history of the Jews that would be remembered in centuries to come. Ha-Cohen, a descendant of exiles from Spain who had settled in Renaissance Italy, turned out the first version of his text in Voltaggio in 1558.[61] The writing of it was inseparable from the degradation of the Italian Jews' situation during the reign of Pope Paul IV, at the end of which Jews were burned at the stake in Ancona. The situation continued to worsen thereafter. In 1558, the crypto-Jews who had taken part in the boycott of Ancona were expelled from Pesaro; that Ha-Cohen produced his text the same

---

60   Yerushalmi, *Zakhor*, 58–9.

61   Joseph Ha-Cohen, *La Vallée des pleurs. Chronique des souffrances d'Israël depuis sa dispersion jusqu'à nos jours,* ed. Julien Sée, 2nd edn, Paris: Centre Abravanel, 1981 [1881].

year was no accident. *The Vale of Tears* is a chronicle of Israel's sufferings since the dispersion. An anonymous scholar known to posterity as the 'corrector' added an appendix to it to cover the misfortunes that befell the Jews from 1575 to 1605. The latter date is that of the complete edition.

Copies of this text long circulated in manuscript form, although it was not widely distributed. The Hebrew version of it did not see print, however, until 1852, in Venice, thanks to the efforts of a leading figure of the Jewish Enlightenment, Max Letteris. The text was subsequently to become an important source for the history of the sixteenth century. A German translation appeared in Leipzig in 1858. The credit for its French publication goes to Julien Sée. He published it in 1881, a date that is obviously not insignificant: 1881 saw the beginnings of the pogroms that followed the assassination of Czar Alexander II in Russia. In France, where the integration of the Jews was nearly complete, Edouard Drumont's *La France juive* would appear barely five years later. In Europe as a whole, the major texts of the history of Jewish suffering once again found favour with the reading public – Jewish history in the modern sense was coming into being.

Letteris, for his part, tells us that *The Vale of Tears* was read out in several different Italian communities on 9 *Av*, the day commemorating the destruction of the Temples, those killed as a result of persecutions, and, later, the expulsion from Spain (the decree announcing the expulsion was said to have gone into effect on this symbolic date). A verse contained in the original text clearly invited Jews to read it then: 'Every Jew should read it on the day the Temple was burned down.' In the same poem, the author asks 'What man is callous enough not to weep upon reading my book?' Yet this poem was not included in the translations of the text into European languages. One explanation for this lacuna is that it stemmed precisely from a desire to divest the book of its liturgical character, inasmuch as the primary reason for publishing it was to call attention to the Jewish people's suffering over the centuries while underscoring the fact that it had been delivered from it by emancipation and integration, deemed the end of this history (of suffering) in the secular sense of the term.

Although the author of *The Vale of Tears* evokes the post-biblical history of the Jewish people, his narrative, too, is governed by theological considerations. For he tells an edifying story about how God puts the Jews through ordeals that vary according to their conduct. There is nothing extraordinary about the way he proceeds, since the theme of the test or ordeal is at the heart of the traditional representation of Jewish history. Was Abraham himself not put through a series of ten ordeals, and did he not emerge victorious from all of them, thus demonstrating the greatness of his love of God? Bound up with the theme of the ordeal is the no less classic theme of 'suffering through love'. Ha-Cohen's work takes its title from a verse in Psalms: 'In crossing the vale of tears, they turn it into a country of springs, which, moreover, an early rain covers with blessings.'[62] For Ha-Cohen, crossing this 'vale of tears' brings consolation. The repetition of the catastrophes that befall the Jews attests the continuity of an epoch; they have to stand and wait for the end of it without wavering. For Ha-Cohen, the expression 'vale of tears' is another way of naming the exile and its tribulations. Thus he says, 'I have called this book "The Vale of Tears", for this title corresponds well to its contents: anyone who reads it will find himself short of breath, his eyes will overflow with tears and, with his hands behind his back, he will say: For how long still, O my God? I implore the Lord to put an end to the days of our grief and send us the Messiah of our salvation and, in his merciful grace, consent to deliver us soon. Amen, amen!'[63]

In the only book he published in his lifetime, *History of the Kings of France and the Ottoman Turkish Sultans* (1553), Ha-Cohen does not simply compare the history of France with that of the Ottomans or evoke the struggle between Christianity and Islam. The background to his narrative is inspired by a war mentioned in Ezekiel. The King of Magog, Gog, the leader of a coalition of the forces of evil, wages this war on the people of Israel, who have returned to their country.[64] Gog's defeat and Israel's survival lead the nations to acknowledge the suffering that Israel has endured as punishment for its transgressions. The terms used in the two chapters of Ezekiel in question, as well as the catastrophic, supernatural nature of the punishments inflicted on Israel's enemies, clearly put this prophecy in the apocalyptic genre. In subsequent literature, the war of Gog and Magog is a sign heralding the imminent coming of the Messiah. The grand military confrontations between nations, such as the struggle between Islam and Christianity, had raised hopes that the Messiah was indeed coming. Let us note that Ha-Cohen also tells the story of Salomon Molkho, who believed that he had been called by God to play a messianic role and was burned at the stake by the Inquisition in 1534. This narrative clearly takes its place among the author's messianic reflections.

In the introduction to *The Vale of Tears*, Ha-Cohen declares that one of the aims of his book is to describe the Jews' sufferings. He treats the history of the Jews as an unending series of persecutions. Indeed, *The Vale of Tears* made its

---

62 Ps 84:7, author's translation from the Hebrew.
63 Ha-Cohen, *La Vallée des pleurs*, 1–2.
64 Ez 38–39.

author the archetypal representative of the lachrymose vision of Jewish history. He was influenced here by narratives of the Crusades as quoted or excerpted in other sources (the originals had not yet been published in the sixteenth century).[65] *A Consolation for Israel's Tribulations*,[66] by Samuel Usque, a crypto-Jew who found refuge in Ferrara Italy after the expulsion, seems to have had an equally profound impact on *The Vale of Tears*.[67]

Usque's book, which was published in Ferrara in 1553, was inspired, in its turn, by the Book of Job, the only biblical text cast in the form of a dialogue. In Usque, three shepherds converse: Icabo, a version of the patriarch Jacob bewailing Israel's fate; Nuinco or Nahum, who takes the comforter's role; and Zicareo or Zechariah, who reminds us of the past, with its consoling promise of redemption. As Usque sees it, whenever the Jewish people is assailed by afflic-tion, it can find consolation by comparing the evils of the past with those of the present.

Usque recounts the misfortunes of the people of Israel because he is convinced that they will soon come to an end. He refers to the Bible in order to show that Israel's worst sin consists in letting itself be assimilated by the Gentile peoples, since assimilation leads to apostasy, idolatry, and marriage with non-Jews. As a result of this sin, Marranism included, the Jewish people has, he says, broken its Covenant with God and brought on the divine chastisement announced in Scripture. Its punishment reflects its sin: it has been reduced to servitude by the nations it sought to imitate. Usque, however, also attempts to show that God has bestowed his favour on the Jewish people despite its sins, at a time when all hope seemed lost. In this way, he urges the Marranos not to abandon hope. After the gloom of winter, the light will again appear, as has already happened in the East: at the peak of its glory, the Ottoman Empire opened its doors to the Jews, who were now free to practice their reli-gion there, and dispatched its armies to humiliate their oppressors. Europe was also growing weaker, according to Usque, as a result of internal strife. Christendom was being torn apart by wars between the different religious camps. Furthermore, Europe's central position in the world had been called into question by the discovery of new continents that were rich and promising. All this strengthens Usque's intuitive sense that the coming of the Messiah is

---

65   Joseph Ha-Cohen, *Sefer 'Emeq Ha-Bakha' (The Vale of Tears), with the Chronicle of the Anonymous Corrector*, ed. Karin Almbladh, Uppsala: Uppsala University Press, 1981, 16–31.

66   In Portuguese, *Consolação às tribulações de Israel*.

67   See Isidore Loeb, 'Joseph Haccohen et les Chroniqueurs juifs', *Revue des études juives*, 16, 1888, 28–56, 212–39; 17, 1888, 74–95, 247–71.

at hand. Thanks to its sins, the people of Israel has to make its way through a sea of suffering. But was the Messiah not supposed to be born amid pain and suffering?[68] Usque's book did not, however, find a large readership, probably because it fell into the Inquisition's clutches immediately after it was published.

In a chronicle known as *Elijah's Little Order*, (*Seder Eliyahu Zuta*) written in 1523, Elijah Capsali, a Cretan Jew of Byzantine extraction, is deeply influenced by the Spanish exiles who arrived on his island. The book is suffused with a messianic tone of biblical inspiration: the Ottoman Sultans are decked out with the features of Cyrus the Great, who restored the land of Israel to the Jews after the Babylonian captivity that followed the destruction of the First Temple in 586 BC. We read, in this chronicle: 'Thus it was that Sultan Bayazet, King of Turkey, heard of all the evils that the Spanish sovereign had inflicted on the Jews and learned that the Jews were seeking a refuge and a haven. He took pity on them, and wrote letters and dispatched messengers to make it known that, throughout his kingdom, none of his governors would dare to deny the Jews entry or expel them. They would, rather, be graciously received.'[69] The Ottomans doubtless offered a haven to the Sepharadim because they could be of use to a capital that had been abandoned by the Greeks after it was captured. Yet the apocryphal declaration attributed to Bayazet is revelatory, first and foremost, of the state of mind of the Jews of the day. It is also an expression of the Jews' great expectations after the terrible shock of the expulsion, which continued to fuel a subterranean messianic current already in existence on the Iberian peninsula. The story of suffering takes its place in this chronicle, against a background provided by words of support and consolation. Throughout it remains within the bounds of a theological framework familiar to the new exiles, who were now in deep disarray.

Ten important Jewish historical works were produced in the sixteenth century. Five of the eight authors were exiles or descendants of exiles from the Iberian Peninsula. Besides the Cretan Capsali, only two came from non-Sephardic communities (Mantua and Prague); one of these, David Gans of Prague, had assimilated the works of his Sephardic predecessors.[70] This corpus, which is historiographical in nature, represented one reaction to the

---

68   Samuel Usque, *Consolação às tribulações de Israel*, Lisbon, Calouste Gulbenkian Foundation, 1989 (1553 Ferrara edition), two vols.; see also Usque, *Consolation for the Tribulations of Israel*, trans. Martin Cohen, Philadelphia: JPS, 5725/1965, 18–29.

69   Elijah Capsali, *Seder Eliyahu Zuta*, eds. Meir Benayahu et al., Jerusalem: The Ben Zvi Institute, 1977, vol. 2, 218 (in Hebrew).

70   Yerushalmi, *Zakhor*, pp. 71–75.

suffering caused by the cataclysm of the expulsion. While some of these works have messianic accents as intense as the despair caused by the expulsion and its multiple consequences, sowing fears of abandonment by God and the attendant end of the Jewish people, a chronicler such as Salomon Ibn Verga considers the misfortunes and survival of the Jews dispassionately. Verga composed his *Sceptre of Judah* (*Shevet Yehudah*) first published posthumously in 1554 in Adrianople, Turkey, by his son, as an historical anthology; it is an early sociological study of the Jewish question. But although he seeks to identify natural causes for the expulsion related to human conditions in this world, he does not conceive of the story of suffering from a strictly secular standpoint.

Verga's panorama retraces the general history of Jewish woes as well as those directly linked to the expulsion; he concentrates, more precisely, on the period that followed the loss of Jewish independence, especially the Middle Ages. The Inquisition also takes its place in this unbroken chain of suffering endured by the people of Israel in exile. Verga opens his chronicle with a sombre account of persecutions, massacres, and mass conversions, taking his information from both Jewish and non-Jewish sources; however he dissipates the gloomy atmosphere thus created by engaging in lengthy considerations of their causes. Only one of these passages reflects the Jews' traditional attitude, explaining the suffering of the moment as punishment for sins long past.[71] 'Lord of the universe!' Verga writes at the end of his chronicle, 'although you have spared me no trial to make me abandon my religion, you should know that, defying the celestial host, I am a Jew and shall remain a Jew, and none of the ordeals that you have made me suffer, and none that you shall make me suffer in future, can help you fulfil your plan.'[72] This determined allegiance to the faith is itself a source of consolation; it enables Verga to find new strength in his own discourse and his resolution to remain Jewish. God's silence does not keep him from persevering in his Jewishness at all costs.

Verga's chronicle was translated into various European languages, including a Yiddish version that was published in Cracow in 1591 and adapted to meet the expectations of an Ashkenazi readership, which felt a need for instructive texts. This brings us to the Ashkenazim's and Sephardim's distinct ways of responding to catastrophe. In the Yiddish translation of *Sceptre of*

---

71   Salomon Ibn Verga, *Shevet Yehoudah*, ed. Azriel Shohat, Jerusalem: Mosad Bialik, 1946 or 1947 (in Hebrew); Abraham Neumann, '*Shebet Yehudah* and Sixteenth Century Historiography' in *Louis Ginzberg: Jubilee Volume on the Occasion of his Seventieth Birthday*, English section, New York: American Academy for Jewish Research, 1945, 253–73.

72   Cited in Yerushalmi, 'Un champ à Anathoth', 96.

Judah, the fall of Jerusalem and destruction of the temple are directly attributed to the Jews' sins, not, as in the Hebrew original, to their rebellion against Rome and the assassination of the Roman governor of Jerusalem. Ibn Verga's chronicle had to be fitted into the traditional explanatory schema, which made disaster divine punishment for Israel's sins. Similarly, an account by the author, found in the second chapter of the original, relates the mass conversion of 30,000 people – in the translation, the number becomes merely 'many Jews'. The 1146–7 conversion of Spanish Jews disappears as well and other conversions in other periods are also removed from the translation. There is no Marrano problem in it either: the Jews of Spain and Portugal are said to have suffered and died as holy martyrs, like their Ashkenazi brothers, preferring the sanctification of the Name of God to the temporal consolation of the baptismal font.[73] What actually transpired was quite the opposite! Thus the discourse on suffering and its therapeutic virtues does not belong to the same register in the Ashkenazi and Sephardic worlds. The Sephardic choice of life over death must also have had an influence on people's behaviour in the long run. At the same time, the Marranos who fell victim to the Inquisition were venerated as martyrs. Thus the sacrifice of Isaac had an important place in the Marrano imagination, in conjunction with mystic ideas.[74] These nuances are not unrelated to the distinct ways in which the story of suffering was interpreted in the Sephardic and, later, Ashkenazi worlds, in the period from modernity today.

Thus, both on the Peninsula and in exile, historiographic writing was one of the Jewish Iberian world's internal responses to its vicissitudes. These chronicles circulated from one community to the other. Others, partial or punctual, were composed on contemporary events; they were not intended as full-length works. Did productions of this sort, which were more frequent among the Sephardim—after the expulsion, at any rate—install the discourse on suffering in a different, more distanced, less emotional register, the more so in that it had rarely been incorporated into the liturgy in the Sephardic world, as it had been among the Ashkenazim?

When, in the nineteenth century, the modern history of the Jews began to emerge, this new form of writing integrated the Sephardic historiography

---

73   Michael Stanislawski, 'The Yiddish *Shevet Yehudah*: A Study of the "Ashkenization" of a Spanish–Jewish Classic', in E. Carlebach, J. M. Efron and D. N. Myers, eds, *Jewish History*, 134–49.

74   Cecil Roth, 'The Religion of the Marranos', *The Jewish Quarterly Review*, 22, 1–33.

produced three centuries earlier. German translations of these sources made them still more accessible, accentuating the panorama of the story of suffering and the memory of it, while reshaping the historical consciousness of contemporary Jews. Paradoxically, however, Sephardic Jews never had direct access to this story of suffering in the version that was sanctioned and identified as modern when it was stamped with the label 'historical'. The Sephardic authors of the Balkan and Ottoman regions, who also wrote history from the nineteenth century on, took greater interest in their local history, which was less turbulent than that of their European counterparts. As for the Jews of North Africa, who were still firmly rooted in tradition, writing history for the purpose of preserving what remained of their Judaism was not a major preoccupation. In the contemporary period, the Sepharadim in fact learned their history by way of the historiography being developed in the Christian West – that is, by way of the lachrymose version of the story of the Jews.

MYSTICISM AS AN ANTIDOTE TO SUFFERING

The historiography produced in the Sephardic world in the sixteenth century left its mark on modern historical writing among the Ashkenazim; the messianic inspiration that partially informed it had considerable impact on the new centre of world Judaism that was to come into being in Eastern Europe. Hasidism, which, with its messianic cast, emerged and developed among the Ashkenazim in the eighteenth century, is reminiscent of the more hopeful currents that appeared in the Sephardic world after the expulsion. The apocryphal legends in circulation about the founder of Hasidism, Baal Shem Tov, credit him with the knowledge and power of an Isaac Luria Ashkenazi, a master of Jewish mysticism who lived and taught in the Holy Land. Again, Hasidic communities adopted a modified version of the Sephardic liturgy, based on the rite produced by this Kabbalist.

More generally, Hasidism popularized, in a certain sense, the doctrines of the Lurianic Kabbalah, for which Israel's exile and dispersion coincided with the exile and dispersion of the divine. Hence it was the Jewish people's mission to bring together the fragments of holiness that had been disseminated among the Gentiles, in a process of redemption that the coming of the Messiah would bring to its term. With his coming, universal redemption would exactly coincide with the redemption of Israel. Jewish mystics accordingly ceased to be merely visionary or contemplative; they were now supposed to influence the course of the world. The diffusion of these doctrines, in combination with the setbacks that the Jews suffered as a result of several historical catastrophes, enables us to account for the emergence and spread, in Eastern Europe, of the movement around the false Messiah Sabbetai Zevi. The failure of Sabbatism – the true Messiah had failed to appear – followed by the failure of Frankism, whose adepts converted to Christianity, sowed profound disillusionment. It is supposed to have favoured the emergence of Hasidism, a new mystical current which, thanks to its emphasis on inner, personal redemption, is said indirectly to have led to the neutralization of a messianism which Sabbateist excesses had made suspect and unsettling.

Some hold that the Hasidic spiritualization of messianism was not just a reaction to certain historical, social, and economic events, but the resurgence of a tendency observable since the thirteenth century. The fact remains that Hasidism emerged in a period that felt a pressing need for consolation. Hasidism was sustained, like other mystical movements, by a hope for deliverance and a desire for redemption and restoration. As a movement that had broad appeal, it sought to offer new responses to suffering in a trying context shaped by war, anti-Jewish decrees, and pogroms. It spread in areas mired in extreme poverty. Half of Polish Jews and a considerable number of Russian Jews joined the movement; as a result of migrations, major outgrowths of Hasidism developed in Western Europe and North America. The Hasidic God is good and compassionate. That said, even within Hasidism, reactions to suffering varied.

One such reaction consisted in an invitation to consider trials and tribulations with serenity, because everything that happens to men is willed by God and, consequently, cannot happen without good reason. According to Pinhas de Koretz, sadness and bitterness result from pride and people's belief that they should not suffer. The humble man, however, accepts what happens to him calmly and with resignation. The *Hasid*[75] does not merely accept the destiny God assigns him; he embraces it with joy. Thanking the Almighty for everything that he sends one's way, without turning against him in anger or despair, is evidence of an unconditional love for God (*ahavat ha-Shem*) of the kind preached by Hasidic doctrine. One can turn to the *Tsadik*, the just man, the charismatic leader and cornerstone of the community, for advice and succour, but he too is ready to suffer for his people. For many *Hasidim*, suffering reminded all men of the need to examine their souls and reform.

Like the movement's founder, Rabbi Nahman of Brastlav concluded, in the eighteenth century, that God visits afflictions upon us to remind us that we should reform our ways and cleanse our souls of the stain of sin. Rabbi

---

75   A follower of Hasidism; literally, a 'pious man' (plural *Hasidim*).

Nahman interpreted adversity as a divine inducement to take the path of repentance. Moreover, God is incapable of inflicting more suffering on us than we have the capacity to bear. The ultimate message of Rabbi Nahman's *Garden of Souls* is that there exists a way to find joy, even amid the woes of this world: the path to it leads through belief in the beyond. Furthermore, suffering and pain can be inflicted on the just man as expiation for the misdeeds of his entire generation. The just man therefore accepts them with love. In expiating the sins of his fellow creatures, he saves them in this world and improves their situation with respect to the world to come. Thanks to the suffering of these just men, the chosen, creation in general is purified and, step-by-step, the world comes closer to perfection.

By closing our eyes on this world and concentrating on the ultimate, eternal goal, we can free ourselves of pain and attain perfect prayer. Since there is suffering in this world, the only place in which we can escape from it is in God and his Torah. 'Yet man is born to trouble', Job declares, 'as the sparks fly upward'.[76] Thus the world is full of pain and suffering. If we seek to live in peace and savour its advantages, we will find only bitterness. On the other hand, by fleeing the struggle in this world and devoting all our energies to the Torah, we prepare ourselves for the world to come, which is eternal; in comparison with it, life in this world passes in the blink of an eye. By conducting ourselves in the prescribed manner, we ensure a better life for ourselves in this world, too.

Adepts of Hasidism could no doubt find a degree of comfort in this rhetoric about the inevitability of suffering in this life and the idea that it led to a beyond which ultimately provided compensation for it.[77] The same did not hold for the nineteenth-century Jews who lived in a world on the way to secularization and bearing the stamp of historicization.

JEWISH IDENTITY IS WRITTEN IN TEARS

The nineteenth century was one of history and nationalism. The emergent nations came to feel a powerful desire for history. Their objective was to affirm their past so as to secure themselves a place in the new state configurations of a Europe caught up in a process of change. The Jews, although they had no

---

76   Jb 5:7.

77   On suffering in Hasidism, see Aviva Weintraub, 'Some Hasidic Responses to Suffering', *Nitzanim*, 3, 1984–5, 98–105; *Garden of the Souls: Rebbe Nachman on Suffering*, trans. Avraham Greenbaum, Jerusalem/New York: Breslov Research Institute, 1990.

specific territorial base nor put forward any well-defined territorial claims, also felt a need to construct their history that was, in a sense, stronger than that of many other groups. They wanted that history to serve as a support for a present that had been turned upside down; and they wanted to create a new Jewish condition.

At this time, the Jews were either familiarizing themselves with all that citizenship implied, as in France, or, as in many other European countries, had set out on the road to emancipation. Like other minorities, they were particularly vulnerable to the vicissitudes, often unfavourable to them, of a century marked by changing borders, the decline of the great empires, and the emergence of new, exclusive nation-states. The year 1848 thus shook the Central European Jews' confidence, confronting them with a very inauspicious political context. The final decades of the century saw numerous pogroms and the growth of modern anti-Semitism. As for the twentieth century, it began with a bloody war that put Jews of the different countries of which they were now citizens in opposing camps.

In these times of far-reaching change, modern Jews could no longer, like their medieval predecessors, look upon history with disdain and treat the study of it as a waste of time, much less proscribe reading it. And, even more than other currents in nineteenth-century Judaism, nascent Jewish nationalism, followed by Zionism, which was one of its variants, felt an imperious need for history – and for biblical mythology as well. Indeed, nationalism and Zionism forged a synthesis of the two in order, ultimately, to justify the creation of a Jewish state on biblical lands that were to be populated by Jews from different diasporas, each possessing a memory and history of its own. The exit from the ghetto had, in an almost physical sense, led to a break in continuity that had previously been based not on history in the modern sense, but, rather, the conviction that the present resembles the past and that the genealogy of individuals and groups has primacy over the merely apparent upheavals of history.

It would, moreover, be a mistake to suppose that emancipation and adaptation to non-Jewish environments were the sole catalysts of historicization among the Jews. Movements internal to Judaism also helped to pave the way for this development. The Jewish Enlightenment current, the *Haskalah*, which emerged in the second half of the eighteenth century in Germany and gradually spread to other regions, was a step on the way to a reformulation of Jewish identity in the context of a new duality that involved being Jewish while also being receptive to the surrounding culture to the point of adopting it fully and without reserve. To get there, the road was long; it spawned questions about Jewish identity and the various modes of being Jewish that continue to be asked today. As soon as such doubts arise, continuity *ipso facto* ceases.

To be sure, there has never been only one way of being Jewish, not even in the pre-modern period. Until the nineteenth century, however, questions of identity were posed in collective, not individual terms. The dominant vision of the world was transmitted through channels that could do without history, in a context in which one was first a member of a religious group, an obligatory affiliation that defined one's place on the political and religious map. Despite a choppy temporal trajectory, the relationship to God did not need history, it required basic texts and rites to sustain faith. The possibility of choosing between one's community and the larger society in which it was embedded, or, simply, the choice of belonging to two groups at once, were both new options; they severed the individual Jew from the chain in which he had previously considered himself a mere link, while obliging the Jew who wished to remain a Jew to construct a form of Jewishness that took the rupture into account. This change did not affect Jews alone; today all of us take it for granted that we must forge an identity for ourselves in a world in which we confront, unaided, a multitude of possibilities, in the knowledge that tradition is no longer capable of telling us who we are.

Among German Jewish intellectuals, an unprecedented current emerged in the first half of the nineteenth century in the wake of the Berlin Jewish Enlightenment: the 'Science of Judaism' (in German, *Wissenschaft des Judentums*). Its adepts sought to forge a new Jewish identity adapted to the contemporary context while promoting a series of reforms in the areas of worship, beliefs, mode of life, social structure, education, and culture that might, in time, lead to legal emancipation. In this vein, they set out to present in a scientific spirit, both within their community and outside it, those aspects of the culture and history of Judaism that they deemed the richest and the most likely to help to win recognition for Jewish values. For this purpose, young intellectuals and scholars in Berlin founded an Association for the Culture and Science of the Jews in 1819.[78] It intended to apply the critical methods of modern scholarship to the canonical texts of Judaism, rather than use the methods of traditional exegesis, as in the past. Judaism as a religion was moribund in the eyes of these European Jews, and a distanced approach was the only one they felt was capable of preventing it from disappearing altogether in the flood of secularization.

---

78   In German, *Verein für Kultur und Wissenschaft der Juden*.

In the process, the Berlin intellectuals showed that Judaism was also a culture and a history. They had, however, to strip it of every last trace of political history to underscore the universal nature of its mission: offering humanity the perfected form of the monotheistic ethic. This mission would be fulfilled in the countries of the dispersion. Any mention of the land of Israel and the ultimate unification of the Jewish people on its territory had to be avoided. This depoliticization of the Jews' history was intended to disarm the foes of Jewish emancipation in Central Europe, while summoning the Jews to remain Jews; they could do so without risk, since all that differentiated them from their Christian entourage was their religion. Henceforth, Judaism was reduced to being a religious community, and Jewish life was inseparable from the Diasporic condition. Gaining citizenship accordingly seemed imperative to these Jews, who had to forget that they had once been a people.

Thus there appeared, in outline, the portrait of an ahistorical Judaism that was basically an object of persecution and oppression, that of a martyred people bereft of power. The history of the Jews had been made by others, not the Jews themselves – they had not been its agents. As late as the turn of the twentieth century, the Jewish German thinker Hermann Cohen was still celebrating the non-existence of a Jewish state as a necessity for the human race, the messianic future of which required that all the peoples of the world come together in a confederation of states. In his *Religion of Reason*, posthumously published in 1918, Cohen interprets the Jews' suffering as a messianic sign addressed to the nations.[79] This picture of an atemporal, ahistorical Judaism recurs in the thought of Cohen's main disciple, Franz Rosenzweig. According to Rosenzweig, the key to the survival of the Jewish people, its essence and mission, depended on its existence outside the parameters of history.

Paradoxically, the Zionists, like those who struggled to win citizenship for Jews, had also made the idea that the Diaspora was condemned to passivity and impotence an integral part of their credo, which was based on a mistaken view of Jewish life in the Middle Ages. Zionists and emancipationists alike wanted to put the traditional condition of the exile behind them, perceiving it as basically negative. For the Zionists, the Jews could regain power and shake off the chains of their passivity only by returning to the land of their ancestors. For the emancipationists, it was the acquisition of citizenship rights that would bring an end to persecution and oppression. It is in this context that we can understand the profound disappointment over the setbacks represented by the defeat of the

---

79   David Biale, 'Power, Passivity and the Legacy of the Holocaust', *Tikkun*, 2:1, 1987, 69.

1848 revolution and the rise of anti-Semitism felt by the generations that had been impatiently awaiting an acceleration of the integration process, a sign of the dawn of a new era.

The idea of the powerless Jew is so widely accepted that many have been led to interpret the Second World War genocide exclusively from the standpoint of the Jews' passivity ('they went off like lambs to slaughter'). This depiction helped shape the mentality of the new combative, victorious Jew; its influence persisted long after the foundation of the state of Israel. In no sense has the notion of Jewish passivity in the Middle Ages been confirmed by historical research however. The medieval Jews demonstrated their economic usefulness to kings and feudal lords and were granted privileges in exchange that ensured them relative autonomy. This principle of alliance, while it of course did not even remotely imply equality between the two allied parties, gave the Jews in exile the security they aspired to. During the Crusades and the pogroms perpetrated by the Cossacks under Bogdan Chmielnicki in 1648–9, some Jews took up arms and defended themselves; only after all hope of repelling the attackers had died did they turn their weapons against themselves. While Jews in the Islamic world were in principle not authorized to bear arms, Muslim Spain nevertheless had its Jewish generals, such as Samuel Ha-Nagid in Grenada.

The Jews' self-perception as passive creatures outside history in fact reaches very far back into the past. The disastrous consequences of the Jewish revolt against the Romans at the beginning of our era led the Jews' rabbinical leadership to expunge the symbol of the Matzada from Jewish collective memory in the second and third centuries and replace it with that of Yohanan Ben Zakkai, an adept of prayer and study. The Pharisees' commitment to quietism rather than military resistance grew in proportion as their power increased. Indeed, Jewish history in these remote times was conceived in strictly theological terms.[80] Because Jews were subject to the changing fortunes of the lands where they had put down roots, and to the will of non-Jewish authorities, this image of the Jew persisted for centuries. It is, however, hard to square with the historical reality of the matter. How are we to explain the Jews' survival in their long years of exile without considering the political strategies they adopted? How can we ignore the impact of the autonomy from which the Jewish community benefited in the Christian and Muslim worlds alike, an autonomy that allowed them, in the confessional framework of the Middle Ages and the modern era, to conduct their religious and familial life in accordance with their own laws (even if they had to pay tribute in exchange)? The

---

80 Biale, 'Power', 1987.

fact of the matter is that their situation oscillated between a community-based sovereignty and dependency, between power and passivity. Yet Raul Hilberg, too, in his great book, *The Destruction of the European Jews*, attributes the Jews' failure to resist during the Second World War to their experience of the previous 2,000 years.[81] Suffering on the one hand and passivity on the other had most assuredly become an inseparable couple in the Jews' long history, or, at any rate, in the dominant representation of it.

In the nineteenth century, it became necessary to write Jewish history – as a rule, a history of subjection and suffering, a cultural rather than political history – not only in response to the crisis precipitated by the ruptures that external and internal pressure had brought about in the Jewish condition, but also as a shield against fears that Jewish identity would be dissolved in this new context. History, or the kind of history that was in question here, became 'the faith of fallen Jews'.[82] It offered a way of remaining Jewish by codifying what being Jewish meant over the long term. To this end, history had to be written differently, following methods that purported to be scientific and, thus, critical. Now that the Jews could no longer content themselves with biblical mythology, what was to be the contents of the history they would write? The ancient memory of the story of suffering was ready and waiting; it was an inexhaustible source of material.

Scholars now not only published or reprinted already existing medieval chronicles; they also took a great interest in the liturgical literature about the persecution of the Jews, and breathed new life into the semblance of historiography engendered in the sixteenth century by the break that the expulsion from Spain had represented. The new Jewish historical consciousness was built up around suffering and the traditional memory of it, prolonging a past in which this memory had been instilled in people's minds and constantly reactivated. Thus the modern history of the Jews was written with tears, inspired by the story of suffering that it would long resemble. Although the methods had changed and the beginnings of historical criticism can be glimpsed in some of these texts, the picture painted in the story of suffering was still valid and would continue to be for a long time to come. Thus was born lachrymose Jewish history – the *Leidensgeschichte* – which found its fullest expression in the

---

81   On the question of passivity, see Ismar Schorsch's excellent essay 'On the History of the Political Judgment of the Jew', *Leo Baeck Memorial Lecture*, 20, 1977, 3–23. On Rosenzweig and his theory of the ahistoricity of Judaism, see his 'Geist und Epochen der Jüdischen Geschichte', in Schorsch, *Kleinere Schriften*, Berlin: Schocken, 1937, 12–25, cited by Schorsch in his essay.

82   Yerushalmi, *Zakhor*, p. 86.

nineteenth century in the work of German Heinrich Graetz, the modern historian of the Jews.

This lachrymose history had the force required to bring together, around the theme of Jewish suffering, the many Jews who slowly but surely abandoned the path their ancestors had followed. How was one to remain Jewish now that belief and transmission no longer existed? Could Jewishness continue to be sustained by the gaze of the Other alone? By returning to the discourse of suffering, the new historiographical writing recreated this community of suffering, although it could not recreate the religious community nor, for that matter, the community *tout court*, which was already a thing of the past or in the process of disappearing. Belief and suffering, Judaism and suffering – they were interchangeable and would continue to bind secularized or secularizing Jews together in a community of trials and tribulations. This transition from the community of the faithful to the community of sufferers presided over the birth of modern historiography, which had so powerful an impact that it consistently drowned out the voices of the handful of resisters who tried then, tried again later, and today are still trying to write a different history, one not tailored to the lachrymose model.

In the nineteenth century, the story of suffering reflected the Jews' self-perception at a time when the horizon was full of promise for Jews in certain countries, while, for others elsewhere, the atmosphere was fraught with threats. The Jewish world – the secularization of broad sectors of it notwithstanding – was still a place defined by the eternal return associated with religion. Nothing could put an end to suffering, even if, here and there, the sun was peeping through the clouds. As in the past, the rhetoric of suffering continued to provide consolation; this time, however, it was consolation for the fact that one was no longer Jewish in the way one had been. These intellectuals of the generation that had left the ghetto behind re-established ties with Judaism by devoting themselves to the study of traditional texts and the writing of history. In the past as well, Judaism's memory had been the memory of suffering; there was no separating the one from the other. God himself suffered for his people; if one suffered as a Jew, it was for love of God. The new discourse simply responded to new demands, those of the groups caught up in a process of secularization and Westernization. Jews could accept this lachrymose history the more easily because the memory of the story of suffering was not yet totally alien to them.

The history of the Jews was thus reduced to this endless vale of tears. When people talk about the Jews, even today, their suffering is mentioned before all else. One of the reasons for this may be that Israel, a triumphant and sometimes oppressive state, like many others, arouses such deep anger. In its turn, lachrymose history generated Jewish victimhood. Yet even if that victimhood is no mere figment of the imagination, but is attested by hard facts, Jewish history cannot be reduced to it. Yet many prefer to dwell exclusively on this aspect of Jewish history, which was tragically reinforced by the events of the Second World War and long muted the voices of those wishing to write differently: their works reached only a cultivated minority. The overwhelming majority remained fixated on suffering and its corollary, victimhood, the two pillars of contemporary Jewish identity, the history of which, as we have seen, goes back a long way. For many secularized Jews, suffering and victimhood now have the status of a virtual dogma. To tamper with or question them is for some a kind of sacrilege.

Memory, even stripped of its religious components, continues to have a greater impact than history on a group for which it long served in history's stead. Nascent history appropriated the memory of suffering, subjecting it to the questions of a critical methodology without recourse to God. Yet the ancient legacy continued to weigh heavily on the present. It was, in the final analysis, this source that was mined by the nineteenth-century scholars and intellectuals who bent themselves to the task of producing a scientific understanding of the Jewish past.

After the genocide, significantly, people no longer spoke of the obligation to preserve history, but of the obligation of memory. But merely proclaiming the existence of a duty will never suffice and never has done to ensure transmission. Should we not rather speak, as far as the present is concerned, of the imperative need for history, something the consumers of memory need urgently to be reminded? Is this a lost cause? Reading Yerushalmi, one might conclude that it is: 'Jewish historiography,' he writes, 'cannot … replace an eroded group memory.'[83] Will the centuries-old sacralized memory of our contemporaries, labouring under the onus of the genocide, have the same future as did, only yesterday, the memory of suffering, bequeathed to the faithful from generation to generation? Once the last survivors have disappeared, the question will be sure to arise in all its acuity. Whence, perhaps, this urgent need for history, necessary not only to universalize the historical experience of the Jews, but also to make it possible to transmit it to a posterity comprised of Jews and non-Jews alike (a posterity whose questions and doubts about identity are not likely to be any less pressing than ours), so that, one day, both Jews and non-Jews can contemplate a rounded picture of the Jews, rather than observing them from the angle of their abiding misfortunes alone.

---

83   Yerushalmi, *Zakhor*, p. 94.

Nineteenth-century Jewish intellectuals and scholars with their special relationship to the discourse of suffering, were able to introduce a new way of dealing with suffering that anticipated contemporary practices. Thus, between the nineteenth and mid-twentieth century, scholars assiduously edited collections of documents in Hebrew that represented the literary responses to the Crusades. Better than any historical narrative could, such compilations made lachrymose Jewish memory available, in condensed form, to men and women of letters and the general public. For the new historians and critics, the Crusades stood as the founding moment of Jewish suffering in the Diaspora. The renowned Viennese preacher and scholar Adolf Jellinek, for example, began publishing the first modern edition of Hebrew sources on the Crusades in 1880. This man of action did not, despite his faith in social integration, disdain the past and its story of suffering. Quite the contrary: he proceeded as if the one was powerless to consign the other to oblivion. Also involved in civic affairs and active in the life of his community, Jellinek feverishly pursued his research on Judaism.

In 1892, Adolf Neubauer, a native of Hungary who had settled in England and become a librarian at Oxford's Bodleian Library, published, with the rabbi and historian Moritz Stern, *Jewish Chronicles of the Jewish Persecutions during the Crusades.*[84] The book, a collection of Hebrew chronicles accompanied by their German translations, helped to promote the professionalization of Jewish historiography. Thus the history of Jewish suffering was made available to Germanophone readers.

Four years later, Sigmund Salfeld published a book that assembled texts bearing witness to the persecutions of the Jews on German territory between 1096 and 1349, along with a list of martyred Jews. In the introduction, he catalogued the 'memory books' (*Memorbücher*) of 55 communities. Let us recall that these publications coincided with the 800th anniversary of the First Crusade in 1896, a date that did not attract much attention from the German public. The late nineteenth century was a period in which the Jews were ardently seeking full integration, and commemorations of this kind were not yet welcome. On the other hand, this anniversary was significant for these scholars because it came at a point when modern anti-Semitism was on the rise. Did this discourse of suffering serve to assuage their growing distress in a period when the Jewish masses, now citizens of their countries of residence, were looking toward what they believed was a bright future?

---

84   In German, *Hebräische Berichte über die Judenverfolgungen während der Kreuzzüge.*

In the late 1880s, Hayyim Jonah Gurland, a rabbi in Odessa, published and annotated an extensive collection of documents on the 1648–9 massacres that had profoundly marked Jews in the waning Middle Ages.[85] In fact, in the copious literature turned out between 1880 and 1890, the medieval period is the focus of attention in cultivated Jewish circles, as if the Jews were advancing on the path of emancipation and integration without abandoning – quite the contrary – this ancestral notion of victimization by their enemies.[86] Was it because they wanted to conjure away the anti-Semitism of their own time? Was it out of a desire to convince themselves that, just as they had in the past, they would soon put this episode behind them, and that better days lay ahead? However that may be, the process of integration into the surrounding society was accompanied by a memory of suffering that these publications revived. Were they read by non-Jewish intellectuals, who could perhaps be moved by what the Jews had borne for centuries? Did these newly erected monuments to suffering constitute a sort of riposte to the anti-Semites of the day? But, if they did, how often did they attain their goal?

Leopold Zunz, a founding figure and eminent representative of the 'Science of Judaism' associated with the Reformed Jews of the synagogue of Berlin, whose official preacher he became in 1821, was a leading specialist in the field of Jewish martyrology and liturgical poetry; he spent much of his time working on the penitential prayers that expressed the suffering of the people of Israel in exile, its faith in the Covenant, and its confident belief in the virtues of repentance and the coming of the Redeemer. The results of Zunz's research took concrete form with the publication of three books between 1855 and 1865. It is no accident that the preface to *Synagogale Poesie des Mittelalters* (1855) appeared in English in 1907, 21 years after its author's death and just a few years after the 1903–5 Russian pogroms in Kishniev – or that it appeared in New York, the city Russian Jews had adopted as their new fatherland. The English title of this slender volume, *The Sufferings of the Jews during the Middle Ages*,

---

85   *Contribution to the History of the Persecutions of Israel*, published in *Otsar-ha-Sifrut*, 1887–1889 (in Hebrew). It should be added that, for some historians of the Jews, the Middle Ages did not end until the eighteenth century in certain areas.

86   Adolf Jellinek, *The Booklet of Mainz and of the Community of Vienna*, Vienna: J. Schlossberg, 1880 (in Hebrew); Adolf Neubauer and Moritz Stern, *Hebräische Berichte über die Judenverfolgungen während der Kreuzzüge*, Berlin: L. Simion, 1892; Adolf Neubauer, *Mediaeval Jewish Chronicles and Chronological Notes*, Amsterdam: Philo Press, 1970, two vols.; Siegmund Salfeld, *Das Martyrologium des Nürnberger Memorbuches*, Berlin: L. Simion, 1898.

leaves no doubt about the permanence of the memory of suffering that was thus carried to the New World.[87]

The author of the preface to the US edition, George Alexander Kohut, wrote:

> The days of the Black Death and the Crusades are again upon us, and in the great Memorbücher of the Nation's sorrow we must now chronicle the martyrdom of the sons and daughters of Judah at Kishineff, Gomel, Odessa, Bialystok and countless other places in the broad empire of the Tsar ... In one Russian town, during the upheavals of 1904, we are informed by an eyewitness, there was a holocaust of Jewish souls, and the martyrs went singing to their doom. Does not this plaintive fact recall the tragedies of the Dark Ages, when the children of Israel, led to slaughter, perished 'as consecrated hosts of the Lord', chanting the *Alenu Prayer*?[88]

Kohut adduces examples of heroism displayed in the darkest moments, mentions the elegies and penitential prayers that had become an integral part of the Jewish liturgy, and adds: 'Suffering is the badge of all our tribe'. For him, Zunz's book, of which he presents only extracts, was the outline of the work of a Jewish martyrologist of the Middle Ages. In the original, Zunz had told a minutely detailed story of persecutions: forced baptisms, the infidelity of apostates, burnings at the stake, torture, exactions, and evidence of slavery in Europe and the East. In this long account, Jews die for their faith or kill themselves for its sake. But, even as Zunz puts the accent on Jewish suffering, he takes care to remind his readers that those who thus accepted death in the name of religion were called saints. If the book is an appeal for sympathy in view of so much suffering, it is also an appeal to share hope.[89]

The rabbi and scholar Shimon Bernfeld published, in his turn, a three-volume anthology entitled *The Book of Tears* (*Sefer Ha-Demaot*) just after the end of the bloody First World War, which led to both the destruction of many Jewish population groups in Eastern Europe and the collapse of Czarism and the accompanying pogroms, notably the 1918–20 pogroms in Ukraine that caused the deaths of 200,000 people or ten per cent of the Jewish population.

---

87   Leopold Zunz, *Die Synagogale Poesie des Mittelalters*, Berlin: J. Springer, 1855–1857, two vols.; Zunz, *Der Ritus des Synagogalen Gottesdienstes*, Zunz, Berlin: Louis Lamm, 1919 [1859]; Zunz, *Literaturgeschichte der Synagogalen Poesie*, Berlin: L. Gerschel, 1865.

88   *Aleinu* is the first word of a prayer that begins, 'it is incumbent upon us [*aleinu*] to praise the Lord of all things'. As a rule, this prayer is recited at the end of each of the three daily services.

89   Leopold Zunz, *The Sufferings of the Jews during the Middle Ages*, trans. A. Löwy, ed. Alexander Kohut, New York: Bloch Publishing Company, 1907, 9 and *passim*.

Bernfeld dates the preface to his book 9 *Av* 5683/1923–9 *Av*, the traditional day of mourning and commemoration of Jewry's great catastrophes. He thereby sets the tone of the book, which is an account of the persecutions and destruction that the Jews have had to endure over the centuries. As in traditional rabbinical literature, he highlights the theme of suffering accepted out of love. Thus he writes that 'The narratives of past torments are also chants of consolation for the future.'

Bernfeld spells out that his aim in writing his book was 'to compile a martyrology of the people of Israel based on the original written sources, with historical commentaries'.[90] To this end, he makes use of narratives and also of liturgical poetry. For Bernfeld the Crusades comprise the timeless foundation of Jewish history, and their Jewish victims are saints. In the preface to the third and last volume of his work, he is at pains to point out that 'The end of this book is not the end of the tragedy known as Jewish history. Even if I had brought my narrative down to the last day, I would not have reached the end. We do not know what the coming days will bring us. Indeed, in the past few years, hatred for the people of Israel has only become more intense.'[91] The well-known historical succession of calamities and suffering is uninterrupted, and has no known end. It is this 'string of interlinked tragedies which make the heart tremble' that the author sets out to bring to the attention of his contemporaries.[92] In his view, anti-Semitism is a constant in Jewish history.

This discourse on suffering revives several themes of the religious literature of earlier centuries, even if the initial intention was to write history, not to resuscitate the memory of the story of suffering. There is nothing surprising about the ambiguity of such a position, inasmuch as the controlling mechanisms of this nascent historiography are still those of the world of religion and because their rhetoric is still heavily religious. Nor is there any doubt that these texts also intended to deliver a message of hope, as their authors themselves declared, even as the skies, heavy with threats, darkened over a Europe that, in the 1920s, vociferously proclaimed its anti-Semitism. The work these scholars did stiffened their resolve to remain Jews in their own way, despite the disappointments of the moment and in defiance of their apprehensions about the future. They built up, brick by brick, this secular Bible: it was an open book on suffering.

---

90   Shimon Bernfeld, *The Book of Tears: Calamities, Persecutions and Massacres*, Berlin: Eshkol, 1923–6, vol. 1, 5–6 (in Hebrew).

91   Bernfeld, vol. 3, p. 5.

92   Bernfeld, vol. 1, p. 80.

A comparable phenomenon could be observed after the genocide, when, in 1946, to mark the 850th anniversary of the First Crusade, Abraham Habermann published an anthology of liturgical poetry under the title *Catastrophes in Germany and Northern France*,[93] while, in 1949, on the occasion of the 300th anniversary of the 1648–9 massacres in Poland and Ukraine, Nahum Wahrmann brought out, in Jerusalem, a collection of liturgical sources on them.[94] Thus the Crusades, the founding event of post-biblical history, with their suffering and their martyrs, loomed up again in these difficult times, like the Cossack massacres, as if what were involved were the activation or reactivation of a memory of solidarity amidst affliction. Today, it is the Holocaust itself which has taken precedence over everything else, and has been elevated in its turn into an unsurpassable founding event. In the first post-war years, however, before the foundation of the state of Israel and the subsequent politicization of the memory of the genocide, the model of the reactivation of the memory of the great massacres, when Jewish suffering was at its height, was still viable; it gave rise to a sort of liturgization that happened to be secular. A collective memory of suffering capable of creating continuity between past and present, yet resistant to history, was once again in demand. It was as if the suffering of the past acted as a sort of antidote that could heal present wounds. Thus this play of mirrors, this *mise-en-abyme* that had come down through the centuries, was repeated when catastrophe struck again, even in the age of emancipation and integration in Europe, and even in the immediate aftermath of the genocide. The dean of what some have called the Jerusalem Historical School, Yitzhak F. Baer, in his introduction to the book by Habermann cited above, once again links the calamities of the past to the tragedies of modern times, especially to the one that culminated in the destruction of the Jews. Indeed, it is the Ashkenazim who, in the past few centuries, have inscribed tragedy at the heart of their historical experience and their literary imagination.[95]

In our day, how many Jews (certain intellectual or religious circles excepted) can still clearly identify the past disasters and instances of

---

93   Abraham Meir Habermann, *Catastrophes in Germany and Northern France: Memoirs by Contemporaries of the Crusades and a Selection from their Liturgical Poems*, Jerusalem: Mosad Ha-Rav Kook, 4706/1946 (in Hebrew).

94   Nahum Wahrmann, *Documents on the History of the Massacres of 1648–1649: Prayers and Penitential Liturgies for 20* Sivan, Jerusalem: Bamberger and Vahrman, 4709/1949 (in Hebrew). On lachrymose and its evolution, see Myers, ' "*Mehabevin et ha-tsarot*" ', 49–64; Schorsch, 'The Lachrymose Conception', 377–80; Mintz, *Hurban*, 115–29.

95   Myers, ' "*Mehabevin et ha-tsarot*" ', 61–2.

martyrdom that so preoccupied the Jewish world for centuries? Who still dreams of commemorating them? Even if someone had the idea of doing so, the commemoration would go unnoticed among the successive wave of commemorations of the genocide that punctuate the life of Jews today, soliciting their participation as either passive spectators or actors. These remarks should not be construed as intending to establish a hierarchy of values among commemorations or magnify one particular catastrophe at the cost of another. The memory of suffering continues to dominate Jewish minds in virtually all the countries in which Jews live, operating in line with schemas that are not very different from those that prevailed in the past. Today, however, it has been reduced to the memory of the genocide, which offers an interpretative grid for all past calamities and all those to come, with the 'irresistible tendency to let the present colour the past'.[96] Before the exclusive domination of the memory of the Holocaust, the memory of suffering served, in the first place, as a means of understanding the present, helping people bear its woes. The uniqueness to which the Final Solution has been confined severs the Jews from other memories of suffering and transforms past misfortunes into harbingers of what was to come, what had to come. Because the genocide is unique, it stands as an isolated instance of suffering, detached from the rest of the history of Jewish suffering. The secularized Jew accordingly approaches it without God or a past, in a present that claims to suffice unto itself, amid an individualistic solitude interrupted only by the commemorations and ceremonies. There, perhaps, lies the source of the despair of contemporary Jews, which one hopes, is only transitory.

We saw earlier that sixteenth-century Sephardic historiographical works such as Joseph Ha-Cohen's *The Vale of Tears* and Salomon Ibn Verga's *Sceptre of Judah* were published and translated in the mid-nineteenth century. These publications were among a flood of collections of historical sources that accompanied the production in Europe, by Ashkenazi scholars, of a modern Jewish history, which, moreover, was clearly rooted in a process centred on defining Jewish identity. In this way, the history of Jewish suffering written by the Sephardic exiles, in which the expulsion from Spain also took its place, made its way into the modern memory of Jewish suffering. Thus the two faces of Judaism, Sephardic and Ashkenazi, and their common heritage, suffering, were joined.

In the nineteenth century, history was written in this fashion to meet the needs of those searching for roots and tradition at a moment when,

---

96   Schorsch, 'The Lachrymose Conception', 382.

paradoxically, because the process of acculturation was in full swing, Jewish memory and the identity that went hand-in-hand with it could not yet be asserted as such. One had to become a 'genuine' German, a 'genuine' Frenchman, and so on, before one could contemplate affirming one's Jewishness. In this context, history appeared, for all those Jews in the process of becoming spectators of their Judaism, as a 'neutral' bond – a bond 'neutralized' by scholarship – between them and their own people.

Graetz, who had a background in rabbinical studies, emerged as the unchallenged architect and ideologue of this lachrymose history. He depicts Judaism's and the Jewish people's struggle to ensure their survival, the uniqueness of this experience, the suffering endured in exile, and the courage of the martyrs in the face of the cruelty of Israel's enemies and persecutors. Graetz treats political and legal developments as, basically, a backdrop, and wholly neglects the social and economic dimensions of Jewish history. In fact, he writes a history of Jewish suffering and a history of the learned/the rabbis.[97] His monumental 11-volume *History of the Jews* had an immense influence on later Jewish historiography, shaping its entire subsequent development.[98]

The many different translations and new editions of Graetz's tome, and the abridged, three-volume version of it released between 1887 and 1889 (which had seen ten editions by 1930) greatly increased its influence. The abridged version became one of the most widely read books in Germany. An 1890–9 Hebrew translation/adaptation had a powerful impact on the Eastern European Jews then learning Hebrew. A number of Yiddish translations also appeared from 1897–8 on. In France, this historical summa was published in five volumes. Rabbi Lazare Wogue helped to produce the translation, to which the Chief Rabbi of France at the time, Zadoc Kahn, wrote a preface.[99] The third volume, entitled *Sinai and Golgotha*, is supposed to have been translated in 1867 by Moses Hess, a Jewish nationalist of German origin and the author of *Rome and Jerusalem*.[100] In 1919, under the significant title *Popular History of the Jews*, the work was made available to the American public in a five-volume edition.[101]

---

97   In German, *Gelehrtengeschichte*.

98   Heinrich Graetz, *Geschichte der Juden von den ältesten Zeiten bis auf die Gegenwart: Aus den Quellen neu bearbeitet*, Leipzig: O. Leiner, 1853–1876, 10 books in 11 volumes.

99   Heinrich Graetz, *Geschichte der Juden: Von den ältesten Zeiten bis zur Mitte des 19. Jahrhunderts*, Berlin: Directmedia, 2002 (reprint).

100   *Encyclopaedia Judaica* (CD Rom), 'Heinrich Graetz', written by another historian of the Jews, Shmuel Ettinger.

101   Heinrich Graetz, *Popular History of the Jews*, trans. A. B. Rhine, with a

The tremendous popularity of Graetz's work is undeniably due to the fact that it was read by Jews who wanted to reformulate an identity that had often been cut off from religious practice. What, indeed, impelled these rabbis to take on the task of translating it? They were, of course, still the keepers of the keys of traditional culture; at the same time, however, aware of the rapidity with which Jewish knowledge and practice were disappearing, they were concerned to provide their co-religionists with access to a heritage that was increasingly absent from people's homes, in countries where they increasingly assumed their roles as full-fledged citizens. It was by means of this historicized discourse of suffering, still a source of consolation, that integrated Jews living outside the ghetto began to construct their new Jewish secular identities.

Salo W. Baron was one of the first Jewish historians to set about vigorously combating the lachrymose conception of Jewish history. He had a different vision of the past, one that was considerably less sorrowful. Thus he refused to take over the post that Graetz had held in the Seminary in Breslau because his own way of writing history differed from that favored by his illustrious predecessor and those who were following in his footsteps. In 1964, after the Holocaust, Baron wrote: 'I have felt that an over-emphasis on Jewish sufferings distorted the total picture of the Jewish historic evolution and, at the same time, badly served a generation which had become impatient of the nightmare of endless persecutions and massacres.'[102] This idea has not lost any of its relevance.

What, however, is to be said, more specifically, of nineteenth-century France, where Jews, after gaining citizenship in 1790–1791, were taking giant steps towards integration? French Jewish intellectuals also wrote the history of Jewish suffering; but, unlike their counterparts in Central Europe, they wrote a history that culminated in a messianic utopia. Scholars such as Moïse Schwab, Elie-Aristide Astruc, Théodore Reinach, and James Darmesteter, who reconstruct a global history of the Jews, had perfect faith in emancipation at the time, regarding it as a direct legacy of the Enlightenment. They cultivated a universalizing discourse. They believed in the virtues of civilization and the enlightened thinking that, they were certain, would ultimately triumph over fanaticism. The Franco-Judaism that Darmesteter proposed was a cross between the principles of the French Republic and those of Judaism. Thus the

---

supplementary volume on recent events by Max Raisin, ed. Alexander Harkavy, New York: Hebrew Publishing Company, 1919.

102 S. Baron, *Essays and Addresses: History and Jewish Historians*, Philadelphia: JPS, 1964, 96.

Jews are supposed to have formulated the basic values of universal morality and justice and to have taught them to the rest of humanity.[103]

Like the architects of the German 'Science of Judaism', French Jewish historians continued to regard Judaism as a religion, nothing more. However, in contrast to their Central European counterparts still waiting to acquire citizenship rights, they were witnesses to, and beneficiaries of, full and total emancipation. For them, the story of suffering was mitigated by the redemption that this emancipation represented, in a figurative sense. It was a movement that promised nothing but the best, a history on the march for the Jews' greater good. In many cases, faith in France and its values did not prevent these intellectuals from being attached to Judaism, because there was no incompatibility between loyalty to the Republic and fidelity to Judaism. Théodore Reinach, in the preface to the first edition of his renowned *Histoire des Israélites depuis la ruine de leur indépendance nationale jusqu'à nos jours* ('History of the Jews from the destruction of their national independence to the present'), published in 1884, gave great play to the persecutions that the Jews had endured, but attributed them first and foremost to 'religious prejudice, encouraged by the Church and sustained by the reigning ignorance'. Thus the Middle Ages were cast as a period of darkness that helped to throw the benefits of emancipation into stark relief. The period of emancipation, in turn, was exalted as a golden age.

The effect of this contrast was, of course, to make the picture of the Jewish past seem still gloomier. Later, Reform Judaism and Zionism, in their effort to distinguish themselves from medieval Judaism, would further darken this picture, making the Middle Ages responsible for all the Jews' woes. In their euphoria, the advocates of Franco-Judaism, Jews who were citizens and fairly well integrated into French society, closed their eyes to the conditions to which other Jews were still subject elsewhere in Europe: 1881–2 also witnessed the great pogroms, the dismantling of Eastern European Judaism, and massive waves of emigration to the Americas. There followed, again in Russia, the interminable pogroms of the early twentieth century – to say nothing of the rise of modern anti-Semitism. Reinach, his faith in progress notwithstanding, declared, in the conclusion to the third edition of his book: 'Everywhere, hatred, persecution, and legal restrictions have led, among Jews, to a physical and moral decline, to all the vices of the oppressed and depressed races; tolerance and equal rights promptly made them men again, citizens worthy of a

---

103   Aron Rodrigue, 'Leon Halevy and Modern French Jewish Historiography', in E. Carlebach, J. Efron and D. N. Myers, eds, *Jewish History*, 413–27.

place among the best and most useful.'[104] While Reinach acknowledged that prejudices against the Jews continued to wreak havoc wherever the conditions for overcoming them did not obtain, he nonetheless counted on the activity of organizations like the Alliance israélite universelle, founded in Paris in 1860, to help to improve those conditions.

The optimism of these writers and their readers inclined them to relegate Jewish suffering to the past. The result was to reinforce their faith in progress and civilization, which slowly but steadily alienated them from the practice of their Judaism. For them, too, history became a harbour in which they could cast anchor, thus striking a balance between the enjoyment of their newly acquired rights and the desire not to be entirely absorbed by the majority. While they were trying to convince their compatriots that they were merely a religious community (and, later, a 'race', but in a sense very different from the one that prevailed in Nazi theories), they themselves were becoming less and less religious. What served them as Judaism was, rather, a reconstructed history that they wished to share as if it constituted a common heritage, even if they had not yet completely cut themselves off from Judaism in the proper sense of the word. The history in question was one of humiliation, persecution, forced conversions, and accusations endured by a group that had been united by a common faith, whereas the members of the generation which they incarnated and addressed were making progress in what they called civilization as individuals who were no longer part of a community, and as citizens who had rallied to a Republic based on principles that they firmly endorsed. The history that they sought to define and establish solidified this form of Jewishness that also looked confidently towards the future. The concern of their German counterparts was to reform their Judaism in order to make it acceptable to non-Jewish society, so that they might at last acquire the citizenship that they so ardently desired. In France, they had already found acceptance, at least in the legal sense; their Judaism and the Republic constituted a viable couple. Was theirs an optimism of convenience? Or was it a strategy of survival in the conditions of a diaspora?

The memory of a history shot through with suffering continued to haunt them, of course. Julien Sée, who translated Joseph Ha-Cohen's *Vale of Tears* in 1881, wrote in his introduction to the book:

---

104   Théodore Reinach, *Histoire des Israélites depuis la ruine de leur indépendance nationale jusqu'à nos jours*, 3rd edn, Paris: Librairie Hachette, 1903, XII and 372.

> I would gladly write on the title page of this book the formula that Jews recite when they enter a cemetery ... a cemetery for martyrs ... Resting here are countless generations of the people of Israel, who, for century after century, suffered every imaginable humiliation and every imaginable insult in order to remain faithful to their beliefs; who consented to be robbed and banished, had their throats cut, and endured torture by fire and water in order to sanctify their God. Sleeping here in eternal peace are husbands full of conjugal affection and fathers consumed by paternal love who, in the madness of a holy delirium, slew the wives they cherished and the children they loved in order to protect them from outrage and save them from apostasy.

Sée goes on to describe Jewish history as a 'bloody, funereal odyssey', 'a history of mourning and oppression, of untold suffering'. He goes so far as to add this confident note: 'it is in the most calamitous periods that the Jews were the most severely persecuted; it is in happier times that they have lived in peace.'[105]

The new definition of secular Judaism was in the process of being born, for better or worse. Elsewhere, other, equally secular voices were raised, voices of those who no longer looked to the classic schema of destruction–redemption or divine intervention for either salvation or consolation. In his poem on the 1903–6 pogroms in Kishniev, 'In the City of the Massacre', the great Hebrew writer Hayim Nahman Bialik, unlike the medieval poet who complains of God's silence during the calamities that befall his people, introduces a note of anger into the literature of destruction. Bialik's 300-line poem urges the inhabitants of the city to defend themselves, proclaims that the death of the victims was pointless, and refuses to mourn them. The poet's anger is directed at the Jews, who, he says, behaved like cowards in the face of their enemy—at the Jews, and also against God. With this poem, Bialik pleads the Zionist cause before the young Jews of the Russian Zone of Residence.[106] By an irony of fate, his poem has become, in our time, part of the martyrology of the liturgy of Yom Kippur, the occasion *par excellence* for solemn religious expiation. Bialik himself had in fact been influenced by the traditional clichés about Jewish passivity, and ignored the acts of resistance that occurred during these pogroms. As for the Hebrew literature produced by immigrants to the Americas or poets living in Russia, it opted for the register of the traditional lamentation whenever it evoked this pogrom.

Thus, for a long time, different responses to calamity co-existed and interpenetrated in Jewish communities across the globe; this was the case in

---

105   Julien Sée, Introduction, Ha-Cohen, *La Vallée des pleurs*, x and lxii.

106   The only territories in which the Jews of the Russian Empire had the right to reside, according to a restrictive decree promulgated by Alexander I in 1804.

Palestine as well, a country that had to cope with new challenges and new trials and tribulations.[107] But the virtually messianic hope that seemed to be incarnated by a Europe which, seemingly at random and more rapidly in some countries than in others, was at last integrating its Jews, was soon to be brutally dashed by the Nazis' assumption of power in 1933, and then reduced to naught by the unprecedented disaster that took place during the Second World War. The promise had become treason.

---

107   Mintz, *Hurban*, 129–48, 150, 165; Roskies, *The Literature*, 145–6.

CHAPTER THREE

Suffering without Hope

The murder, on European soil, of six million Jews by the Nazis and their collaborators during the Second World War not only constituted a radical historical break. It was also a catastrophe destined to eclipse all the earlier calamities that had contributed, in the course of centuries, to the compilation, from generation to generation, of a liturgized story of suffering.

This ancient liturgy of suffering, as we have seen, made it possible for Jews to solidify as a group and protect the faith of its members against the temptations of apostasy. It had, in the process, forged a long-term collective identity by means of what had become classic schemas of punishment/retribution and destruction/redemption.

These paradigms did not, to be sure, cease functioning altogether in the contemporary period, when the Jews had to confront the worst consequences of anti-Semitism, the death camps, and then face up to the challenges of a period of reconstruction of a Jewish life shattered by persecution, the death of loved ones, and incomparable suffering. Inevitably, the survivors were haunted by existential questions, such as: what had God been doing at Auschwitz, the symbol of absolute evil? The question recalled others that Jews had asked themselves in past times of profound distress; they had responded with consoling answers of many different kinds, including the idea of collective punishment for sin.

After the genocide, this answer seemed senseless, as did others that had long served as the benchmarks of Jewish life. Many Jews now rejected the traditional vision of a providential God who was active in history and watched protectively over his people, whom he had chosen from among the nations. Many of those who had entered the death camps without God and had survived, and even some of the survivors who believed in Him, had to ask themselves these kinds of questions and try to find answers in order to overcome their grief or continue to live with it. Some survivors who had originally been atheists embraced the faith; others abandoned Judaism. Many opted for one or the other of the various attitudes between these two extremes. Before the genocide, the majority of survivors had believed in the existence of God; thereafter, only 38 per cent did. The belief that the Jews were a chosen people proved tenacious: 41 per cent held this view before the war; one-third still did after it.

Six per cent of the survivors even declared that the creation of Israel had been worth the sacrifice of six million Jewish lives.[1] At all events, Judaism and the survivors, the most secularized included, were disoriented by the ordeals that they had experienced during the war.

Elie Wiesel cites a Hasidic Jew who is supposed to have said: 'for the faithful there are no questions; for the non-believer there are no answers'. Yet was it possible, during and after the genocide, to accept the explanation put forward by the great thinker Hermann Cohen, who died in 1918, to the effect that 'misery and pain are needed in order to awaken the conscience of men and thereby to advance the cause of ethical progress'?[2] Is evil, as Cohen suggests, a backdrop for good, the condition for its unfolding? 'The suffering of the poor is a kind of sacrifice for the sins of all mankind ... as the price of progress,' he adds. 'It is the saints who suffer; God loves the miserable.'[3] Indeed, if the question of good and evil ceaselessly haunted the Jewish world throughout its history, the question of theodicy, as old as Judaism itself, now took on crucial importance for Orthodoxy, which had to adopt a position in response to those seeking explanations for their suffering, even while remaining faithful to the commandments. Joseph Klausner would accordingly define the problem of the theodicy of the genocide as 'the question of questions'.[4]

DYING FOR GOD IN AUSCHWITZ

In Nazi Germany, the ultra-Orthodox had already produced theological responses to anti-Semitism. Thus the two most important ultra-Orthodox leaders in this period, Hayim Ozer Grodzensky, known by the acronym Ahiezer de Vilna, and Elhonon Wasserman, Grodzensky's brother-in-law, both of whom died before the genocide but lived to see *Kristallnacht* (9–10 November 1938), summoned the Jews to prayer, fortitude, and a return to the practice of their religion in 1939, after the destruction of Jewish synagogues, homes, and stores that presaged a dark period for the Jews of not only

---

1   Lewis Feuer, 'The Reasoning of Holocaust Theology', *Judaism*, 138:35, 1986, 201.

2   Cited in Baruch Cohon, ed., *Jewish Existence in an Open Society: A Convocation*, Los Angeles: Jewish Centers Association, 1970, 41; also cited in Charles Steckel, 'God and the Holocaust', *Judaism*, 20:3, 1971, 280.

3   Cited in Steckel, 'God and the Holocaust'. See also Laurence Kaplan, 'Suffering and Joy in the Thought of Hermann Cohen', *Modern Judaism*, 21, 2001, 15–22.

4   Joseph Klausner, 'The Question of All Questions and All Answers', in Yehuda Burla, ed., *About Home: A Literary Anthology by Writers from the Land of Israel for their Brothers Still Living in Europe*, Tel Aviv: Agudat Ha-sofrim Ha-ivriim Be-Eretz Yisrael, 1945 or 1946, 7–30 (in Hebrew).

Germany, but all Europe. Their response took its place within the paradigm of the Covenant. The whole of history unfolds under God's aegis; the Nazis themselves, said these ultra-Orthodox thinkers, were his instruments. De Vilna held the Reformed Jews responsible for what was happening. Wasserman blamed the abandonment of the Torah, assimilation, and Zionism, which he regarded as an act of normalization and proof of lack of trust in religion and God. Both de Vilna and Wasserman maintained that, at such moments, men's first duty was to turn, by way of the Torah, to God, who relieves suffering. The more the apparent increase in the power of evil and the sterner the chastisement, the closer one was to redemption. Thus Nazis, Zionists, heretics, the assimilated, and Reformed Jews were all instruments of the divine plan of salvation. Had Wasserman not accused both socialism and nationalism of being two forms of idolatry which, in Heaven, combined to produce national-socialism? Indeed, many people who frequented the circles of which these two teachers were representative criticized the Jewish Enlightenment for alienating the Jews from their traditions, thus bringing on this fatal outcome. Modernity, too, was accused of all manner of evil. Personal sacrifice would, however, bring Judaism closer to redemption. Although all indications are that redemption is not yet on hand, this kind of theological response to calamity has survived down to our day.[5]

Ahron Rokeah, the leader of the Hasidic dynasty of Belz, whose eldest son was burned alive in a synagogue that the Germans had put to the torch, expressed his grief in terms of sacrifice for God: 'It is indeed a kindness of the Almighty that I also offered a personal sacrifice.'[6] Suffering, in this conception, was a process of continual sacrifice, an act of religious devotion that had begun with the sacrifice of Isaac; it enhanced the sanctity of God and redeemed man. It was a form of God's 'hidden grace' (*hesed nistar*) that prayer and study of the Torah could transform into manifest, 'revealed goodness' (*hesed nigleh*). Thus God is supposed to have offered men an opportunity to draw closer to him.

Shem Klinberg, the leader of the Hasidic dynasty Zaloshizer, cited, as he presided over the third Sabbath meal in the Plashow death camp, Psalms 72:17: 'May his name be blessed for ever, and endure in the sight of the sun. In him shall be blessed every race in the world, and all nations call him blessed'. He

---

5   Gershon Greenberg, 'Faith, Ethics and the Holocaust: Orthodox Theological Responses to *Kristallnacht*: Chayyim Ozer Grodzensky ("Achiezer") and Elchonon Wassermann', *Holocaust and Genocide Studies* 3:4, 1988, 431–41.

6   Pesach Schindler, *Hasidic Responses to the Holocaust in the Light of Hasidic Thought*, Hoboken NJ: Ktav, 1990, 27.

then made a Hasidic commentary on these verses that mobilized a classic defensive justification of God which had it that his ways, and the current genocide, remained incomprehensible to man. If God is truth, his justice is not open to question. We serve him not only in love, enthusiasm, and joy, but also through grief. Someone who accepts suffering with love does not speculate about the reasons for God's decrees. According to rabbinical tradition, the divine attribute of judgement, the stern, wrathful face of God, is necessarily tempered by another of his attributes, grace and sovereign indulgence. In this interpretative framework, evil and suffering themselves have their origins in good and, in the end, are transformed into good. Recognizing God as father and king of the whole human race, the Hasidic teachers urged the faithful to accept suffering and (if necessary) death with love, even during the Final Solution.

Between 1940 and 1942, Rebbe Piazesner, Kalonymus Kalmish Shapiro, delivered a series of Sabbath sermons in his home in the Warsaw ghetto, which had been transformed into a synagogue and soup kitchen.[7] He translated them into Hebrew and buried them early in 1943. Discovered by a Polish worker after the war, they were published in 1960 under the title *Sacred Fire* (*Esh Kodesh*). Shapiro, who was himself murdered by the Nazis, considered the Jews' suffering to be a form of suffering that came from God. It had not been caused by their sins, but was part of his plan for humanity in general and the Jews in particular. In situations of extreme suffering, it was possible to share God's suffering; out of this mystical communion would emerge a new, active commitment, expressed in study of the Torah or observance of the commandments. For Shapiro, the destruction of European Judaism was part of a war against God in which the Jews were soldiers. However onerous this suffering, it bore an ancillary relationship to God's. The people of Israel no longer suffered for its misdeeds, but for its identification with the divinity.

For his part, Rebbe Razvirter, Shalom Eliezer Halberstam, reminded Jews, who were bemoaning their fate in this sombre period, of the principle of belief and confidence in God (*emunat ha-shem*), urging them to follow the ways of the Lord. The central doctrine of Hasidism preaches joy in the face of extreme adversity, which, in turn, reinforces faith in God. Thus the spiritual head of the Spinker dynasty, Yitshak Weiss, danced and sang in the train that brought him to Auschwitz. 'Purify our hearts', he exclaimed, 'and we shall serve you in truth!' Similarly, Rebbe Dombrower, Hayim Yehiel Rubin, recited the Sabbath

---

7   *Rebbe* is the Yiddish equivalent of the Hebrew *rabi* (teacher) and the title given to the heads of the Hasidic dynasties.

prayer with great fervour, sang the Sabbath songs recited at meals, and led 20 other Jews in a Hasidic dance before all of them were killed and buried in graves that they had dug with their own hands.

It is only when man does not admit that God is the source of suffering and shares this suffering with the people of Israel that suffering is tainted with despair. These acts of joyful acceptance of death are also bound up with the notion of the sanctification of the Name of God, which finds expression in martyrdom; that idea resurfaced during the dark years of the genocide. Maimonides' classic summary of the different ways in which Jews should or could fulfil the commandments was often evoked in these circles. In the Warsaw ghetto, Hasidic leaders extended this teaching by applying the term 'sanctification of the Name of God' to every victim of the genocide. For Maimonides, indeed, 'a Jew who is killed, though it may be for reasons other than conversion but simply because he is a Jew, is called *kaddosh*'.[8] In the Talmud, it is generally agreed that there is sanctification of the Name of God only when the Jew killed had had a choice in the matter. Thus, in ancient Jewish martyrology, the martyrs as a rule had been in a position to choose life, often by repudiating Judaism. But the martyrs of the Final Solution, while they hardly had the option of choosing life and faced certain death, nevertheless found themselves confronted with a choice – about the *way* in which they would accept and prepare their deaths. It was now a question of choosing between a death amid degradation and death with inner peace, nobility of soul, and self-respect. That new alternative emerged in this period as an attribute of the martyr's. But, like all commandments, it also required not only preparation in order to be properly carried out, but also concentration on the significance of the religious act accomplished. Thus Rebbe Grodzisker, Yisrael Shapira, demanded that Jews accept martyrdom in joy before entering the gas chamber. And, putting himself at their head, he sang the *Ani maamin* 'I believe'.[9]

The sanctification of the Name of God also manifested itself in the 'sanctification of life' (*kidush ha-hayim*): in physical resistance, whether it took the form of modest, spiritual, passive resistance or personal sacrifice made to help others in these times of distress. Jews were supposed to face death in a dignified way and to live with equal dignity, bearing in mind the divine element in man. Pride emerged as a response to the physical and spiritual degradation

---

8   Maimonides, cited in Schindler, 'Hasidic Responses', 60.

9   This is a short credo by an unknown author; it is based on Maimonides' articles of faith. In most Ashkenazi prayer books, it appears at the end of morning prayer.

inflicted by the enemy. Thus, to avoid the prostitution into which German soldiers were trying to force them, 93 young women of the Orthodox school Beit Yaakov in Cracow committed suicide by taking poison, after reciting one last prayer in order to 'sanctify the Name of God by their deaths as well as their lives'. Their sacrifice was immortalized by the Hebrew poet Hillel Bavli in a poem which has today been incorporated into the liturgy of Yom Kippur, the Jewish Day of Atonement, in a spirit reminiscent of the medieval custom of liturgizing catastrophes and acts of martyrdom for the instruction of future generations.[10]

Dying in order to sanctify the Name of God is deemed to be a selfless act: one dies for God, for the love of God, not in order to receive a reward. Yet even those who consent to make this ultimate sacrifice are aware that the final purpose of the creation of man and the justification for the Covenant come down to observing the Torah and living with it, not, exceptions aside, dying for it. As God's partner in creation, man is committed to the process of life; he thus bears witness to God's grandeur. Hence Jews had to accept everything with love, inspired by their confidence and faith in God's benevolent relationship with man. In this case, they responded to God by clinging to him in mystical union, amid joy. This process leads to the dissolution of the forces of the ego and indifference in the face of material want or physical adversity. God's privileged relationship to his people is thus forged amid shared suffering.[11]

That said, ultra-Orthodox discourse by no means freed itself of the idea that the calamity which befell the Jews was justified by their sins against the commandments. Hitler was the new Nebuchadnezzar sent by God to chastise his people. Yoel Teitelboym, a genocide survivor and the head of the Hasidic Satmar dynasty, which remains an anti-Zionist current even today, cursed the Zionists for behaving in such a way as to precipitate and legitimate the Final Solution – the just punishment for an act of insolent blasphemy, that of initiating a return to Zion on their own and, thereby, acting as substitutes for the awaited Messiah. One of the most recent expressions of the paradigm of punishment/retribution is to be found in a 2001 declaration by a Rabbi from Iraq, Ovadia Yossef, the spiritual leader of the Israeli political party known as the *Shas*, which rallies Orthodox Sepharadic Jews, especially from Morocco.

10　On this episode, see Zev Garber, 'The Ninety-Three Beit Ya'akov Martyrs', *Shofar* 12:1, 1993, 70–3.

11　Schindler, *Hasidic Responses*, 27, 60–4, 68–70, 115–6; Yehuda Bauer, *Rethinking the Holocaust*, New Haven: Yale University Press, 2000, 201–2.

For Yossef, the six million victims of the genocide were 'reincarnations of earlier souls, who sinned and caused others to sin'.[12]

Thus the massacre elicited a wide range of responses from the ultra-Orthodox, who, if only because of their visibility, paid an especially heavy toll to the genocide. Some Hasidic thinkers even saw the mass murder as 'the labour pains' that are to precede the coming of the Messiah, supposed to bring the exile and its vicious influence to an end. Indeed, the Hasidic Lubavitch movement *Habad* established a connection between its messianism and the Final Solution.[13] The modern period and twentieth century were perceived as the dawn of the messianic age, which could only be preceded by cataclysmic events. In the 1940s and early 1950s, this current considered the Holocaust to be the culmination of this period of distress; it would be directly followed, they believed, by the coming of the Messiah. In the view of many of the movement's adepts, its charismatic leader, Menahem Mendel Schneerson, himself incarnated this hope, inasmuch as God was to send the Redeemer directly after the disaster. His coming depended, however, on whether the Jews once again began observing the precepts of their religion. Schneerson accordingly set out to popularize the *Habad* teachings that could accelerate the process. The genocide was also thought to have saved the people of Israel by amputating one of its gangrenous members. Again, the suffering endured by pure, holy beings in this period had been merely temporal. What did it matter when measured against eternal life? The Orthodox who had endured the ordeal were martyrs; their martyrdom had to be understood as an immense privilege. When Yekutiel Yehudah Halberstam, the leader of the Hasidic dynasty of Sanz-Klausenburg, who had lost his wife and 11 children at Auschwitz, was asked whether he still believed that the Jews were a chosen people, he answered that he did. The reason was simply that it was not the Jews who had perpetrated these horrors, but the Gentiles. His family had been singled out by God to make this sacrifice. To suffer for the love of God – therein lay the significance of being chosen. Schneerson, for his part, went even further, suggesting that the genocide had

---

12   Berel Lang, *Post-Holocaust: Interpretation, Misinterpretation, and the Claims of History*, Bloomington: Indiana University Press, 2005, 40–1; Aviezer Ravitzky, *Messianism, Zionism and Jewish Religious Radicalism*, trans. Michael Swirsky and Jonathan Chipman, Chicago: University of Chicago Press, 1996, 124.

13   *Habad* is an abbreviation for *Hokhmah, Binah, Daat* ('wisdom, discernment, knowledge'). The movement of the same name was founded by Shneur Zalman of Lyadi (1745–1813) and is based in New York today. The death in 1994 of the last rabbi of the dynasty, Menahem Mendel Schneerson, who died with no heirs, by no means put an end to the messianic fervour that surrounded him in his lifetime.

been the work of a just God, that it had been caused by the sins of the Jews, and that God had carried out his work with the help of Hitler, his messenger.[14]

While the promise of immortality, an acute sense of sin, and a certain conception of election paved the way for some, the most devout, to reconcile faith in a just and loving God with the horror of the death camps, this path was closed to many others who lacked such convictions or even regarded them as particularly inhuman. It should be noted, however, that this fundamentalist vision of the massacre generally put *all* the victims of the genocide in the category of holy martyrs, whatever the precise circumstances surrounding their deaths. It is in fact not certain that Nazi persecution can be described as 'religious' or that it is legitimate to assign special importance to measures such as the 1942 decree promulgated by the Germans in the Kaunas ghetto, which made study of the Talmud a capital offence. Yet the fact remains that in 1990, long after the genocide a Hasidic leader such as Schneerson was still asserting that every Jew who had died in it had to be considered a holy martyr.

While Rebbe Halberstam, as we have seen, was indeed capable of transforming the death of his family into martyrdom and even finding an infinitely precious reinforcement of his faith in it, few laymen were capable of doing the same. And many believers refused to be satisfied by such interpretations. Thus, in the post-Holocaust period, alongside the ultra-Orthodox responses to the event, deemed unsatisfactory by some, there developed a new theology that sought to arrive at a better understanding of the Jews' suffering.

DID GOD HIMSELF DIE AT AUSCHWITZ?

The theology just evoked brought two visions face to face. One suggested God had been *hidden* during the genocide. The other proclaimed God had been *absent* from Auschwitz and elsewhere, because God was dead.[15]

The theology elaborated by Eliezer Berkovits, an Orthodox rabbi, fell into the first category. Although Berkovits took due account of the anti-Semitism that had preceded the Final Solution and led up to it as a specific historical reality, he did not abandon ancient religious explanatory models. Auschwitz was not unique, inasmuch as it put the same questions to faith as the disasters of the past had. Unlike some ultra-Orthodox thinkers, however, Berkovits did not attribute the existence of the death camps to Israel's sins. He acknowledged that the genocide had been an absolute injustice, and appealed to a concept

---

14   Steckel, 'God and the Holocaust', 284; Bauer, *Rethinking the Holocaust,* 204–15.
15   Steckel, 'God and the Holocaust', 284.

more sophisticated than those usually cited by the adherents of the old paradigms. This concept, present in the Bible, was that of the 'veiling of the face' of God (*hester panim*). Berkovits elaborated his interpretation of theology in a trilogy, the first volume of which appeared in 1959. In the third, published in 1973 entitled *Faith after the Holocaust*, he applied his theories of suffering to the genocide.

When God 'veils his face', he withdraws from history, thereby allowing certain events that he could have prevented to take place. This withdrawal by no means indicates that God *wanted* these events to occur; simply, it proceeds from his desire that man should have greater spiritual freedom. Such 'veiling' is the price to be paid for the emergence of a moral humanity. This view of history breaks it down into two parts, one divine, the other human, one subject to God's action, the other to man's. God could also control the human side of history, but chooses not to in order to provide a guarantee of human freedom. Moreover, he abstains from reacting to moral evil. In this way, Berkovits reiterates the classic theme that free will is the necessary premise for authentic morality. It would be impossible to be humane if God were rigorously just. He chooses to act in this manner, although he is not compelled to. Every theodicy is confronted with such a choice, since everything that occurs, God's withdrawal from history included, is bound up with a divine intention. The 'veiling' of god must accordingly be understood as one sign of his presence. God did not die at Auschwitz, but the 'veiling' of God made the horror possible. It was not God who brought Auschwitz into being, but man, who, as a result of this 'veiling', enjoyed total freedom of action, the freedom to do good or evil.

In his 1979 book *With God in Hell: Judaism in the Ghettos and Deathcamps*, Berkovits tries to show that the feeling that Judaism died in the death camps is based on a false idea. Quite the contrary: the camps can be regarded as a spiritual Matzada preceding the final act of suicide, which strengthened Judaism in the worst of hells. This offers a lesson to the engaged Judaism of the present and future. The 'absence' of God is nothing new, for every generation has had its Auschwitz. Suffering, for Berkovits, is a consequence of man's free will. God ensures the possibility of evil in order to ensure that of its opposite, good, harmony, and love. What is good is good because evil exists; evil is evil because the possibility of good exists. So that man can exist, God must suffer for a long time with him. God's long period of suffering is oriented toward evil people as well as good ones. To ensure the individual's spiritual independence, it is necessary that God veil his face. As a creator, God is obliged to create an imperfect world, to create darkness and evil. At a personal level, suffering is positive. Properly borne, suffering purifies and deepens the personality. The fact that the face of God had to be veiled does not explain God's silence during Auschwitz, yet it justifies it.

The crucial question that Berkovits raises is whether, after the genocide, Jewish belief in the God of history still makes sense. For him, the Final Solution had been an attempt to dethrone God. The affirmation of the presence of a God of history is the antithesis of the Nazis' repudiation of universal human values. The Nazis had understood that the destiny of such a God is inseparable from the Jews'. The nature of Jewish existence was a prophetic witness to the moral degeneration of human beings and nations. Auschwitz showed not only what man was capable of doing to the Jews, but also what he was capable of doing to his fellow man. For Berkovits, the fact that Israel was reborn on its territory after the genocide proves that God is not absent from history; rather, the vocation of the terrestrial world is truly to become the kingdom of God. The genocide was only the most recent and most terrible of the occasions on which the Jewish people has had to suffer in order to make God's existence manifest. The Holocaust, followed by the creation of the state of Israel, was a new, extraordinary example of the basic oscillation between a God who veils his face and a God who reveals himself.[16]

Like Berkovits, other traditionalist thinkers, such as Harold Fisch and Irving Greenberg, recast the doctrine of necessary suffering without legitimating persecution. Greenberg makes use of models drawn from Job and Lamentations, even while contending that, after Auschwitz, the central religious affirmation is the creation of life. He, too, identifies the state of Israel as a religious institution, despite its secular character, regarding it as the Jewish people's supreme response, a response that generates life, to the will of those who wanted to annihilate it.

For his part, the rabbi and reformed theologian Ignaz Maybaum, in his famous book, *The Face of God after Auschwitz*, maintains that Hitler nursed special hatred for the Jews because they were the witnesses to the existence of God and a divine plan in the world. The primary task incumbent on them was

---

16 Eliezer Berkovits, *God, Man and History: A Jewish Interpretation*, New York: Jonathan Davis, 1959; Berkovits, *Faith after the Holocaust*, New York: Ktav, 1973; Berkovits, *With God in Hell: Judaism in the Ghettos and Deathcamps*, New York: Sanhedrin Press, 1979; Reuven Bulka, 'Different Paths, Common Thrust: The "Shoalogy" of Berkovits and Frankl', in Bernhard Rosenberg and Fred Heuman, eds, *Theological and Halakhic Reflections on the Holocaust*, New York: Ktav, 1992, 165–87; Eugene Borowitz, 'Confronting the Holocaust', in Jacob Neusner, ed., *Faith Renewed: The Judaic Affirmation Beyond the Holocaust*, Macon GA: Mercer University Press, 1994, vol. 1, 175–96; Leaman, *Evil and Suffering*, 190–1.

to lead the Gentiles toward God; the calamities that befell them were merely steps on the way to the accomplishment of this mission. If the destruction of the Jews was the result of divine intervention, it was nevertheless not a divine chastisement. Jesus was an innocent victim whose death led to the world's salvation. In the same way, the victims of the genocide were sacrificial offerings chosen by God himself. Every act of destruction had been bound up with a divine intervention of decisive significance for the course of history. All such acts had ushered in new historical periods, the succession of which had progressively brought the nations closer to God. The two major disasters prior to the genocide, the destruction of the First and Second Temples, had helped to create a Diaspora and inspired the invention of the synagogue as a substitute for the Sanctuary. The destruction of the First Temple benefited the human race, because, in dispersing the Jews, it allowed them to spread the divine message among the nations. That of the Second Temple established a purer form of worship, led to the abandonment of sacrifices, and promoted a growing awareness of the omnipresence of the divine. The third disaster, the genocide, marked the end of the medieval period, which had been dominated by a narrow conception of religion and community, and hastened the advent of a new world, based on reason and modernity. Thus the ferment of progress lies in destruction. One-third of Jewry was destroyed, but the remaining two-thirds outlived Hitler. It was now up to the survivors to grasp that it was their duty to persevere in the effort to transform society. Hitler had been God's tool, as had Nebuchadnezzar before him; the six million slain were simply innocent victims who had died for others' sins.[17]

Other theologians developed similar theories in an attempt to ensure the continuity between the calamities of the past and the suffering associated with the genocide. It was in the Anglo-Saxon world and, in particular, the United States that the theology of the Holocaust attained recognition and stature. In France, even at the heart of a Jewish world that had felt the full force of the genocide, little of this work has been translated, and there has been no comparable theological effort, Emile Fackenheim's writings excepted. This is doubtless not unrelated to the fact that pre-war France did not produce Jewish thinkers comparable to the grand figures who emerged in Germany, such as Hermann Cohen, Franz Rosenzweig, Walter Benjamin, Martin Buber, and others. The separation of church and state, elevated to the rank of one of the

---

17 Ignaz Maybaum, *The Face of God after Auschwitz*, Amsterdam: Polak and Van Gennep, 1965; Dan Cohn-Sherbok, 'God and the Holocaust', in Maybaum, ed., *Theodicy*, Lewiston NY: Edwin Mellen Press, 1997, 85–7; Leaman, *Evil and Suffering*, 191–2.

supreme principles of the French Republic in 1905, probably also curbed interest in theology or Jewish thought; Judaism as a religion remained confined to the private sphere. Only Jewish historiographical writing had some success in France – from the nineteenth century on, as we have seen. The Jewish philosophy that developed in France after the war, although it broached the question of the Holocaust, did not confront it as in the Anglo-Saxon world, whether by extending or reviving traditional theology or experimenting with less conventional approaches. Few French Jewish thinkers apprehended the event as intensely as Anglo-Saxon theologians did.

From this standpoint, one of the most original representatives of what would eventually be given the name 'Shoalogy' in English is, undisputedly, Richard Rubinstein, whose ideas had soon sparked discussion and debate. In his well-known *After Auschwitz*, published in 1966, and in subsequent writings as well, Rubinstein breaks with the classic theology of an omnipotent, benevolent God and, echoing Nietszche's *Zarathustra*, sounds the theme of the death of God. This theme was already in circulation among American theologians such as Thomas Altizer, Harvey Cox, and William Hamilton. For Rubinstein, Auschwitz destroyed the foundations of belief in Judaism's traditional historical God and made any theology espousing this belief intellectually untenable. How could one continue to believe, after Auschwitz, in a providential God who was active in history and watched over his people? Rubinstein calls for replacing traditional theology with a positive affirmation of the value of human life for its own sake, with no specific theological references. Joy and personal fulfilment have from now on to be sought in this world, rather than in a mystical, eschatological future. There is no hope of salvation for the human race, whose ultimate fate is to return to nothingness. Rubinstein, rejecting the biblical conception of the divinity along with Jewish theodicy, subscribes to a form of paganism of the kind that prevailed in Canaan. In his view, the only possible response to the death camps is rejection of God. As for the Jewish people, Rubinstein considers it to be a people whose religion has been successively influenced by divergent cultural and historical events. He also grants that Judaism's ethical content guarantees its longevity even in the absence of religious convictions, as long as it is not reduced to a mere system of beliefs.[18]

In the nineteenth century, many Jewish thinkers revised their conception of a supreme God supposed to be the omnipotent agent of history and avoided establishing a direct relationship between this God and human suffering.

---

18   Richard Rubinstein, *After Auschwitz: Radical Theology and Contemporary Judaism*, Indianapolis: Bobbs Merrill, 1966.

They did not, however, opt for the rupture represented by Rubinstein's thought, a radical rupture, to be sure, yet doubtless one of the most honest answers it was possible to give after the genocide. That said, Rubinstein snatched theodicy away from those who needed it most, those who had suffered and were now waiting for a justification or explanation of God's silence during the Second World War. Elie Wiesel, although not a theologian himself, was not very far from Rubinstein when he admonished himself never to forget that the flames had destroyed his faith forever; the genocide, he added, was incomprehensible with God, although it was also incomprehensible without him. Similarly, Wiesel confessed that he would be lying if he said that he believed in God, and lying if he said the opposite.[19] Thinkers who, after the genocide, refused to ground their faith in a traditional approach to God were by no means rare.

In his writings during 1968–70, especially in *The Human Condition after Auschwitz* and *God's Presence in History*, the theologian Emil Fackenheim, a German refugee who fled Nazism and acquired Canadian citizenship, echoes Rubinstein's view that Auschwitz had greatly imperilled traditional belief and the idea of a redemptive God. Fackenheim, too, makes Jewish ethics and Jewish survival fundamental objectives and values in the post-Auschwitz period. He insists that it is the Jews' imperative duty to remain alive, resistant, and united as a distinct, identifiable people. He repeats in his own name a statement made by a secular Israeli journalist on the left: 'After the death camps, there remains only one supreme value: existence'. Fackenheim makes survival a commandment, the 614th, proclaimed by God after the genocide.[20] The Jews are under an obligation to survive as Jews so as not hand a posthumous victory to Hitler, who planned to destroy them, and to destroy Judaism in the process. For Fackenheim, the state of Israel is a riposte to Auschwitz; it is a response based on life and new construction cast in the teeth of destruction and death.[21] The creation of Israel becomes 'reparations' (*tikun*) for all the suffering endured. This concept, borrowed from the Lurianic Kabbalah, traditionally designates 'reparations' for damage done to the universe at its inception; the people of

---

19   Elie Wiesel, *Night,* New York: Bantam, 1982, cited in Dan Cohn-Sherbok, 'God and the Holocaust', 75–6.

20   Rabbinical Judaism maintains that there are 613 commandments in the Torah.

21   Emil Fackenheim, *The Human Condition after Auschwitz: A Jewish Testimony a Generation After,* Syracuse NY: Syracuse University Press, 1971; Fackenheim, *God's Presence in History: Jewish Affirmations and Philosophical Reflections,* Northvale, NJ: Aronson, 1997; Seymour Cain, 'The Question and the Answers after Auschwitz', *Judaism,* 20:3, 1971, 271–2.

Israel is actively involved in making such reparations, which lead to redemption. Thus the sacred character conferred on the creation of Israel began to fuse with the theme of the genocide. Gradually, the two themes came to pervade the new Jewish attitudes that, from the 1970s on, marked the transition from relative silence about the Holocaust to its progressive entry into the public sphere. This connection, once made, was as effective in the Diaspora as in Israel; functioning in surprisingly well co-ordinated fashion in both, it provided a twofold source of support for the reconstruction of Jewish identity, even more conspicuously among secular than among religious Jews. This osmosis increasingly induced Israel and the Diaspora to define themselves as a single community united by indissoluble bonds.

The fact remains that placing the genocide in a theoretical framework which ensured its continuity with previous ordeals sanctified it, while rendering it incomprehensible for as long as it remained outside the traditional genealogy of misfortune. This type of interpretation and appropriation stripped it of its uniqueness, a uniqueness that is today, let us add, most often proclaimed by secularized Jews. For the genocide effectively became part of the long line of calamities that have befallen the Jews over the centuries. It was solidly anchored in this story of suffering handed down from generation to generation, a story which, sufficient unto itself, divided the world up into those who suffer, namely, the Jews, and those who inflict suffering, the Gentiles. At the same time, this story of suffering once again removed an event, here the genocide, from the course of a History constituted by ruptures and continuities and evolving in a direction determined by, not a ubiquitous God, but fallible men and women.

The Orthodox, armed with the explanatory models and/or the theological justification of the massacre that they had forged, did not participate as fully as secular Jews in promoting the ever more conspicuous penetration of the public sphere and public debate by the Holocaust. It was as if the millennial schemas had assuaged people's grief, putting the genocide in perspective alongside other disasters in whose wake the Jews had continued to exist while respecting the commandments. The Orthodox theologian Berkovits writes that the difference between the calamities of the past and the genocide resides in the exceptional magnitude of the latter, but that the scope of an event has little importance in theology: the problems raised by the death of a single innocent person are identical to those raised by the death of six million. In his view, the Jews have experienced countless Auschwitzes.[22]

---

22   Cited in Lang, *Post-Holocaust*, 38.

Moreover, the effect of the continuity established by this sort of theological thinking, its ahistorical nature notwithstanding, was, undeniably, to open the present to the future. If this catastrophe was not one of a kind, it solicited further interpretation rather than circling round itself amid the despair engendered by closure. To accept continuity, however, one had to have kept the faith.

THE JUDAISM 'OF THE HOLOCAUST AND REDEMPTION'

Those who had been seeking non-religious responses to the Holocaust were left with their questions. Nonetheless, non-Orthodox and even secularized circles also contributed, if in a different way, to 'theologizing' the event. Over the years, on a foundation provided by the millennial history of Jewish suffering, the Holocaust itself has been erected into a new secular religion without a God, a self-sufficient religion with its rites, ceremonies, priests, places of pilgrimage, modern martyrs, rhetoric, and one supreme commandment: the obligation to remember. At the centre of this religion stands Auschwitz: for, curiously enough, 'Auschwitz' has become *the* symbolic name for all the ghettos and camps, although, at Auschwitz itself, 70,000 prisoners, the overwhelming majority of them Soviet prisoners-of-war or Poles, were put to death, whereas, at Auschwitz II, the death camp that the Germans called Birkenau, between 1,100,000 and 1,600,000 people were gassed, 90 per cent of them Jews.[23] The classic theological exegeses of the past were no longer satisfactory. From now on, everything human had to be interpreted in the light of this symbol.

The new religion began to take form with the 1961 Eichmann trial and the 1967 Six Day War, a war that some feared would culminate in a second genocide. Auschwitz was eventually transformed into a new Sinai: the place where a new Judaism, a Judaism made to order – less constraining, without the onus of Jewish religious practices or Jewish culture – was revealed to man. Jewishness was thus no longer a religious category, properly speaking, but, rather, an ethics adapted to the demands of a modern society in which mixed identities co-exist without discomfiture, while difference becomes a plus, as long as it remains acceptable to the social majority. Thus was born a new Judaism, one that Jacob Neusner has called the Judaism 'of the Holocaust and Redemption'; this secular religion raised the destruction of the European Jews – from now on, the 'Shoah' – to the level of an event possessing intense transcendental

---

23   Henryk Grynberg, 'Appropriating the Holocaust', *Commentary*, 74:5, 1982, 54–5. I have corrected the figures cited by Grynberg in the light of the estimates generally accepted today.

meaning, while conferring qualities of the same order, redemptive in this case, on the creation of the state of Israel.[24] The genocide thus became a unique species of suffering which, by virtue of its uniqueness, told the Jews why they had to be Jews. Furthermore, the existence of the state of Israel ruled out a repetition of this founding event.

The genocide certainly does not have the same significance for those who survived it as for those who did not, yet it is through this event that Judaism's genealogical lineage is reconstructed, and it is suffering that is supposed to hold everything together. For the survivors, suffering had the reality of a tragic experience; for others, it generated Jewish identity at a time when Judaism had thrown its substance and religious practice overboard. If Jews were to be Jews without Judaism, it was urgent that a memory be elaborated that could be shared by the survivors and those who wished to remain Jewish by assuming the Holocaust victims' history. It was as if the fear of losing its Jewishness compelled each generation to find, at all costs, a catastrophe that could serve it as a support.

In the nineteenth century and the first half of the twentieth, the story of suffering had been painted on a broad canvas, with the Crusades and their contingent of martyrs as its central motif. In the post-war period, the story of suffering would again be pressed into service as a support, but, this time, the Holocaust was put at the centre, with, as its pillars, the witnesses to it who were still alive. The obligation to remember evolved accordingly. Initially, it was nothing more than an obligation to honour the dead and the survivors. It was placed under the sign of a twofold injunction: 'never again!' and 'do not forget that you are Jews'.

The Holocaust did not, finally, have to be included in the long line of past calamities. It rose to the rank of the Catastrophe with a capital 'C', to which everything that happened later would inevitably be geared. The result was that secular Jews were deprived of a promising, meaningful future. It is true that Levinas spoke of the genocide as a 'paradigm' of suffering, but he did not isolate it from the Gulag and other twentieth-century places of suffering, which is to say that he reinserted it in the course of history.[25] The modern ethnic Jew, in contenting herself with memory, deliberately deprived herself of answers capable of explaining the genocide. Rejecting the theologians'

---

24   Of Neusner's works, see esp. *Stranger at Home: 'The Holocaust', Zionism and American Judaism*, Chicago: University of Chicago Press, 1981, 79–90; *Formative Judaism: Religious, Historical, and Literary Studies, Sixth Series*, Atlanta GA: Scholars Press, 1989, 18–21; 'Stranger at Home: Myths in American Judaism', *Forum*, 39, 1980, 34.

25   On this question, see Lang, *Post-Holocaust*, 43–4.

'rationalizations', or quite simply unaware of them, she also rejected history in the strict sense of the word—the history in which the Jewish genocide, if ranged alongside other genocides and catastrophes, could have acquired new meaning as a result of comparison and contextualization. Because the genocide was unique, it belonged to the Jews and to them alone. This obsession with uniqueness was in fact an unpleasant secular version of the idea that the Jews were a chosen people.[26]

As for Isaac Deutscher and Elie Wiesel, they advocated silence, on the grounds that the genocide would remain forever beyond the grasp of the human mind. In fact, in the 1950s and 1960s, the event acquired a certain normalcy, and the fact that it had occurred so recently helped to keep it outside the field of history. Of course, the passage of time and the distancing that comes with this paved the way for an attempt at historicization. It then became possible to affirm, at least from a historical point of view, that the catastrophe was an intelligible event that could be critically analyzed. However, the historicization attempted in the late 1960s gave way, shortly thereafter, to a tendency to politicize discourse about the genocide and exploit it to ends foreign to it. This historicization had little effect on those who had seized on the Holocaust as a religion, and on its central article of faith, the obligation to remember. As had repeatedly happened in the course of the Jewish experience, history and memory again entered into a relation of tension, a tension that, in the case of the genocide, is probably unlikely to diminish before the death of the last of the survivors. Memory will probably pursue its path for some time yet; there will, however, come a day when history will be the only means of transmitting it. In the meantime, the Holocaust as a religion of suffering has quite clearly been adopted by the Jewish masses, who remain deaf to historicization, which has essentially been restricted to scholarly circles. This 'conversion' has profoundly changed the face of Judaism, except among the Orthodox and, especially, ultra-Orthodox, who did not need this new religion in order to continue to be Jewish or become Jewish again. One may wonder, indeed, how long this secular religion can provide the grounds for a viable Jewish identity, when one considers that it has been erected mainly on a foundation of suffering and victimhood and makes of its followers eternally vigilant Jews plunged into a permanent state of insecurity.

Whereas Deutscher and Wiesel called for silence as the appropriate response to the sacred, Claude Lanzmann directed Shoah, a movie 9 hours and 23 minutes long and produced in 1985 that is based mainly on interviews with

26   Ismar Schorsch, 'The Holocaust and Jewish Survival', Midstream, 27/1, January 1981, p. 39.

survivors or non-Jewish witnesses. In the director's estimation, this is the only acceptable avenue of approach to the theme. In his view, a fiction film on the subject would be a major transgression, for it is impossible to imagine what happened, and representing it is taboo. If it is true that Lanzmann's work avoids Hollywood conventions, it is not free of artifice, to say nothing of the self-dramatization its director – omnipresent throughout – indulges in. Some, indeed, have even criticized Lanzmann for engaging in tactical manipulation of his interviewees. Moreover, in American academic circles, *Shoah* was not exempt from criticism of a kind unimaginable in France, so closely is Lanzmann's person identified with the event itself in his native country. Since his film and the genocide are one, the sacralization of the event could not but draw the film's creator into its aura.

That sacralization is due in large measure to the choice of the film's title. Lanzmann borrows it from the Bible, from the prophets Isaiah and Sophonia.[27] In the scriptural sources, *Shoah* means destruction, defeat, exile, and individual misfortune, of the kind that flows from a punishment imposed by God on an individual or group for sinning. Thus the Hebrew word *Shoah* signifies a disaster brought on by God's wrath. In the Book of Job, the term is used, for the first time, to refer to a catastrophe of cosmic dimensions; here, too, catastrophe is linked to the punishment of sin. In 1938, the word was current among Zionist circles in Palestine, where it was used to designate the tragic events of *Kristallnacht*. In Continental Europe, especially in France, it is gradually getting the better of the English word Holocaust. What is more, *shoah* is today the Hebrew term used in Israel to name the Jewish genocide. Incomprehensible for someone who does not know Hebrew (Lanzmann has pointed out that he initially chose it precisely because he did not know what it meant),[28] the word 'Shoah' not only de-universalizes the Jewish genocide, but also takes the event out of its historical context. And while its official adoption in Israel has, together with its secularization, helped to blot out its original connotations of 'sin' and 'punishment', the fact remains that it refers, despite itself, to one of the Orthodox theological interpretations of suffering in the camps. Thus all the basic elements of a secular theology of the Holocaust are already present in this term.[29] To this it must be added that Lanzmann, who rejects fiction and even

---

27   The word 'Shoah' occurs in the Hebrew Bible in the following verses: Is 47:11; So 1:15; Ps 35:8 and 63:10; Jb 30:3, 30:14, and 38:27; Pr 1:27 and 3:25.

28   'I chose this name because I didn't understand what it meant' (*Libération*, 24 January 2005).

29   For critiques of Lanzmann's movie, see Alan Mintz, *Popular Culture and the Shaping of Holocaust Memory*, Seattle: University of Washington Press, 2001, 145–9; Claude Lanzmann, 'Holocauste, représentation impossible', *Le Monde*, 3 March 1994.

rules out the use of archival documents, in fact seems to endorse, with his conception of the only kind of film it is possible to make about the genocide, the biblical prohibition on figurative representation.[30] Nothing of what has just been said diminishes the value of his work, which, as hardly needs to be pointed out here, is rich and compelling. The fact remains that these choices, made by a secular Jew such as Lanzmann, clearly took their place in the then rising wave of sacralization of the Holocaust in France. Lanzmann's movie played an important role in this process, if only by virtue of the fact that its title entered into general usage there. He himself, moreover, states the matter without reserve: 'It's a film in the present tense. It doesn't contain a single archival document, a single photograph, a single commentary. I tried to annul all distance between the past and the present so that viewers would experience the Shoah again in an almost hallucinatory sort of timelessness.'[31] Thus he puts us outside the world of human time – indeed, in the realm of the unthinkable.

Elie Wiesel was no less suspicious of aesthetic representations of the genocide, fearing the trivialization to which they could lead. He was equally suspicious of historical explanations, since it was a short step from explanation to excuse. Theodor Adorno himself affirmed that it was not possible to write poetry after Auschwitz. He reconsidered, however, after reading 'Death Fugue', a poem by Paul Celan, who had lost his loved ones in the genocide.[32] Celan had begun writing this poem, with its many allusions to the camps, in Czernowitz, completing it in Bucharest at war's end. His poem was a call for hope; it affirmed that poetry was capable of reconstructing humanity after the disaster, thus contradicting the theses about the incommunicability and ineffability of the annihilation.[33]

All the talk about ineffability and the impossibility of representation after Auschwitz contributes to the mythologization of the event. In traditional Jewish theology, the ways of God are inscrutable. The ways of Auschwitz now became inscrutable as well. The survivors and their descendants suffered, but were not authorized to *understand*. The genocide was on its way to becoming an essentially religious mystery. Similarly, those who treated it as such became new Jobs – the Job who was not supposed to try to discover the reasons for his suffering – but were inevitably deprived of the consolation provided by a belief

---

30   Ex 20:4.
31   Halpérin and Lévitte, eds, *Mémoire et Histoire*, 73.
32   In German, *Todesfuge*.
33   Esther Cameron, 'Post-Holocaust Poetry of Paul Celan', *Tikkun* 2:1, 1987, 38–43; Enzo Traverso, *L'Histoire déchirée: Essai sur Auschwitz and les intellectuels*, Paris: Cerf, 1997 (see esp. the section entitled 'Paul Celan et la poésie de la destruction').

in the just God who reveals himself at the end of the biblical dialogue. Suffering, on this approach, was to be irrevocably condemned to silence. It was shut up in a solitude that bordered on election, a solitude and an election deliberately chosen by the group itself: a self-election of the human, by the human, and for the human, without God. That said, it is, paradoxically, hard to identify with something that one can neither explain nor understand. Yet the genocide was a human event, perpetrated by human beings, and rationally planned; it can be rendered intelligible, despite the difficulties inherent in such a programme and the understandably powerful emotion involved. It is not wrong to say that the immensity of the pain and suffering that it caused imposes an extremely arduous task on any artist, novelist, philosopher, or poet attempting to account for it. Yet this does not put it in the realm of the unrealizable, unless we are to assume that the event had nothing human about it, so that it must be treated as a metahistorical or extrahistorical occurrence.[34] If we do, then what hope is there that it can take on universal significance, or that one can say, for the whole human race, 'never again'?

Conceived outside history, the Final Solution becomes a tragedy that defies all comparison or analogy: it appears as a black hole bereft of a past or future that annihilates all explanatory models, including the traditional symbols and archetypes which, earlier, enabled the Jews to cope with suffering. Of course, the new religion of the absolute exception nevertheless found itself constrained to borrow some of its substance and cultural forms from the ancient Jewish theological models. Paradoxically, however, it did not find adequate responses to suffering in them. It tended to reduce the entire millennial Jewish experience to this insurmountable and always imminent 'tragedy', as if the history of the Jews were nothing more than an interminable cycle of disasters. So interpreted, Jewish history would begin with the genocide and, in the worst case, end with a similar tragedy. Thus to the suffering actually endured there corresponds an imagined suffering, a suffering to come.

The event, once it became the object of a cult, was rendered sacred, and the memory of it was elevated to the level of the absolute. Not by accident does a historian of the Holocaust such as Alvin Rosenfeld demand that we treat the memoirs, poetry, and prose about this subject as 'holy,' not simply literary, texts. Arnost Lustin, for his part, contends that some of the fiction produced on this theme 'can stand comparison with the best written parts of the Bible'.[35]

---

34   Yehuda Bauer, 'Essay: On the Place of the Holocaust in History: In Honour of Franklin H. Littell', *Holocaust and Genocide Studies*, 2:2, 1987, 209–20.

35   Alvin Rosenfeld, *A Double Dying: Reflections on Holocaust Literature*, Bloomington: Indiana University Press, 1980; Byron Sherwin and Susan Ament, eds,

Elisabeth de Fontenay adds: 'It seems to the Jews that, without pathos and tears, the dead die a second death ... To write the history of the catastrophe, on this view, is to be as cold, after the fact, as those who allowed it to happen.' This is a way of abolishing all possibility of historicizing the event, while associating those who harness themselves to that task with the passive observers, if not, indeed, the accomplices. It is a perspective which has it that the genocide cannot be rationally understood, but only grasped emotionally, through a story of suffering. Albeit secular, this vision of the genocide is, no less, an authentic theology. Has the historian Saul Friedlander himself not declared that the Holocaust stands in need of the historian's discourse, more than any other?[36]

In the popular vision of the matter, as we have had occasion to note, the genocide and the foundation of the state of Israel are linked. If one assumes that redemption has already come about thanks to the creation of the state, then there is little reason to await the arrival of a Messiah and Saviour. The Jews, their eyes fixed on Israel, now expect it to save them. The emergence of this country was perceived as the dawning of the light after the dark night of the catastrophe. Purified by suffering and bloodshed, the Jews were entering a new era, of which Israel was supposed to be the expression. There was now a post-Auschwitz era, which gradually began to relegate the pre-Auschwitz era, with all its cultural richness and diversity, to the shadows. The post-Auschwitz era, the time of memory, was placed under the sign of 'never again', which in fact meant 'never again for the Jews'.

What had become of those who had been personally affected by the Final Solution? For the survivors, the attempt to transmit this experience flowed from a desire to confer a meaning, however minimal, on what had happened, and to warn against the possibility of new dangers. For the generations whose memory of the event had been bequeathed to them by the media's treatment of it, however, that memory served to construct a transnational community made up of Sepharadim and Ashkenazim alike, both in Europe, where the horror had occurred, and outside it. Israel and the Diaspora found themselves united in a new shared religion that outsiders could immediately recognize and

---

Encountering Holocaust: An Interdisciplinary Survey, Chicago: Impact Press, 1979; Edward Alexander, *The Resonance of Dust: Essays on Holocaust Literature and Jewish Fate*, Columbus: Ohio State University Press, 1979. For the citations, see David Roskies, 'The Holocaust According to the Literary Critics', *Prooftexts*, 1:2, 1981, 209.

36   Elizabeth de Fontenay, in Halpérin and Lévitte, eds, *Mémoire and Histoire*, 70; Saul Friedlander, cited in Régine Robin, *La Mémoire saturée*, Paris: Stock, 2003, 294.

that was easy to practice. It was a religion of those chosen by suffering, an ersatz for Judaism that protected them from anti-Semitism, at least for a time, and acted as a brake on assimilation. Somewhat in the same way that, in the past, the memory of the suffering that their ancestors had endured in order to remain Jewish had served to maintain the cohesion of the group and tended to curb the inclination to defect, the memory of the genocide breathed new life into Judaism and reinforced fidelity to Israel. Such fidelity became, after the Six Day War, a new commandment, for there continued to loom on the horizon, for both survivors and other Jews, the spectre of inevitable persecution and the dogma that the world was divided into Jewish victims and everyone else. It was if those faithful to the dogma wished to confirm the views of those who attributed the survival of the Jews and Judaism over the centuries to anti-Semitism.

Was it impossible to be a Jew in a positive sense? Had Spinoza not already said, with reference to the fifteenth-century expulsion from Spain, that the Jews had been preserved, in large measure, by the Gentiles' hatred? Later, in the eighteenth and nineteenth centuries, had the Jewish advocates of emancipation not feared that equality between Gentile and Jew would precipitate the end of Jewish life? Finally, in the twentieth century, had a number of European intellectuals – Karl Kautsky, Jean-Paul Sartre, Arnold Toynbee, Max Frisch – not continued to maintain that, once the persecution of the Jews came to an end, the Jews would cease to exist as Jews? They had anticipated neither what the memory of the genocide would come to represent, a New Sinai that encountered the New Jerusalem after the Six Day War, nor the perfect communion that followed.[37] Yet nothing requires that we inevitably chalk the continuity of Jewish existence up to anti-Semitism, unless we wish to ensconce ourselves in the 'lachrymose history' that produces more tears than history, more suffering than consolation, and, what is more, reduces the Jews to the status of eternal victims – indeed, passive spectators of their own suffering.

In suffering, there is no future. Judaism preaches life. At least, it does so if one is to believe the Deuteronomist: 'I have set before you life and death, blessing and cursing: therefore choose life, that both thou and thy seed may live.'[38] The Jews have been actors of history and made a positive contribution, at their level, to building civilization. To confine them within the gaze of the anti-Semitic Other and that Other's rejection of them is a way of situating them outside history and erecting them into archetypes of the absolute victim, who,

---

37   For an overview of Ismar Schorsch's ideas on Jewish survival and anti-Semitism, see his article 'The Holocaust and Jewish Survival', 244.

38   Dt 30:19.

it must be admitted, enjoys many more rights than duties in our society. It is also a way of sucking the marrow from Jewish life, of divesting it of its inner wealth, which thrives through its interaction with the Other.

We might also ask how well the religion of the Holocaust preserves the memory of those who perished in the camps and those who survived in them – the task it originally set out to accomplish, remembering the dead so that they would not die a second death. This original intention has been perverted in order to serve the need to safeguard an identity; political objectives; the interests of the high priests of the new religion; and a long string of causes unrelated to memory in the proper sense of the word, even if, at the individual level, that religion is for many Jews intimately bound up with the memory of their dead and the suffering that they themselves experienced in the years of the nightmare. The uses to which memory has been put border on expropriation. In fact, the religion of the Holocaust that was put in place after the Six Day War rang in the era of being Jewish without Judaism and, of course, without God; it leaned for support, to be sure, on glorified tutelary spirits, the survivors, and on their accounts, founding texts situated outside history.

In the face of the broad range of traditional responses to suffering, the one that secular Jews proffer might seem reductive. And, in fact, the Judaism 'of the Holocaust and Redemption' that developed alongside the Judaism based on the written and oral Torah cheated itself of perspectives. In every part of the world in which Jews live, it has helped to create a community based not on Jewish practice, but on a shared history of grief, the sole ground for which was the suffering endured in Auschwitz. It made the Jew the archetypal sufferer – indeed, an incomparable, unmatchable paragon of suffering. Henceforth, as Jacob Neusner writes, Judaism was 'cast in extreme emotions of terror and triumph'.[39]

The new religion required Jews constantly to imagine that they were in the gas chambers or on the threshold of them. From this point of view, a visit to the various holocaust museums in the United States is edifying. These museums attribute to their visitors, for as long as their visit lasts, the identity of Jews who were gassed or died of other causes in the camps. The gas chambers, crematoria, and entrances to the camps are recreated in them. Moreover, the messages put out by some of these museums, places where the ritual of the memory of the genocide is celebrated, are transmitted amid emotion and produce more emotion in their turn. The visitor is asked to feel the event, not to understand it. Pathos dominates consciousness. Yet, in order not to forget,

---

39   Neusner, *Formative Judaism*, 21.

we need to understand; in order to understand, we need to put the event back in the context that made it possible in the first place. Indeed, in order not to forget, we need history, not emotions, which are always fugitive and must constantly be revived, with greater intensity each time. What is more, in such a state of mind, it becomes impossible to envisage bringing Jews and non-Jews face-to-face with their responsibilities, so as to prevent such episodes of human barbarity from recurring. In the process of being converted into a universal religion with a message that is easy to understand, the memory of the genocide contributed, paradoxically, to de-universalizing the Jews, distancing them from others who suffered and gradually shutting them inside their own pain.

THE CHRISTIAN RESPONSE

The Christian theology produced after the genocide naturally confronted the event with a religious approach. This is not the place to study the various aspects of this rich theology, which, however, merits brief comparison with the theologies, religious or secular, developed by Jews. We can gain some sense of it by considering the symbols it has secreted, setting out from existing archetypes about the necessity of suffering and the suffering of the innocent. Jews, in this theology, are treated as models of the suffering servant. Some currents of Christianity even endeavour to confer Christian meaning on the genocide, which is conceived on the mode of the Christian mysteries of the crucifixion and resurrection.

The crucified Jew is not a new symbol, but, after the Holocaust, Jesus was treated as a metaphor for the genocide by way of his identification as a Jew. At the end of the war, the martyrdom suffered by those interned in the camps was often likened to Christ's Passion; when Dachau was liberated, the Avenue of the SS in the camp was renamed 'The Way of the Cross'. In 1979 did Pope John Paul II not describe Auschwitz as the 'modern world's Golgotha', a statement that was perceived as a Christian annexation of Jewish suffering? One ultra-Orthodox Jewish interpretation of the genocide, which has it that the Jews were sacrificed to hasten the coming of the Messiah, is not all that different from the Christological vision promoted by certain Christian scholars and thinkers, who draw a parallel between the Jewish people's sacrifice and Christ's. The two interpretations converge in treating the genocide as a religious event in which the victims were martyred for their faith, thus becoming, to some degree, heroes.

After the war, this Christological representation was frequently adopted by artists, among them Jewish painters such as Chagall, who had made use of it even earlier. In Chagall's work, the crucified Jesus is surrounded by other symbols of persecution and the genocide: a village in flames, a fugitive mother and child, refugees, the wandering Jew, and so on. Post-war artists such as Corrado Cagli or Hans Grundig emphasize the similarities between the corpses in the camps and Holbein's *The Body of the Dead Christ in the Tomb*. The last allusion is also to be found in Marcel Janco's *Genocide of 1945*. This identification was reinforced when corpses were found in the camps with their arms outstretched, as if on the cross. Some of these bodies were immortalized by photographers, whose work was published under the title *Ecce Homo – Bergen Belsen*. These visual representations were invitations to see the Holocaust victim as a Christ figure. The theme of the 'pietà', represented in postures inspired by Renaissance painting, also acquired universal popularity after the war. Indeed, in the commemorative sculpture of the 1950s and early 1960s, the 'Pietà' became, in a sense, a standard motif. Thus art transformed Christ's Passion and the Crucifixion into enduring popular symbols of the genocide. Some painters also made use of Christian symbols as a means of accusing Christianity in general and the Church in particular of having done nothing to save the Jews. Thus an entire mode of artistic representation came into being, sustained by a modern utilization of the Passion, symbol of the suffering of humankind. Artists who draw heavily on Christian symbolism such as Otto Dix, Francis Bacon, or Rico Lebrun broadened the meaning of the Crucifixion by employing detail to link it to the genocide, whereas the treatment of the genocide by Jewish artists such as Ben Zion or Hayim Gross borrowed details from the Crucifixion. Toward the end of the 1960s, the link between Crucifixion and Holocaust again came to the fore in German and Austrian art – for example, in what Herbert Falken accomplishes in his series 'Scandalum Crucis' (1969).

The history of this Christological symbolism no doubt reaches back to ancient declarations by Christian and Jewish theologians who, from the late eighth century on, recalled that Jesus was a Jew who addressed the Jews in their own language—an idea which, at the time, stirred up a storm of protest from Christians as well as Jews.[40] As for the long-term consequences of this Christological approach to the genocide, it contained a number of elements that served to sustain and reinforce the (Jewish) religion 'of the Holocaust and Redemption' that emerged in the 1970s.

---

40   Ziva Amishai-Maisels, ' "Faith, Ethics and the Holocaust", Christological Symbolism of the Holocaust', *Holocaust and Genocide Studies*, 3:4, 1988, 457–81.

NAMING 'THE UNNAMEABLE'

The history of the successive, competing names for the genocide is no less revelatory than painting, cinema, or theology of the evolving approaches to the
event. Lanzmann's *Shoah* is not the alpha and omega of this story, the richness
of which shows just how high the stakes of the forms of commemoration that
emerged in the post-war years were.

During the war, in Palestine under the British mandate, the traditional
Hebrew word *hurban* was used to designate what had befallen the European
Jews. Pronounced *khurbun* in Yiddish,[41] the word means 'destruction' or
'catastrophe', and was employed to designate the destruction of the two
Temples, in particular the destruction of the Second Temple in AD 70. In the
Middle Ages, it evoked various persecutions and pogroms. The word made its
way to the United States with the emigrants, but remained essentially confined
to the Yiddish-speaking community; Anglophones did not use it. The new
massacre in Europe was known as *der driter khurbun*, 'the third destruction'.
Thus the term itself created a continuity with previous calamities, re-estab-
lishing the uninterrupted chain of Jewish suffering.

In 1944, Polish-Jewish lawyer Raphael Lemkin, who had found refuge in
the United States after losing his whole family, became an advisor in the
Foreign Affairs Section of the United States Department of War. He coined the
term 'genocide', derived from the Greek *genos*, 'race', and the Latin *caedes*,
'murder', 'massacre', 'carnage', to designate the crimes being perpetrated in
Europe. His knowledge of the anti-Jewish persecutions and the 1915 Armenian
massacres led him to define 'genocide' as any 'coordinated plan of different
actions aiming at the destruction of essential foundations of the life of national
groups, with the aim of annihilating the groups themselves'. The term was used
from time to time during the Nuremberg trials of 1945 and early 1946 and was
adopted by the UN General Assembly in its 9 December 1948 Convention for
the Prevention and Punishment of the Crime of Genocide. It could be equally
well applied to the destruction of the Jews, the Armenians, and the Roma. It
was of course unlikely that this universalizing use of the term would be
accepted by those who proclaimed the uniqueness of the Jewish genocide
and were opposed to seeing it put in the same category as other massacres
committed in the course of history (or that would be committed in the future).
Yet the use of the term 'genocide' in no wise diminished the specificity of each
genocide, the Jewish genocide not excluded. Nothing prevents us from

---

41   Also *khurban*, *khurbn*, and so on.

supposing that, if this term had triumphed in the war of words, it would have been harder to confer a religious dimension on the genocide of the Jews.

In the late 1950s, the expression 'Final Solution' (*Endlösung* in German) was also in use, along with a panoply of other terms: 'event', 'cataclysm', 'disaster', 'apocalypse', 'destruction of the European Jews', and 'world of the concentration camps', together with, of course, 'Auschwitz', the place that came to symbolize the event (even if the use of the name seemed to exclude the victims who had not been deported to this particular camp or, more generally, to a death camp). At the same time, in these years when the word 'genocide' was coming into ever wider circulation and the Yiddish equivalents of 'disaster' and 'catastrophe' were also still in use, the word 'Holocaust' made its appearance.

The word comes from the Greek *holokauston*, 'wholly burned'. Previously, it had traditionally served as, in both Greek and a variety of other European languages, an equivalent for the Hebrew world *olah*, which, in Leviticus,[42] designates a particular kind of offering to God – as a rule, a 'wholly burned' animal. In French and Italian, 'holocaust' had long retained its 'sacrificial' meaning and only appeared in religious contexts. In English, in contrast, the word evolved in peculiar fashion from the nineteenth century on. The *Oxford English Dictionary* attests its use in 1833 to mean 'complete destruction; a great slaughter or massacre'. In the 1930s and 1940s, the word was occasionally used of massacres in general. After the war, 'holocaust' also served to designate the hecatomb at Hiroshima. It was between 1957 and 1959 that 'Holocaust', with a capital H, became the equivalent of the Hebrew word *Shoah*, replacing the words 'destruction' and 'catastrophe'.

The specialized press was the first to use the term. Hannah Arendt employs it in the reports on the 1961 Eichmann trial that she published in the *New Yorker*, albeit only when quoting Israeli sources (the rest of the time, she continues to use words such as 'Jewish catastrophe', 'great catastrophe', or 'Final Solution'). Beginning in 1960, the term made its way from the Jewish–American mass press into everyday American usage. Jewish writers had also employed it in their debates and conferences before it was taken up by the general press. The word's sacrificial overtones surely had something to do with its popularization in the United States (although some maintain that Anglophones took it to mean nothing more than the destruction associated with war and fire). But was it not falsifying the Jews' history to say that they had been killed like martyrs and, willy-nilly, to make their massacre a 'sacrifice'? Did this religious–mythical characterization of the event, albeit indirect and

---

42   One of the several occurrences of the word in Leviticus may be found in Lv 1:13.

even unconscious, make the massacre more acceptable by locating it squarely in the series of disasters that had befallen the Jews?

Elie Wiesel would later claim that he had pioneered the use of the word 'Holocaust' in the meaning it has today, which does not carry, for most of those who use it, any connotation of sacrifice. Wiesel did play an important role in propagating it. He was also, of course, quite familiar with its biblical roots. As he explains, the use of this word in his writings derives from his comparison of the biblical sacrifice of Isaac to the destruction of the Jews.[43] God asks Abraham to sacrifice his son to him in the form of a 'holocaust' (*olah*), that is, immolation to the point of complete destruction by fire. For Wiesel, Isaac is the first survivor; he teaches others to survive, begin again, and continue to believe. Thus the annihilation is perceived as a sacrifice that opens the way to a new life.

This is not unlike certain Orthodox Jewish interpretations, and is quite similar to the Christological vision. The motif that seems to prevail here is that of self-sacrifice, destined, according to some, to hasten the arrival of the Messiah, and, according to others, to precipitate the birth of the state of Israel. The Catholic writer François Mauriac, who helped to ensure Wiesel's entry into the world of French letters, was one of those Christians fond of the analogy between the sacrifice of the Jewish people and Christ. He first referred to the genocide as a self-sacrifice in an article published in the 7 June 1958 literary supplement to the French daily *Le Figaro*. This text would later serve as the preface to the French edition of Wiesel's *Night*, the version destined for a Christian European public, very different in tone from the original Yiddish version, which is filled with rage at the—Christian European—persecutors.[44] For Mauriac, the young survivor Wiesel recalls the resuscitated Lazarus, while the Jewish victims of the genocide are reminiscent of Christ, who let himself be nailed to the cross to save humanity. This translation of the genocide into self-sacrifice inevitably found echoes in the Christian world, because it conferred meaning on an event that seemed to lack all meaning. The idea established itself at a time when there did not yet exist more distanced historical works capable of guiding reflection, seemingly giving the theological approach free rein.

The Hebrew word *korban*, which is also used in Yiddish and means 'sacrifice',[45] had already made its appearance in memoirs of the genocide written by pious survivors and in inscriptions on the first monuments erected in memory

---

43   Gn 22.

44   Naomi Seidman, 'Elie Wiesel and the Scandal of Jewish Rage', *Jewish Social Studies*, 3:1, 1996, 1–19.

45   In a perfectly neutral sense, free of religious overtones, *korban* can also designate individual 'victims', including the victims of ordinary accidents.

of slain Jews from Eastern Europe. The English word 'martyr', long used during the war to designate genocide victims, was also adopted by secular Jews. For example, the site dedicated to the memory of the genocide in Jerusalem, Yad Vashem, under construction from the 1950s to 1980, bears the official name 'Holocaust Martyrs' and Heroes' Remembrance Authority'; it thus pays even-handed tribute to martyrology and the exaltation of heroism. The use of the word 'martyr' in a secular sense is no doubt something of a cultural distortion, but it also brings the victims within the compass of non-Jews' understanding, giving content to their suffering and death while surreptitiously re-injecting religion into it, since a martyr dies, first and foremost, for her faith. The insistence on this dimension of martyrdom, accentuated over the years, and the use, in Hebrew, of another term, *kedoshim* – the 'saints' or 'sanctified' – to designate the victims are further signs of the gradual constitution of the new Holocaust religion.

Nevertheless, upon examination, it becomes clear that religious overtones did not dominate the secular approach to the genocide adopted in the immediate post-war period. Ben Zion Dinur, a historian of the Jerusalem School, and, at the time, the Israeli Minister of Culture, who was a supporter of the project to create Yad Vashem and a co-founder of the journal *Yad Vashem Studies*, was instrumental in making the English word 'Holocaust' the official translation of the Hebrew word 'Shoah' during the 1953 parliamentary debate on the draft law for a project to commemorate the Shoah and Heroes which also spelled out Yad Vashem's mission. The 'sacrificial' dimension was, however, foreign to the secular version defended by the minister. The draft law created an indissoluble link between the genocide, the state of Israel, and Jerusalem. The Hebraic name of the commemorative site was taken from Isaiah.[46] In his speech defending the project, Dinur retraced the history of the persecution, putting the accent on the heroism of the victims who stood up to Nazism. These were the years in which Israeli identity was still under construction and heroes were still needed to flesh it out. Dinur considered not only the rebels of the Warsaw ghetto to be heroes, but also all the Jews who had struggled daily to survive. The solidarity among the persecuted, their faith that justice would triumph, and their efforts to preserve their human dignity—all this constituted heroism, in his estimation. Moreover, Dinur did not pass up the occasion to draw a connection between the Holocaust and the state of Israel; he likened the

---

46 'For thus saith the Lord unto the eunuchs that keep my sabbaths, and choose the things that please me, and take hold of my covenant; Even unto them will I give in mine house and within my walls a place and a name [*yad va-shem*] better than of sons and of daughters: I will give them an everlasting name, that shall not be cut off.' Is 56:4–5.

Warsaw ghetto fighters to the valiant soldiers who had fought for Israel's independence. It is clear that the rebels of the ghetto were hero models for young
Israelis. Let us also not forget that, in this period, the victims of the genocide
elicited not only compassion, but also anger and incomprehension, because
they had let themselves be led off 'like lambs to slaughter', as the Israeli poet
Abba Kovner put it. How could these Jews of the Diaspora, given such a
perception of them, serve as examples for those who were building the new
state? It was necessary to counter this negative aspect by highlighting individual
or collective acts of courage and resistance; it was, above all, such acts that now
moved centre-stage.[47]

The word 'Shoah', which incorporated the passive dimension, was thus
counterbalanced by the word *gevurah*, 'heroism'. The use of 'Shoah' was made
official by a resolution, passed by the Israel parliament on 12 April 1951, which
made the 27th day of the month of *Nisan* a 'day of memory of the catastrophe
and of heroism'.[48] This date was chosen because it fell between the one
commemorating the revolt of the Warsaw ghetto and the one commemorating
the Israeli war of independence, but also because it coincided with a period
of mourning, *omer*, as that period was traditionally reckoned.[49] Mordechai
Nurock, the member of Knesset who proposed the date, called the event to be
commemorated the 'third destruction', after that of the two Temples. In 1953,
the law officializing the creation of Yad Vashem charged the institution with
commemorating this Day of Memory, which ultimately became an important
landmark in the national calendar, a sacred day in the Israeli secular religion.

The English word 'Holocaust' nevertheless continued to progress, thanks
to the television series 'Holocaust', based on Gerald Green's book of the same
name. First broadcast in 1978, the series made both the term and the event
familiar to the general public. More than 100 million Americans watched at
least part of this series, which then crossed the Atlantic and introduced the
word 'Holocaust' into the European press. It was taken up in French and Italian

---

47   See Edith Zertal's excellent *Israel's Holocaust and the Politics of Nationhood*,
Cambridge: Cambridge University Press, 118–23.

48   In Hebrew, *Yom ha-zikaron la-Shoah ve-la-gevurah*.

49   The word *omer* designates the offering of new barley that would be taken to the
Temple on the second day of Easter, in line with Lv 23:9–14. The Bible also enjoins the faithful
to celebrate, seven weeks after this day, the feast of *Shavuot*, which marks the end of the
barley harvest and the beginning of the wheat harvest. After the destruction of the Sanctuary,
only the practice of the daily reckoning of *omer* was maintained. This period became, moreover, a period of semi-mourning. The reason usually invoked is an epidemic which, between
Easter and the 33rd day of *omer*, is supposed to have swept away 24,000 of Rabbi Akiba's
students.

with its new meaning, now divested of the notion of 'sacrifice'; in the United States, it eventually eclipsed all the other names used for the event. The term 'Holocaust' spread worldwide; in time, even Elie Wiesel regretted having contributed to its propagation. The French linguist Gilles Pétrequin has suggested that it be replaced by 'Judeocide', a neologism proposed by the historian Arno Mayer that more closely resembles the word 'genocide'.

The success of the word 'Holocaust' in French was, however, short-lived. It is in no way comparable to the exceptional good fortune the term has enjoyed in the Anglo-Saxon world. In North America it is omnipresent, in the names of university chairs, the titles of books, or the labels on certain shelves in the libraries ('Holocaust Studies'), to say nothing of the famous *United States Holocaust Memorial Museum* in Washington, DC. In English, as we have seen, the 'sacrificial' overtones had, by this time, vanished without a trace. But this was not the case in French, where these lingering echoes continued to be troubling. It was, however, the considerable impact of Lanzmann's movie, in France and other countries as well, which ultimately imposed the use of the word 'Shoah' in French. The screenplay was published by Fayard in 1985, with a preface by Simone de Beauvoir, which invested it with immense moral authority.[50] In the end, this Hebraic term thrust all the other names for the genocide into the shadows, particularizing to an extreme the destruction of the Jews during the Second World War and thus forestalling its inclusion in a broader framework.

This phenomenon is specifically French. Elsewhere, the diffusion of the word 'Shoah' met with powerful resistance from its Anglo-Saxon competitor, 'Holocaust'. The dominant position of English as the international language cemented the victory of the latter term. Without a doubt, the 'exotic' ring of the word 'Shoah' partly explains the fascination it exerts in France. Entering into ordinary usage, contributed to calling a halt to the French debate on the question of the uniqueness of the event, on which a great deal of ink has been spilt on the other side of the Atlantic; the US debate helped to advance the discussion of this question, which is crucial if the 'ghettoization' of the Jewish genocide is to be avoided. The Hebraic designation left little room for deeper analysis of this aspect of the genocide. While 'Holocaust' continues to be widely employed across the globe, 'Shoah' remains, essentially, a sort of French exception, even if, in the last few years, it has also made progress in various places outside France.

---

50   On the terminology of genocide, see Anna-Vera Calimani Sullam's very rich essay, 'A Name for Extermination', *The Modern Language Review*, 94, 1999, 978–99.

Yet there is no good reason for refusing to maintain a large variety of names – genocide, Auschwitz, Final Solution, extermination, Judeocide, catastrophe, destruction, and so on. On the contrary, using such a broad array of designations would help to prevent the appropriation of the event by a single word. The circulation of varied terms would remind us of the difficulty of apprehending the single event they all name, underscoring both its particularity and what it has in common with the other twentieth-century genocides. It might also contribute to stripping it of its theological–religious trappings with and restoring it to the status of a reality born of human barbarity and always capable of being brought back to life.

CHAPTER FOUR

A Secular Redemption: The Holocaust, Israel, and the Jews

In Israel, in the post-war years, the Jews who had fallen victim to the Nazis did not escape the general interpretative schema divided up the populations of Europe into heroes and collaborators. Rapidly, the genocide, known in this period as the 'destruction' of the Jews, provided a focal point for political quarrels: every party appropriated the heroes for itself and abandoned the victims to its adversaries. When the Israeli state was established, 650,000 Jews were living in the country, of whom more than 100,000 were genocide survivors. Between 1948 and 1952, 720,000 people emigrated to Israel, more than half of whom were also survivors. The 'destruction' was perceived by those constructing the young country as a Jewish defeat that violated Zionism's moral code, based on negation of the Diaspora and the heroism of the new sons of the Jewish people, whose history began in Eastern Europe and culminated in the new state. That history served, in some sense, as the backdrop against which the redemption brought by Zionism could be thrown into relief.

Zionist rhetoric, which found its inspiration before the war in the traditional rhetoric of Judaism about the transition 'from destruction to redemption', now dwelt on the transition 'from the Holocaust to Redemption'. In the post-genocide period, conceived as an opportunity to create a national renaissance in the midst of tragedy, Israeli literature from the survivor Ka-Tzetnik, through Yoram Kaniuk and the poetry of Uri Zvi Greenberg to Abba Kovner, tended to voice aspirations to reconstruction and redemption. For Shmuel Yosef Agnon or Haim Hazaz and others like them, the hope of redemption made itself felt even in their writings that did not take the genocide as their theme. Thus, in the nascent national consciousness, traditional religious expectations converged with the aspirations of the young state, which had taken on the task of finding a response to the destruction in order to continue to build a new country.[1]

---

1   Alan Yuter, *The Holocaust in Hebrew Literature: From Genocide to Rebirth*, Port Washington NY: Associated Faculty Press, 1983, 121–2.

A NATIONAL SAGA PICKING ITS WAY BETWEEN HEROES AND VICTIMS

In Israel, the memory of the genocide was evoked even in the Declaration of Independence, which cast the state as the ultimate response to the event. The message was clear: Jews could never return to the lands of the dispersion. There was no salvation outside the Jewish state, the key to their future. However, in this period, the Israelis were singularly lacking in empathy and sympathy for the survivors. Their attitude was, rather, critical and cold, even contemptuous, despite the fact that these survivors constituted one-third of the population. Young Israelis often wondered how the Jews had managed to end up in such a state.

During these formative years, Jewish history was nationalized in order to provide the Hebrew state with a solid base and invest it with its new function, the features of which gradually swam into focus: namely, to serve as the guarantee for the security of the Jewish people throughout the world. On the one hand, those busy re-appropriating this history evoked the memory of the Warsaw ghetto heroes, succeeded by the fighters who had laid down their lives for Independence. On the other, they ignored the genocide, which clouded the glorious image of a triumphant people on the march. The hero who had fallen on the field of battle defending his country was elevated to a central figure of the Israeli renaissance; he became a leader and symbol of unity in a society seeking to strike roots in its newly adopted land. The glorification of the fighters who died so that Israel might live is a story of sacrifice that holds a dominant place in Jewish historiography, from the Matzada through the Warsaw ghetto and traditional Jewish martyrology to Tel-Hai.[2]

This mythologization of soldiers who lay down their lives for the fatherland emerges early in the ethos of modern nation states. The young state's fighters differed from the martyrs of an earlier day in that they incarnated the new Jew's active heroism; passive religious heroism belonged to the Diaspora.[3] Yet an ambivalence remained in the link forged between these two forms of

---

2   It was at Tel-Hai, in the Upper Galilee, that, on 1 March 1920, Joseph Trumpeldor (1880–1920) and five of his men were killed in unequal combat against their Bedouin attackers. A hero of the Czarist army in the Russo-Japanese War, which cost him an arm at Port Arthur in 1904, the initiator and second-highest commanding officer of the Zion Mule Corps, a Jewish unit of the British army that was engaged in combat around Gallipoli during the First World War, Trumpeldor, whose last words were, 'What the hell, it's worth dying for one's country', was the immediate embodiment of the values of modern Jewish heroism and patriotism.

3   Yoram Bilu and Eliezer Witztum, 'War-Related Loss and Suffering in Israeli Society: An Historical Perspective', *Israel Studies*, 5:2, 2000, 3–5.

heroism, a link that made it possible to return to Jewish history, reconstruct it, and homogenize it over a long period. It is rather reminiscent of the way secular Zionists tailored biblical Israel to modern Israel's needs, or worked out an accommodation between the religiosity of the new fatherland and the secular character of the country, affirmed in the image of it cultivated by its founders.

The cult of the soldier who had fallen in battle counted as patriotism, whereas the discourse on suffering and mourning imported by the survivors as well as immigrants from Muslim countries was shunted into the social and cultural margins, if only because these immigrants had not gone through the process of initiation required of the good Israeli. Israel's 1956 victory over the Egyptian army during the Sinai campaign raised the state to the level of a regional superpower and made the army the focus of the hero cult. Between 1947 and 1956, some 150 monuments were erected to celebrate the 6,000 victims of the War of Independence – a monument for every 40 soldiers killed. These soldiers' status began to crumble starting in the 1970s, and their memory gradually ceased to serve as the cement of social and national solidarity. In the wake of this erosion, the image of the Warsaw ghetto fighters lost its pre-eminence as a symbol of the commemoration of the genocide. It was replaced by that of victims and survivors.

In response to the ideological demands of the day, public discourse on the genocide began to be politicized in the Israel of the 1950s. The controversy came to a head around the issue of the indemnities that Germany had to pay Israel, supposedly in order to finance absorption of mass immigration from Europe. It was only with great reluctance that the opposition parties and the population at large accepted the principle of these indemnities. The law was finally ratified in 1952 and diplomatic relations were established with Germany. In 1950, the Knesset had already passed a law about prosecuting the Nazis and their collaborators; the following year, it established a day of commemoration for the Holocaust. There followed the trials of Jews accused of collaborating with the Nazis, which culminated in a political crisis and a change of government. Nasser's 1956 nationalization of the Suez Canal, the Suez campaign, and the forced departure of Jews from Egypt helped reinforce the place of the memory of the Holocaust in political discourse and the press. Egypt was depicted as a 'rising Nazi power', the nationalization of the Suez Canal was likened to *Anschluss*, and Nasser was compared with Hitler. The genocide was now in the process of shaping Israel's ideas about its security.

The Eichmann trial, which opened in 1961 with the testimony of the survivors, introduced the Holocaust into Israel's collective consciousness and then the collective consciousness of Jews in the Diaspora. From this point on, people identified with the victims and genocide survivors, who now began to abandon their silence in order to relate what had happened in their own words. It was an act of revenge on their persecutors, through whose discourse they had existed until now. The victims in the country became accusers and, thanks to this transformation, the survivors, yesterday's 'sheep', were promoted to the rank of modern 'heroes' and 'saints'. At the same time, there unfolded a process of remembering that now clearly distinguished between the personal and national dimensions of the commemoration. Eichmann's trial culminated in a renewal of national unity brought about by such rememoration, which erected a bridge between the living and the dead. The trial also reinforced the image of the supremacy of Israel, which, by bringing the enemies of the Jewish people to judgement, showed that it was incumbent on the new country to lead the struggle to prevent a similar catastrophe from ever happening again.

The survivors were there to testify to the horrors of their impotent exis-tence in the Diaspora. 'Never again!' took on sacred significance, that of a duty assumed by the people of Israel. The state was sacralized in one and the same movement. All this prefigured the future sacralization of the Diaspora's fidelity to the country, in the name of those who had died in the camps and the better future to be offered to coming generations. The moral significance of the foun-dation of the Israeli state was thus enhanced. Every sacrifice was now justified, as was all the suffering inflicted on the Palestinians. This state was holy, and its holiness was inseparable from the genocide. The Eichmann trial legitimated this narrative model in both Israel and the Diaspora. The narrative was any-thing but insignificant. For the survivors, it was the story of their suffering; for young Israelis, it was a way of renewing their Jewish identity, negated in the first years of the foundation of the state; for the Jews of the Diaspora, it was a means of loosening tongues and encouraging the expression of personal misfortune, but also an incitement to construct memories around the genocide and use it to strengthen their identity so as to be able to continue being Jewish. At the same time, the catastrophe legitimated the supremacy of the Ashkenazim in Israel, even while maintaining their cohesion vis-à-vis the Sephardim, who, before the immigration of the Russian Jews, were a majority in the country, although they were virtually invisible in the machinery of the state and occupied a precarious socio-economic position.

Subsequently, the direct link forged between the genocide and the state of Israel on both the moral and political level bore down with all its weight on what is known as the obligation to remember, which was conflated with the defence of Israel at whatever price and in any and all circumstances. Indeed, reactivation of the theme of the Holocaust is a constant, recurring every time

Israel is in trouble or at war. The year 1963 marked the beginnings of the practice of making visits to Poland along a route leading from camp to camp: it was inaugurated on the eve of the Six Day War, when the Israelis felt that they were under siege and thought their existence was in jeopardy. It was at such moments that they expressed a desire to learn more about the world of their parents and grandparents, about what they had experienced or how they had been murdered, in order better to understand the survivors' situation and appreciate their concerns. Thus the young renewed their bonds with their elders and, by the same token, with the Diaspora. Such were the first symptoms of this identification that began to confer meaning on the Holocaust in the context of a permanent state of war and in the face of the situation of instability and anxiety that war engendered among the generation born on the soil of the young state.

It was also possible to observe among survivors in Israel, at a very early stage, the resurgence of religious models in commemorations of the genocide. Genocide survivors were organized in more than 500 immigrant associations corresponding to their native European towns and villages. These associations published 'memory books' about their community, a practice similar to that common in the Middle Ages, and placed memorial plaques in the synagogues. This was still the period of personal commemoration of the genocide, before the transition, in the wake of the 1961 Eichmann trial, to a collective dimension marked by monuments and ceremonies that also gradually borrowed ritual elements from the traditional liturgy. The Eichmann trial itself took on the character of a holy story recounted by survivors who, thanks to the trial, were briefly sacralized. It was a holy story which, from now on, stood in lieu of history and constructed the memory of the genocide much more powerfully than any book ever could.

There thus came about an encounter between a nascent memory that took on religious overtones and collective rituals with a non-negligible religious dimension. In this perspective, survivors' organizations were soon opting to erect monuments rather than publish 'memory books': the number of such books published sank from twelve in 1975 to four in 1984. The same organizations built unusually big, architecturally rich monuments to commemorate the dead in the avenues of the cemeteries in central Israel, in memory of their destroyed communities and 'holy martyrs'. 'Sacred ashes' were brought back from the death camps and buried under most of these monuments.

The correlation between the Holocaust and Israel authorized an over-dramatization of existing conflicts, eliciting powerful emotional reactions which testified to the fact that the process of mourning the Holocaust had not yet reached its term. It is this unfinished mourning which makes possible permanent reactivation of the memory of the Holocaust to political ends that actually have nothing to do with it. Israel will, no doubt, be incapable of taking into account the suffering of the peoples with whom it finds itself in conflict until this work of mourning comes to an end. Only on that condition will the Jewish people find its way back to a healthier form of Judaism; only on that condition can the state of Israel cease to exploit the fears of a population, trau- matized by the genocide and its narration, and stop brandishing the spectre of annihilation as the ultimate justification for a belligerence that goes far beyond the legitimate defence of its right to exist.[4]

The way the obligation to remember used was not, then, inherent in it. What is more, it ultimately led to the situation of veritable solitude for the survivors themselves, the true guardians of the living memory of the suffering undergone and the pain endured. If, when such suffering and pain are trans- formed into a spectacle, they are diverted (in Pascal's sense of the word), it is to be feared that, once they disappear, a veil will be cast over the real importance of the event, that profound rupture of the human that is perhaps the only real lesson the genocide has to teach, if it can teach us anything at all. Unless, of course, their disappearance effectively brings the period of mourning to a close, neutralizing memory in a transition to history that will make it harder to instrumentalize memory.

'EVERYBODY IS AGAINST US'

In this regard, 1967 constituted a turning point in Israel's history. After the Six Day War, the occupation of new territories by Israel raised a set of new ques- tions about identity among the population as a whole. Expansion to Israel's biblical frontiers could no longer be justified on the grounds that a persecuted people had a right to exist – a people seeking to create a state in order to gather together its sons and daughters from across the globe and offer them refuge in a land whose memory had accompanied them throughout their exile. With the occupation came a return of repressed origins. The new conquest of course recalled the first, the fruit of the War of Independence, which had culminated in the massive expulsion of the Palestinians. This time, however, Israel had to administer the populations of the occupied territories, populations that had

---

4   Mooli Brog, 'Victims and Victors: Holocaust and Military Commemoration in Israel Collective Memory', *Israel Studies*, 8:3, 2003, 65–122. Brog's essay provides a very good description of the successive stages of the commemoration of the genocide victims, explaining, in their light, the evolution of attitudes toward the event. See also Zertal, *Death and the Nation*.

not fled and, simply by virtue of their presence, reminded the conquerors of their right to the land. Thus immorality was introduced into the sacred; it now had to be justified. The two Intifadas and, in particular, the Palestinian suicide-bombers ultimately made the new situation still harder to bear, since the struggle was now brought to the heart of the country and to territories that had hitherto been considered authentically Israeli. This war within the country's borders served as an unmistakable, permanent reminder of the 'original sin' of the War of Independence.

Since 1967, as a general rule, whenever justifications based on the need for security prove insufficient, the spectre of the Holocaust leaps into the breach. Thus, after Israel's lightning victory in the Six Day War, Abba Eban, a member of the Labour Party, called the country's old borders, in the course of remarks on its new ones, 'the Auschwitz frontiers', thereby associating the Israeli–Palestinian conflict with the legacy of the genocide. Menachim Begin, who assumed power in 1977, made skilful use of this rhetoric time and again, in an attempt to lend the conquest a moral character; it was Begin who made 'Israel the Holocaust victims' heir'.[5] Such talk never failed to raise apocalyptic fears. In 1992, Prime Minister Yitzhak Shamir, adopting the terms of Eban's rhetoric, claimed that any territorial negotiations with the Palestinians would be suicidal, because Israel's pre-1967 borders were simply those of Auschwitz. Gradually, the genocide came to legitimate the occupation. Its primary meaning was perverted, preventing it from making its way into people's consciences as an appeal directed to all those who bore the memory of it: an appeal to save other human beings and other peoples, elsewhere, from onerous oppression. The lesson that Israel's leaders draw from the Holocaust is, in fact, a pessimistic one: given the magnitude of the tragedy that befell the Jews, they must trust to nothing but the strength of their own arms. Israel, which had become powerful, and possessed, in the estimation of the whole world (at least until the 2006 invasion of Lebanon and the army's relative discomfiture in the face of the Hezbollah), one of the most sophisticated armies in the Middle East, spoke and acted as if it were a victim – as if it were still on the defensive. Yitzhak Rabin alone, another Prime Minister who, unlike his predecessors, was born in Israel, succeeded in bending this lesson in the direction of compromise.

A passage in the Haggadah, a ritual text read out in Jewish homes during the Passover meal, recalls that 'in each and every generation they stand against us to destroy us'. Every situation that is or seems to be truly dangerous arouses

---

5   Robin, *La Mémoire saturée*, 155

ancestral fears. Thus the peril in which Israel found itself in the 1973 Yom Kippur War profoundly shook the nation. Immediately thereafter, there arose a different understanding of the Jews' desperate plight during the genocide, accompanied by renewed resolve never to fall back into such a situation. From this moment on, Begin started to make use of the 'lessons' of the past to point to the existence of a constant, serious threat, anti-Semitism, and affirm the absolute necessity of accumulating power in order to meet that threat. The *goyim*, Begin maintained, hated the Jews; in traditional terms, Esau hated Jacob. Israel, in its isolation in the face of the enemy, had an imperative need to be powerful. It was the Jews' impotence that had made them victims. The essential thing was to prevent that from ever happening again. Thus, during the 1982 invasion of Lebanon, Begin would compare Arafat in his bunker in besieged Beirut to Hitler in his bunker in Berlin under the Allied bombs. Other Israeli statesmen, such as Shamir, followed him in drawing analogies of this kind, which were aired again during the in 1986 trial of John Demanjuk, accused of being the 'Ivan the Terrible' of the camp in Treblinka. The opposition interpreted this trial as the right's attempt to stage a trial of its own, in hopes of scoring something of a 'success' like the one that the Eichmann trial had earlier netted the left.

Until the mid-1970s, schoolbooks unsurprisingly focused, in discussions of the Holocaust, on the heroism of the partisans and the fighters in the ghettos. Not until the late 1970s did they begin to include more information on the suffering and destruction of the Jews. The same tendency is observable in academic research, which long focused on Jewish resistance, to apologetic ends. Now it broached the role of Palestine's Jewish community in rescuing and providing a home for the survivors, a role that was not among the most glorious.[6] In 1980, the Knesset passed an amendment to the law on public education, requiring all secondary schools to teach the Holocaust. Twenty per cent of history courses were now to be devoted to the subject.[7] When we add the time allotted to teaching Zionism, it becomes clear that little remains for teaching the long history of the Jews, most of which has taken place in the Diaspora, to say nothing of the history of the rest of the world. It would of course have been unacceptable to leave the genocide out of Israel's history books. The reasons for its large place in the curriculum, inseparable from that devoted to Zionism, are obvious; the one serves the other's cause.

---

6   On the activity of the Jewish community in Palestine during the Holocaust, see, for example, Tom Segev, *The Seventh Million: The Israelis and the Holocaust*, trans. Haim Watzman, New York: Henry Holt, 2000.

7   Brog, 'Victims and Victors', 84.

After the failure of the 1982 Lebanese campaign, it became evident that people in Israel were incapable of distinguishing the political conjuncture of the 1980s from that of the 1940s. Despite the profound differences between the two periods, it was imperative to find a link between them. Israel returned to the history of the Holocaust in order to shape and reinforce its national saga. The teleological interpretation of the event that had triumphed in the period of the state's foundation was extended. Life in the Diaspora had inevitably led to genocide; the creation of the state would prevent that from ever recurring. This teleologization – classic, after all – was enriched with new elements, drawn, this time, from the political realities of the day, the need for security among them.

In the same spirit, the genocide began to be presented in theological terms, as if it were an impenetrable mystery. The ideologization of it now went hand-in-hand with its sacralization and the reinforcement of the teleological inter-pretation, thus justifying Israel's policies vis-à-vis the Palestinians while also affecting the self-perception of the Jews of the Diaspora. By the same token, the history of the Jews ceased to be part of universal history, even as studies of it multiplied. An extensively Judaized memory of the genocide gained the upper hand. It was in this context that the religion of the Holocaust, which is also a religion of identity, came into its own.

Regarded as a consequence of, and a response to, the genocide, the state of Israel arouses the guilt feelings of the whole world, which is awash in empathy for it.[8] It is only right that this feeling should act as an obstacle to the develop-ment of anti-Semitism; but the use that is made of it diverts it from its natural function. The increased awareness brought about by the Jewish genocide could have led to a heightening of the whole world's sense of responsibility; all victims of oppression, persecution, and massacre would have been the natural, legiti-mate beneficiaries. But the ideologization and sacralization of the genocide have limited the effects of the message, without in the least preventing its trivialization or, for that matter, trivialization of the memory of the event. With increasing frequency whenever the country is confronted with serious ques-tions or dilemmas, the memory of the destruction of the Jews is moved centre stage. During the 1991 Gulf War, the 39 missiles that fell on Israel reawakened existential anguish at both the private and national level. The fear of annihila-tion is intense among people native to the country. During this war, it was reflected in evocations of Saddam Hussein, Yasser Arafat, or the Arabs in

---

8   Moshe Zuckermann, 'The Curse of Forgetting: Israel and the Holocaust', *Telos*, 78, 1988–9, 45–50.

general in terms borrowed from the Holocaust period or the Second World War. Arafat, once again, was cast in the role of a new Hitler, and the Palestinians in that of the Nazis; their demand for an independent state was regarded as another step toward annihilation, and Rabin's recognition of them at Oslo was branded treason. The opposition, at the time, distributed photos of Rabin dressed like Arafat or in an SS officer's uniform.

While the Israelis born on Israeli soil once served as models for the survivors, it is now the survivors whom the natives take as their examples. Yesterday's victors feel that they have become today's victims, whereas yesterday's victims are today's victors.[9] The Diasporic past and its bloody experiences invest Israel's present and future with meaning. The genocide is not only an essential component of Israeli identity, but also a unifying factor in Israeli society. It fills the void created by the weakening of Israeli identity and testifies to a partial return to a more traditional Judaism, one consisting, in this case, of negative elements.

In the face of a development of this sort, the first question that comes to mind is: how can Israel base a national identity on the genocide and bind its youth to this history of suffering, which turns peace with the country's neighbours into an increasingly abstract notion? Israelis visit Auschwitz and go back home with the conviction that Israel owes it to itself to be a powerful state, equipped with a strong army and imbued with a patriotism ready to meet any challenge. The Israeli Minister of Justice and Tourism, Avraham Sharir, once again comparing Arafat to Hitler, said that a people that had experienced the Holocaust could take no risks. It could live without peace, but if it did not have security, no existence was possible.[10] Do Israelis have the right to speak in the name of those who died in the genocide? Have the dead ever mandated the Zionists who built the state to speak on their behalf? Have they ever approved of the use that some make of their tragic destiny, bending it to the service of nationalist aspirations at the expense of the Palestinians, who are in no way responsible for the catastrophe that befell the European Jews?[11]

In 1988, during the first Intifada, university professor Yehuda Elkana published, in the Israeli daily *Ha'aretz*, an article entitled 'In Praise of Forgetting'. A great deal of ink has been spilt over it since. Elkana put forward the thesis that Israeli leaders have no task more important than to forget, to learn to put themselves on the side of life and in the service of the future, rather than

---

9   Brog, 'Victims and Victors', 91, 94.

10   Zuckermann, 'The Curse of Forgetting', 52.

11   Shlomo Aronson, 'The New Historians and the Purpose of the Shoah', *Ha'aretz* (supplement), 24 June 1994 (in Hebrew).

endlessly cultivating their relation to the symbols, ceremonies, and lessons of the Holocaust. Israeli society's relationship with the Palestinians, Elkana said, is mediated by a profound existential fear sustained by one particular interpretation of the genocide, according to which the whole world is against the Jews and Jews are eternal victims. He sees in this a tragic, paradoxical victory for Hitler. Without denying the historical importance of the collective memory, he maintains that shaping a relationship to the present and constructing a future on the sole basis of the teachings of the past is catastrophic for a society wishing to live in peace and serenity. Under no circumstances, Elkana argues, can one accord the past the right and the power to decide a society's future or a people's destiny. Democracy is endangered when the memory of yesterday's victims makes up an active part of the democratic process. Democracy and absorption in the past are antithetical. Of course, no nation completely forgets or ought to forget its past; but it is naturally inclined to use other important myths to construct its future, such as the myths of excellence and creativity.[12] In issuing this call to forget, Elkana was attacking the most important element of legitimization in Zionist ideology. Indeed, has Israel really remembered the genocide and its universal import? The intellectual and university professor Moshe Zuckermann answers that, from the outset and at every stage in its history, the post-1967 occupation included, Israel has repressed the Holocaust, while utilizing the image of it as a more or less concrete illustration of the right of a Zionist state to exist and develop.[13]

Today, the genocide – or, rather, the image of it – has become an essential factor in young Jewish Israelis' perception of their Jewishness. On the basis of a poll carried out in the 1990s among more than 500 young men and women studying in a teacher training college, Yair Auron came to the conclusion that the genocide was taught in such a way as to draw lessons, messages, meanings, and interpretations from the past and put them in the service of the present and future. This corroborates Elkana's theses. The lessons in question are Zionist ones: all Jews should emigrate to Israel; Jews cannot be safe in Diaspora; Israel is the safest place for Jews to live. Such lessons lead on to the decisive principle: the imperious need for a strong, self-confident, sovereign state for all Jews. At the same time, lessons not bearing directly on Israel are also drawn from the Holocaust, lessons that point to the omnipresent fear so often observed among the Jews of the Diaspora in the past few years. Among them are the need for

---

12 Yehuda Elkana, 'In Praise of Forgetting', *Ha'aretz*, 2 March 1988 (in Hebrew).

13 Zuckermann, 'The Curse of Forgetting', 45. See also Zuckermann, *The Shoah in the Padded Chamber: The 'Shoah' in the Israeli Press during the Gulf War*, Tel Aviv, privately printed, 1993 (in Hebrew).

solidarity among Jews; the importance of self-defence; and the obligation, for Jews, to rely only on their own strength and remain vigilant in the face of any manifestation of anti-Semitism, so as to be ready to combat it as soon as the first signs of it appear.

In this perspective, there is little reason to be hopeful about the future, whether Israel's or the Diaspora's. Rather, the future is fraught with elements likely to lead to self-absorption and a defensive retreat to an exclusively Jewish milieu, whereas the universal conclusions that ought to be drawn from the genocide are the need to struggle for minority rights across the globe while combating all forms of racism (and anti-Semitism) everywhere, as well as all anti-democratic tendencies. Above all, the genocide should lead us to the conclusion that if human nature is essentially evil, its evil is not directed against the Jews alone.[14] In the final analysis, the Jews advertise, by way of the Holocaust, their innocence and rectitude, which make them insensitive to the injustice inflicted on the Palestinians or, more recently, the Lebanese trapped between the Israelis and the Hezbollah. Thus the Jews' suffering confines them in a moral ivory tower.

Former Israeli Foreign Minister Shlomo Ben-Ami, in the 27 January 2007 speech that he gave at a Spanish ceremony marking the International Day of Remembrance of the Holocaust, called on Jewish Israelis to renounce the mentality of the victim and the ghetto and stop comparing Arafat, Sadam Hussein, or even Ahmadinejad to Hitler. He added: 'If the strongest nation in the Near East speaks of each war and each threat as if it harboured a danger of Holocaust, then it is we ourselves who are trivializing the Holocaust.' He concluded that Israel was 'the prisoner of a form of paranoia: the memory of the Holocaust'.[15]

Israeli society, and the Diaspora as well, remain in the powerful grip of the obligation to remember, with all its ramifications and its perversions as well. For many secularized Israelis, the genocide is the sole tie binding them to Judaism, and they are often tempted to appeal to it as the crowning argument in defence of one or another political position, particularly with regard to the Palestinian question. The settlers in the occupied territories, including – indeed, above all – the Orthodox settlers, did just that in summer 2005, when they had to leave Gaza. They even put the Holocaust on stage, as it were, before the media of the whole world. Thus they wore orange stars of David (the colour

---

14   The results of the poll may be found in Yair Auron, 'The Holocaust and the Israeli Teacher', *Holocaust and Genocide Studies*, 8:2, 1994, 225–57.

15   *Yediot Aharonot*, 30 January 2007.

was inspired by the Orange Revolution in the Ukraine); held up posters bearing the word *judenrein*; presented children holding their hands over their heads and wearing a star of David on their chests, in imitation of a famous photograph, often reproduced as a symbol of persecution, of a little boy in the Warsaw ghetto; wrote their identity card numbers on their forearms, recalling the numbers that the Nazis tattooed on the arms of concentration camp prisoners; and refused to move until soldiers dragged them off to buses and packed them into them. Thus they did everything in their power to make the authorities who were expelling them look like Nazis, while casting themselves in the role of the Nazis' innocent victims. Ariel Sharon, assigning his enemies the part of a new Hitler or the head of a new *Judenrat* (the notorious Jewish councils that the Nazis set up in the ghettos), was thus hoist with the petard of the rhetoric that his own party had used and abused in the past when, at demonstrations, party members pinned the label *Judenrat* on the Rabin government. The political exploitation of the Holocaust and the whole panoply of symbols associated with it becomes routine once it is set in motion, and it can easily change camps. What happened when the settlers were evacuated from Gaza is just one example among many; it illustrates the gulf between the reality of the genocide and the uses to which it is put today.[16] Similarly abusive use of historical references may be observed among detractors of Israel as a state. Nazi metaphors had already been bandied about in the media after the 1982 Israeli invasion of Lebanon, and manipulation of this sort continues to colour a certain anti-Israeli rhetoric. In the past few years, this has happened, notably, in Iran, a country that enjoys the sinister distinction of having organized, in 2006, a Holocaust caricature competition, followed by a 'scholarly conference' of Holocaust deniers.

Victimization, in its collective political form, is the pendant to the defeat of the universal. This cult is not the exclusive prerogative of Israel and the Jews. It is regularly celebrated by the Arab media as well, including the television network Al-Jazeera, something made possible by the fact that the ideology currently dominant in the Arab world brings this rejection of the universal in its wake and takes refuge in a culture of death of which Jihadism embodies the last, convulsive avatar. But if Jihadism is clearly the extreme expression of this ideology, this culture of death and cult of the victim, paired with hatred of Jews, Israel, and the West as metaphors for everything that is going badly, also circulates in diffuse, pernicious form in states characterized by dire poverty and the absence of democracy and controlled by corrupt regimes. In such countries,

---

16   Esther Benbassa, 'Les brouillages sémantiques de Gaza', *Le Figaro*, 29 August 2005.

death, sanctified and held up for admiration – death as the ultimate challenge – confers meaning on a present that is bereft of hope and paralyzed by its daily dose of suffering.[17]

A PLAY OF MIRRORS: PALESTINIAN VICTIMHOOD

The victimization that bears the closest resemblance to that of the Israelis and Jews is the Palestinians'.

In the 1940s, Palestinian public discourse did not ignore the genocide; frequent reference was made to it in various political and ideological movements, although no coherent narrative was ever produced on this theme. Arab and Palestinian leaders initially acknowledged the Jewish catastrophe; however, after the 1948 War of Independence, the Palestinian defeat, and the ensuing expulsion, the Palestinians, who considered themselves the victims of Zionism, denied their enemy the status of victim. With the consolidation of the Palestinian Liberation Organization from the 1970s on, PLO-subsidized publications began to produce a narrative on the genocide in which the denunciation of the collaboration between Zionists and Nazis emerged as a major theme. The most important text in this regard is the doctoral dissertation of Mahmud Abbas (whose *nom de guerre* is Abu Mazen), published in 1984, which tends to credit the thesis of Zionist–Nazi collaboration. Abbas cites the Holocaust denier Robert Faurisson and, in airing doubts about the figure of six million victims, treated as a Zionist invention, cites, very oddly, *The Destruction of the European Jews* by the Holocaust historian Raul Hilberg. What is more, according to the champions of this thesis, the two partners did not collaborate for merely pragmatic reasons, but also because of the affinities between Nazism and Zionism. Supporters of this view base what they say on, notably, the transfer (*ha'avara*) agreement signed in 1933 by the German government and the Zionist leader Haim Arlozorov with a view to facilitating Jewish emigration to Palestine. Their accusation is, of course, intended to counter the emphasis that the Zionists put on the collaboration between the Nazis and the Mufti of Jerusalem, Haj Amin al-Husayni.[19]

---

17   Samir Kassir, *Considérations sur le malheur arabe*, Arles: Actes Sud–Sindbad, 2004, 24–5, 90–1, 101.
19   Meir Litvak and Esther Webman, 'Perceptions of the Holocaust in Palestinian Public Discourse', *Israel Studies*, 8:3, 2003, 126–7. See also Rashid Khalidi, *Palestinian Identiy: The Construction of Modern National Consciousness*, New York: Columbia University Press, 1997.

Indeed, this counter-image signals the similarities between the constructed representations of the Holocaust and the *Nakba*, the Palestinian tragedy. The word '*Nakba*' itself, which evokes the severe trauma occasioned by the foundation of the state of Israel and the expropriation and massive expulsion of the Palestinians, means, simply, 'catastrophe', as does one of the first names given to the Jewish genocide. To be sure, there are substantial differences between the two events; these were, however, ignored by those who exploited them to political ends. In fact, the terminology and discourse of the Holocaust have, from the outset, profoundly influenced the elaboration of the Palestinian narrative of the *Nakba*. To 'Shoah and redemption'[20] and 'Shoah and renaissance'[21] there correspond *Nakba* and resistance'[22] and 'perseverance and resistance'.[23] The *Nakba* has been reconstructed as a founding myth both to shape the memory of the past and provide a springboard for a radiant future. Victimization and victimhood, which are central to the representation of Jewish experience and identity, are also central to the Palestinian narrative. In the 1980s and 1990s, the 'culture of victimhood' was erected into a basic component of the Palestinians' ethnic and national identity. Jewish victimhood served as a paradigm. In this period, Palestinian militants demanded that a special tribunal be created to judge Israeli war criminals. More generally, laying claim to the status of victims, the Palestinians effectively demand recognition and reparation for their past misfortunes; this implies that Israel should pay them indemnities and make a place for their ordeal in its national memory. The Palestinians, who tend to see themselves as the victims of the greatest injustice of the twentieth century, also demand recognition for the twofold responsibility, in the *Nakba*, of Israel *and the West*, which is charged with compensating for its own sense of guilt after the genocide by guaranteeing the Jews a state.

In the wake of the peace process of the 1990s, however, there has emerged a new tendency that calls for recognition of both the Jewish and Palestinian tragedies. Among its representatives are intellectuals such as Edward Said, who demanded that the Jewish experience be acknowledged, with all the horror and fear associated with it. Said invited the Arabs to show their 'comprehension and compassion'. A move of this sort might have led Israelis and supporters of Israel to show a similar desire to comprehend and pity the Palestinians.[24]

20   In Hebrew, *shoah u-geulah*.
21   In Hebrew, *shoah u-tehiyah*.
22   In Arabic, *nakba u-muqawama*.
23   In Arabic, *israr wa-nidal*.
24   Litvak and Webman, 'Perceptions of the Holocaust'. (Said's thoughts are also inspired by this essay.) On Said's remarks, see also *Ha'aretz*, 20 February 1998; *Le Monde Diplomatique*, August–September 1998.

Unfortunately, the reciprocal attempts at recognizing the Other's suffering, an essential condition for the reconciliation of the two peoples, largely evaporated in the renewal of tensions that set in 2000 and have intensified since. Yet there are still Palestinians who clearly reject the option of Holocaust denial. They are exemplified by Mahmud Al-Safadi, a militant of the Popular Front for the Liberation of Palestine who, shortly after his release from an Israeli prison, wrote to the Iranian President Mahmud Ahmadinejad in the spirit of the late Edward Said. 'As for my people's struggle for its independence and freedom', Al-Safadi said in his letter, 'perhaps you consider denial of the Holocaust to be an expression of support for the Palestinians? In that, too, you are mistaken. We are struggling for our existence and rights, and struggling against the historical injustice to which we were subjected in 1948. We will not gain our victory and independence by denying the genocide perpetrated against the Jewish people, even if the forces that, today, occupy our country and dispossess us of it belong to that people'.[25]

THE CONVERSION OF FRENCH JEWS TO THE RELIGION OF THE HOLOCAUST

On 2 June 1967, in an article entitled 'Five Left Intellectuals Violently Denounce the Arab Countries' Political Course', the French daily *Le Monde* quoted a declaration by Claude Lanzmann: 'The destruction of Israel would be worse than the Nazi Holocaust. For Israel is my freedom. I have, to be sure, been assimilated, but I lack confidence. Without Israel, I feel naked.' Be it noted that Lanzmann did not yet use the word 'Shoah', which he would later choose as the title of his film, quite simply because the period of the particularization of the genocide had not yet begun. Here, Lanzmann was in some sense echoing the way French Jews interpreted the Israeli–Arab conflict. The genocide and Six Day War had been so closely intertwined that it was impossible to understand the one without the other. Each, necessarily, implied the other. The theme of Israel as a fallback position and shield against hard times – which would often be sounded in the following years – was already in the air. At the same time, between the lines, another idea was making itself felt: that the fatal rupture represented by the genocide had profoundly shaken Jews' confidence in the countries they lived in.

French Jews, who identified with the Israelis and Israel, followed the course of the war with great emotion. Raymond Aron expressed their fear of the

---

25   Mahmud Al-Safadi, *Le Monde*, 5 December 2006.

the state might be destroyed; he used the word 'stateocide' ...elled on 'genocide', which he would use again in his book *De* ...*nd the Jews*.[26] Wladimir Rabi, a Jewish intellectual who, unlike ...he left, evoked, in the Catholic journal *Esprit*, the impossibility of ...second Auschwitz in one and the same generation.[27] From this point ..., genocide weighed ever more heavily on the minds of French and also American Jews. In this regard, the year 1973, which was also that of the *Yom Kippur* War, marked a decisive turning point in the United States. A consensus emerged on the need to preserve the memory of the Holocaust; university courses and programmes, publications, conferences, and, eventually, museums proliferated in consequence. In his book on the subject, Peter Novick dwells at length on the growing hold that the theme had over American Jewry and American culture.[28]

In France, too, the Holocaust now served to mobilize support for the state of Israel. In 2003, during the second Intifada, when the Administrative Council of the University of Paris VI called for a boycott of Israeli universities, Claude Lanzmann was not loath to draw comparisons with the Nazi period in his successful bid to have the decision annulled. In a speech read by Bernard-Henri Lévy at a demonstration called to the same end, Lévy declared:

> The word 'boycott' has a sinister, intolerable connotation, which the good bureaucrats of the Administrative Council of Paris VI would have recalled, if they had the least semblance of memory and awareness. On 1 April 1933, the Nazis declared a pan-German boycott of Jewish businesses and merchants. Countless slogans and appeals were pasted up on the windows and doors of every Jewish shop: 'Don't buy from Jews', 'The Jews are our scourge'.[29]

More recently, in summer 2006, during the war waged by Israel against Hezbollah in Southern Lebanon, Lanzmann spoke out yet again. This was a war that may have been legitimate at the outset, but in which Israel soon got bogged down; it caused immense material damage and great loss of life, especially among Lebanese civilians. It did not leave Israel unaffected, either, inasmuch as the population of the northern part of the country was targeted by Hezbollah's missiles. As the fighting raged, Lanzmann wrote in *Le Monde* on 4 August 2006: 'What is taking place at the moment is the first act, the great

---

26   Raymond Aron, *De Gaulle, Israel and the Jews*, trans. John Sturrock, New York: Praeger, 1969.
27   Wladimir Rabi, *Esprit*, April 1968, 581–2.
28   Peter Novick, *The Holocaust in American Life*, Boston: Houghton Mifflin, 1999.
29   Bernard-Henri Lévy, *Le Monde*, 7 January 2003.

overture of this war, the *final* purpose of which, as in the *solution* of the same name sixty years ago, is the destruction of the state of Israel.'[30] As this declaration again attests, the indissoluble bond between the Holocaust and its 'redemption', Israel, comes regularly to the fore in situations of crisis, great or small.

We will be struck by the contrast if we recall that in 1955, when, in Paris, the question of whether to erect a Monument to the Unknown Jewish Martyr alongside the Centre of Contemporary Jewish Documentation[31] (CCJD) was put on the public agenda, the *Conseil représentatif des institutions juives de France* (CRIF: the Representative Council of French Jewish Institutions) and the Consistory opposed the project. In spring 1955, 19 Jewish associations publicly rejected the idea, while Paris's Yiddish press voiced the opposition of the city's East European Jewish community. For his part, Guy de Rothschild, the reporter of the Committee to Create the Monument, announced that he was hostile to the project, on the grounds that it had sentimental, but no social value. He advocated creating a modest memorial associated with a community centre. In the end, the American Claims Conference, which had negotiated the reparations agreement between Germany and Israel, footed the entire bill for the building, which eventually included both the monument, finished in 1956, and the CCJD itself (ten per cent of whose budget, be it noted, was also provided by the Claims Conference).[32] In January 2005, half a century later, in a radically different context, the Memorial to the Holocaust was solemnly inaugurated on the site of the Monument to the Unknown Jewish Martyr; it formed an ensemble with this Monument and the CCJD itself. Its president, Eric de Rothschild, Guy's cousin, called it a 'museum of vigilance' and a 'bulwark against forgetting'.

By itself, the history of this institution shows how a policy of commemorating the genocide finally gave way to the demands of the obligation to remember, transforming the museums of the genocide into virtual temples, new places of worship of a secular religion. The Memorial to the Holocaust erected in 2005, with its wall covered with names – the same names that are ritually read out during commemorations – provides the perfect illustration of this shift. Curiously, in France, a country that vociferously declares its allegiance to the separation of church and state, a place of worship such as this one

---

30   Emphasis added.

31   This Centre was founded in 1943 as an underground organization.

32   Ronald Zweig, 'Politics of Commemoration', *Jewish Social Studies*, 49:2, 1987, 155–9.

does not strike anyone as an incongruity. On the contrary it enables indirectly a country that finds it difficult to acknowledge the sombre pages of its history to put off admitting the harm it has done to other groups in other periods. It is as if fulfilling one's obligation to remember in the case of the Holocaust implied at least temporary exemption from the obligation to perform other 'duties' of the same order.

In 1961, even before the Six Day War, French Jewry's reaction to the Eichmann trial provided a harbinger of the tone and scope of its future identification with Israel. One can name various reasons for this mobilization, in France, of the memory of genocide in defence of the Jewish state. To begin with, thanks to Nasser's repeated calls to destroy Israel and wipe it off the face of the map, the young state, which Jews regarded as vulnerable at the time, feared the worst. There also existed a fear that de Gaulle would abandon his Jews as Pétain had earlier. Similarly, the repatriated Algerian Jews who had only recently left Algeria for France itself, like other *pieds-noirs* (the name given to French citizens repatriated from Algeria), harboured a certain bitterness towards France for relinquishing its former colony. They also knew that de Gaulle had, for a time, nursed the project of acceding to the demands of the Algerian National Liberation Front on the question of the 'Algerian' nationality of the country's Jews – that is, he had contemplated stripping them of French citizenship, which France had accorded them with the 1870 Crémieux Decree. All this helped fuel the real hostility that the Jews who had left Algeria for France felt for de Gaulle in particular and the Gaullist regime in general. This hostility increased during the Six Day War thanks to the attitude that de Gaulle adopted towards Israel and his indirect support for the Arab countries. Many of the repatriates from Algeria saw connections between this attitude and the abandonment of Algeria to the Arabs. The Jews accordingly conceived their relationship to the French nation as that of Holocaust survivors and, consequently, Jews. In a rhetoric laden with emotion, they expressed their fears that a second genocide might occur in the Middle East; in their estimation, the singular, incomprehensible horror of such a catastrophe required that they make a public show of their Jewishness and, what is more, manifest unconditional support for the state of Israel.[33] In Jacobin France, this was unprecedented.

Between 1956 and 1967, some 235,000 Jews from Northern Africa settled in France, fleeing Egypt after the Suez Crisis as well as Morocco, Tunisia, and

---

33   Joan B. Wolf, *Harnessing the Holocaust: The Politics of Memory in France*, Stanford CA: Stanford University Press, 2004, 17.

Algeria during the period of decolonization. They were extremely resentful of the Arabs, whom they blamed for their exile. What is more, the North African Jews had extensive family ties to Israel and projected their own experience of exile onto the Israelis, who, they feared, would also have to leave their country after an Arab victory. The Israeli–Arab conflict also gave rise to a wave of pro-Israeli opinion in non-Jewish circles, inspired sometimes by admiration for the accomplishments of the new state and sometimes by anti-Arab sentiment, a legacy of the war in Algeria. This had its impact on the French Jewish population, which now considered itself legitimated and felt as if it constituted an integral part of French society. Thus France's approval of Israel was doubly internalized by the French Jews as a group. A poll taken during the first two days of the Six Day War showed that 58 per cent of Parisians sympathized with Israel, while only two per cent sympathized with Egypt and the Arab countries. Another poll conducted throughout France between 8 and 11 June revealed that only six per cent of the French considered Israel to be the aggressor, against the 54 per cent who blamed the Arab countries for the war.[34] Alongside the findings of the pollsters, however, we must range the famous November 1967 declarations of the French President, de Gaulle, who called Israel a warlike state, adding that the Jewish people was 'self-assured and domineering'; these statements sparked fears of a resurgence of anti-Semitism.

It was in this complex, wholly new climate that the connection between Israel and the Genocide crystallized in France. Most North African Jews learned about the Holocaust in metropolitan France. Thus for them it was in exile that Israel and the Genocide came to be associated, an association which, it may be added, also served to inhibit expression of these exiles' own suffering, faced as they were with Jews who had gone through the traumatic experience of the Second World War and the deportation. The North African Jews' exile was thus consigned to silence, whereas the silence about the Holocaust was gradually broken beginning in the 1970s.

Several of the elements that surfaced in the debates of later years had their origins in the Israeli–Arab conflict. From this point on, the Holocaust justified publicly asserting one's Jewish identity. In France, the Jews had always striven not to let their Jewishness come into conflict with their French citizenship; being French made it necessary to downplay being Jewish. The Six Day War led to a break in this tradition. French Jews were not disloyal French citizens. From now on, however, they were also Jews who declared that they were Jews and

---

34   Joan Wolf, 'Anne Frank is Dead. Long Live Anne: The Six-Day War and the Holocaust in French Public Discourse', *History and Memory*, 11:1, 1999, 117.

cultivated political commitments bound up with their Jewish identity. This led them to consider new ways of being simultaneously French and Jewish. By the same token, the new turn announced the demise of the 'Israelite', that is, the Frenchman of Jewish faith; gradually, he gave way to the Jew *tout court*, to the French Jew. In the following decades, the Jews of France sought to structure this plural identity, which, moreover, eventually acquired the status of a paradigm for the construction of various other sorts of identity.

The other persistent element that traces its beginnings to this war has to do with the direct relation established between Israel and the genocide. The genocide stood as proof that there had to be a Jewish state, that it had to be defended at all costs, and that any encroachment on Israel's moral or territorial integrity had to be combated, even in the Diaspora. Many people simply ignored the origins of Zionism – which took shape in the nineteenth century in the wake of the major European nationalist movements of the period and engaged in a long-term effort (lasting several decades) to bring a Jewish state into existence – and perceived Israel as a triumph over the Holocaust. But, while it is true that the genocide did indeed accelerate the creation of the state, Israel was by no means a direct outgrowth of it. Yet the two now formed a whole, occupying the same niche in the memory of the Jews of the Diaspora. This facilitated the task of Israeli statesmen, who could play on this dyad as often as they wished in order to fan the Diasporic Jews' Zionism, even while playing on the West's guilt feelings in order to 'neutralize' Israel's share of the responsibility for the Israeli–Palestinian conflict. With Auschwitz as backdrop, the Palestinians were assigned the role of merciless executioners of a people that had been victimized from time immemorial. Thus in 1967 large numbers of Jews, the diversity of their political commitments notwithstanding, pointed to the genocide to explain their unconditional support for the Jewish state. When, in 1973, the French government chose to support the Arabs and the French public failed to rally to the Israeli cause, or, again, when in 1982, the media criticized Israel during the invasion of Lebanon and the massacres at Sabra and Shatila, comparing the country to Nazi Germany, the Jews invoked their past suffering in the attempt to show that Israel was above criticism. Defending it under all circumstances and praising its mission and virtues subsequently became a mandatory constant in Jewish public discourse, discordant voices here and there notwithstanding.

In the 1970s, while Jews were trying to find content for their Jewishness, France confronted its Vichy past and its collaboration with the Nazis, shattering the myth about it as the country that had resisted. As part of the same process, the developing memory of the genocide sparked reconsideration of the Vichy regime and the role of French anti-Semitism in the 1930s and 1940s. It was in this context a film such as Marcel Ophüls's *The Sorrow and the Pity* was produced and that the emblematic work by the American historian Robert Paxton, *Vichy France, 1940–1944*, was published in French translation. Trials staged between 1973 and 1997 helped restructure the memory of the genocide: the 1987 trial of the former SS captain Klaus Barbie; the 1944 trial of Paul Touvier, who had executed seven hostages in Rillieux; and, finally, the trial of the former secretary-general of the prefecture of the Gironde, Maurice Papon, which began in 1997 and resulted in a ten-year prison sentence for the accused. Let us also note the well-known indictments that did not result in trials: the 1991 indictment of René Bousquet, the former secretary-general of Vichy's police force and one of the organizers of the 16–17 July 1942 round-up of Jews interned in the stadium known as the Vel' d'Hiv, or the 1979 indictment of Jean Legay, Bosquet's representative in the Nazi-occupied zone. Legay died in 1989, before he could be tried. As for Bousquet, a personal friend of President François Mitterrand's, he was assassinated before he could be brought to court. Parallel to these developments, commemorations were held, monuments erected, and memorial plaques put in place, helping to perpetuate the memory of the event.

The 1970s also saw the creation of activist memorial associations. One, founded in 1979, Les Fils et Filles des Déportés juifs de France ('The sons and daughters of Jews deported from France'), supported the work of Beate and Serge Klarsfeld, who sought to end the impunity then enjoyed by Frenchmen and Germans responsible for the deportations. Mention should also be made of the sometimes very sharp polemics of the day, including the one that sprang up around the 'Jewish files' that Klarsfeld discovered in the French Veterans' Ministry in 1992. These were, he maintained, the files that had been assembled by the police in 1940 and used in the round-ups of Jews. A commission of experts was charged with determining the exact nature of these files; it concluded that they were not the 1940 files, which, it said, had been destroyed in 1948–9.

On 3 February 1993, François Mitterrand issued a decree making 16 July a national day of commemoration of the 'racist and anti-Semitic persecutions carried out under the *de facto* authority known as the "government of the French state" (1940–4)'. For the first time in the history of the French Republic, a national day of commemoration was established by decree, that is, without benefit of the procedure of a parliamentary discussion and vote. Thereafter, the state erected steles and monuments in tribute to the victims of the persecutions: they were admonitions not to forget.

Another national debate about Vichy was sparked by President Jacques Chirac's 16 July 1995 speech on the occasion of the 53rd anniversary of the Vel' d'Hiv round-up. Chirac acknowledged 'the responsibility of the French state' and spoke of a 'collective offence'. France, he said, had contracted a debt of guilt toward 76,000 murdered Jews. The leaders of the organized Jewish community expressed their satisfaction, as did 72 per cent of the French polled by the magazine *L'Événement du Jeudi* and the Institut français d'opinion publique. This recognition from above now made it possible to consolidate a badly mutilated memory, while gradually establishing a place for Vichy within the French collective memory and, in the process, buttressing a Jewish identity of which the genocide was now one of the main markers. The far right accused Chirac of 'dragging the nation through the mud'. Maurice Papon's trial sparked a new round in the debate, centred on the question of the trial's educational value, on which a good deal of ink was spilt. On 20 July 1997, finally, in direct continuity with Chirac's previous declarations, the Socialist Prime Minister Lionel Jospin also acknowledged the French state's responsibility in the Vel' d'Hiv' round-up, and announced that the government would 'fully support' the work of the commissions charged with making an inventory of the despoliation, under the German occupation, of real estate, works of art, and financial holdings belonging to Jews living in France. Jospin added that the government would also help found a 'Museum of the Shoah' in Paris. With the help of compensation payments for the Jews' confiscated property, a Foundation for the Memory of the Shoah was created in 2000.

These events and declarations acquired the value of moral reparations for the genocide victims; they also gradually helped engender national awareness of the extent to which the French government of the time was implicated in the catastrophe. Ultimately, that catastrophe became an essential component of the identity of French Jews, including those who had no experience of it, such as the younger generation or the North African Jews. One might even speak of a veritable crystallization of Jewish identity around the genocide in the past few years, among young people in particular. In the 1970s and 1980s, the French Jews' quest for identity also made itself felt in cultural form: people studied the various Jewish languages, founded cultural reviews, and organized conferences. In the absence of a rich, creative Jewish culture, the obligation to remember advocated by community institutions and their organs made it possible to bring back into the fold Jews who had long been dispersed in struggles for various civic causes and in the ideologies of the post-war period. They were thus drawn into the exclusivity of a memory that shunned the universalism of the modern Jew's vocation to change the world, an inseparable part of being Jewish until then. This turn had been prepared by the breaking of the contract between the Jews and the countries in which they resided during the Second World War; it became still more conspicuous with the stalemate in the Israeli–Palestinian conflict.

In *The Imaginary Jew*, first published in French in 1980, Alain Finkielkraut had already declared:

> I thought I was living up to Israel's calling, and played the role of the Jew, the black, the colonized, the Indian, or the impoverished of the Third World. These were happy, boisterous years, when I stuck to my origins like glue. It doesn't work anymore: the drama's mainspring has unsprung ... Even the affirmation 'I am a Jew' quickly produces a painful sense that I'm appropriating the Holocaust as my own, draping myself with the torture that others underwent.[35]

It was in a vale of tears that this memory was constructed, tallying, one after the other, all the misfortunes and grievances of the Jewish people, summed up in the final destruction that figured as the inevitable culminating point of an unbroken continuum of persecution and hatred. It was in this fashion that one was drawn into a teleological story that resembled religion more than history. Because everything conduces to disaster, nothing can ever change; the Jew has always been and will always be a victim. In a certain sense, the history of the Jews, which goes back thousands of years, finds itself reduced to Zionism, the Holocaust, and the creation of the state of Israel; untold, crucially important aspects of what Judaism really was at other moments in history are thus shrouded in darkness. Moreover, even when such aspects are brought out from the shadows, they are interpreted through the grid provided by these three new components of what might fairly be called modern Judaism, especially that of the secular Jews. Between Jewish victimization and Israeli victory, everything takes its place in an emotional and rhetorical framework that leaves no room for more finely shaded discourse. Thus modern Judaism condemns Jews to living in a sort of perpetual *Sturm und Drang* that does not leave them the leisure to assume their identity without mediation. (This is less true of religious Jews: one can, without idealizing them, acknowledge their capacity to draw on more positive sources.) The whole of Judaism – for secular Jews, at any rate – is strained through this filter. Can a Jewishness that has become synonymous with victimhood perpetuate itself indefinitely, even after the survivors have

---

35   Alain Finkielkraut, *The Imaginary Jew*, trans. Kevin O'Neill and David Suchoff, Lincoln NE: University of Nebraska Press, 2nd edn, 1997, 32.

disappeared, which will soon be the case? Admittedly, the various memorial constructions appear able to do without direct witnesses, as would seem to be shown by recent calls in France for recognition of the memory of slavery, an institution that ended in that country a little less than two centuries ago.

Until that day comes, the eternal victim can pride themself on their impregnable, morally elevated position, towering above all others. Yet the victim is not more virtuous simply because they have been victimized. Those who have endured the greatest horrors are not, for that reason, always right. If immorality is plainly always on the murderers' side of the divide, it is not enough to be or to have been a victim in order automatically to find oneself on the other side. Morality is not a status that one acquires for good and all; one has to conquer it anew in everyday moral action. Victims are not ennobled by their suffering. On the contrary, the perception of one's own victimhood is likely to breed a desire for compensation and an inclination to play the tyrant with others. It is time to abandon the idea that the Holocaust is the one and only founding event of Jewish history and that being Jewish comes down to regarding oneself as the victim of non-Jews. No individual or group identity can be sustained on such grounds.[36]

If the genocide is treated as the alpha and omega of Jewish history, then Judaism is inevitably doomed to disappear. 'Holocaustmania', as Jacob Neusner calls it, is impoverishing Jewish spiritual life. Just after the war, the Holocaust occupied a minor place in Jewish American life; the same held for France. The book by the great American sociologist Nathan Glazer, written in this period, refers to the destruction of European Jewry only in passing.[37] The contrast with the 1970s, especially in the United States, a country in which the Jews were not directly confronted with the genocide, is overwhelming. Today, it is not possible to address the Jewish world without referring to the Final Solution. Does this not create a situation, particularly in Europe, in which the only way the younger generation can learn about the Jews is by way of the genocide – by way of their destruction rather than their long existence on the continent and the contributions they have made and continue to make to their respective countries? Thanks to the obsession that surrounds it and the civil religion it has spawned, the genocide has become the main theme of public discourse about the Jews and Judaism. One episode in the Jewish experience, a most fateful one,

---

36   See Michael Andre Bernstein, *Foregone Conclusions: Against Apocalyptic History*, Berkeley: University of California Press, 1994, 85–9, 90–4, 126–7.

37   Nathan Glazer, *American Judaism*, Chicago Chicago University Press, 1957. See also Neusner, *Stranger at Home*, 84.

has taken the place of a millennial Jewish history.[38] Genocidal undertakings seek to put an end to the spiritual, cultural, and artistic life of an ethnic or religious group, and, indeed, to its life *tout court*, thus depriving humanity of their contribution to it. The desire of those who have been affected by the experience of genocide, whether directly or from afar, might well be not to be imprisoned by it, to promote life, precisely, to open themselves to the rest of the human race and struggle shoulder-to-shoulder with it to prevent the evil from ever recurring. Not to do so amounts to betraying, in the same act, Judaism and humanity.

To confine the Holocaust to the prison-house of a secular religion in no way ensures that the lessons to be drawn from it will be universal ones. To be sure, in the present era of globalization, the memory of the genocide is becoming ever more cosmopolitan; its rites, codes, and memorials are increasingly familiar and conspicuous in diverse places across the globe. Yet, at the same time, the Holocaust is perceived as a disaster that happened to the Jews, not really as a catastrophe that could befall other groups. The apparent cosmopolitanism of this memory does not make its message universal; the reason is the failure to put the accent on its universal aspect. The globalization of the memory of the Holocaust, in a period in which our intellectual landmarks are constantly shifting amid the disappearance of the ideologies that once furnished us discourses that clearly distinguished 'good' from 'evil', answers to our need for a moral touchstone.[39] Yet only History has the power to universalize the message of the event; a memory that functions 'narcissistically' does not. Sanctification and narcissization have dissociated this genocide from the other disasters that humanity has known in the course of its history. This segregation, deliberately sought by those responsible for the institutionalization and politicization of the Holocaust, is fraught with dangers. One of the most conspicuous, common today in France as elsewhere, has been called by Michael Marrus – the great Canadian historian whose 1981 book *Vichy France and the Jews*, co-authored with Robert Paxton, brought France face-to-face with one of the sombre pages of its history – the 'triumphalism of pain'.[40] This triumphalism is the source of the indifference of the victims, draped in their voluntarily assumed, incomparable pain.

---

38   Neusner, *Stranger at Home*, 84–7.

39   Daniel Levy and Natan Sznaider, 'Memory Unbound: The Holocaust and the Formation of Cosmopolitan Memory', *European Journal of Social Theory*, 5:1, 2002, 87–106.

40   Michael Marrus, 'The Use and the Misuse of the Holocaust', in Peter Hayes, ed., *Lessons and Legacies: The Meaning of the Holocaust in a Changing World*, Evanston IL: Northwestern University Press, 115–6.

CHAPTER FIVE

Outside Suffering, No Salvation!

One of the best illustrations of the mechanisms that I have tried to analyze in the preceding chapter is also one of the most recent. Here I propose to discuss the Jewish responses to the rise of anti-Semitism observable in the wake of the second Intifada in Europe and, especially, France, where North Africans and Jews of working-class origin from the Maghreb often inhabit the same lower-income suburbs and sometimes even the same housing estates.

The relative success of these Jews, which has to do with the fact that they possess tools of adaptation inherited from the long Diasporic history of the Jews in general, exacerbates the resentment that the other North Africans feel toward them as a result of the present Israeli–Palestinian conflict. The North African Jews who live side-by-side with the Arabs also harbour resentment, not only as a result of their traumatic departure from North Africa, but also because they project their own experience, which they interpret today as an 'expulsion', onto what is going on in the Middle East between Israelis and Palestinians. As they see it, their fellow Jews in Israel are threatened with a similar fate. Let us add that one finds the same type of projection in Israel itself, where the eastern Jews have transformed the rancour engendered by their exile and the trials and tribulations that they face as easterners in their new country into hostility toward Palestinians and Arabs in general.

Jewish and Muslim Arab community loyalty, which has grown more intense above all since the second Intifada, taking concrete form as diasporic nationalism, has obviously helped bring these mutual hostilities into being. All Jews and Arabs, wherever they constitute large diasporas, in France and elsewhere, are affected to one degree or another by this nationalism. It is a nationalism that makes no territorial claims and accommodates a marriage of loyalty toward one's country of residence with unwavering support for a cause external to it, support of the kind capable of cementing a diasporic identity. Such causes are transnational. By defending the Palestinian struggle, the Muslim Arabs of the diaspora have reconstructed a certain unity that transcends their or their parents' particular national affiliation; they have put by latent internal disagreements in the process. This identification endows the young, among whom it is more conspicuous, with a genealogy, despite the slackening of their ties to their country of origin and their parents, who are criticized for having passively put up with the humiliations and sacrifices imposed by immigration.

In the volatile powder-kegs that the suburbs of the big French cities have become, with their large immigrant populations, identification with the Palestinians or all those who defy the West is, more than religion, the means by which the younger generation seeks to restore its elders' lost honour. The spectacular operations of the heroes of the Palestinian cause have become acts of bravura and objects to appropriate, while Israel, associated with the West that has relegated these immigrants to its margins, incarnates the enemy *par excellence*, and the persecutor of their brothers, the Palestinians, who have been dealt a similar fate. In this schema, Israelis are not, as a rule, dissociated from Jews. Jews, for their part, have long since developed a Diasporic nationalism centred on Israel. It has been reinforced by the course of the conflict in the Middle East.

What, in such a context, is to be said about Muslim Arab anti-Semitism in France, which is an active expression of diasporic nationalism set in the context of membership in a community? There can of course be no denying either the sharp increase in the number of anti-Jewish actions, serious and less serious, or the existence of sharp hostility to the Jews in certain Muslim Arab circles; what is more, it is not limited to these circles, since anti-Semitism has increasingly become a metaphor for all the ills of French society. The anti-Semitism that affects certain Muslim Arab social strata is not, for its part, unrelated to certain social ills: the absence of effective policies for integrating immigrants and their descendants, a social and professional mobility that is still in its early stages, and the attendant problems.

Between 1 January and 30 June 2004, 135 anti-Semitic acts were reported to the French authorities, as against 127 in 2003. Dominique de Villepin, then interior minister, stated that there had been 160 anti-Semitic attacks on people or property in the first seven months of 2004, as opposed to 75 in the same seven-month period in 2003. In the first half of 2005, however, the number of anti-Semitic attacks plunged by 48 per cent in comparison with the first half of 2004. Two hundred and ninety acts of an anti-Semitic nature were reported to the French authorities in 2005, as opposed to 561 in 2004; this drop is probably down to the government's campaign against anti-Semitism.[1] Finally,

---

1   See online lesrapports.ladocumentationfrancaise.fr.

according to statistics emanating from the Direction Générale de la Police Nationale, 2006 witnessed a further (albeit slight) decrease in anti-Semitic acts: there were 3.5 per cent fewer than in 2005.[2] Given these facts and the trends that they reveal, and taking into account the general context briefly described above, can it be said that the fear that has come over French Jews and the public attention it has been given is commensurate with the level of aggression to which they have in fact been subjected?

Some, such as Alain Finkielkraut, have not hesitated to speak of a 'Year of Crystal'. The phrase seems both typical and, to say the least, exaggerated. The 1938 *Kristallnacht*[3] was directly encouraged by the Nazi regime. In contrast, in contemporary France, politicians of all stripes have, as everyone knows, outdone each other in defending the Jews. Should we not therefore take the Jewish reaction to the recent rise in anti-Semitism as one more expression of the new Diasporic nationalism that is based on past Jewish suffering, illegitimately exploits the genocide, is oriented toward the defence of Israel, and is quick to brand the criticisms that come its way anti-Semitic – all this against the backdrop provided by the reactivation of its traumas in a tense climate?

Anti-Arab racism is also on the rise; conflating Islam and terrorism, it is grafted onto a conflict, inherited from the period of colonization and decolonization, that has resurfaced in the wake of the 11 September 2001 attacks. Statistics on racist abuse are, however, harder to produce, since its victims are less inclined to lodge complaints for fear of being rebuffed because of their origins or skin colour. The problem is compounded by the absence, among groups of immigrants and their descendants, of veritable institutions rooted in non-religious civil society that are capable of defending victims of racism in such situations or of stepping in with the state authorities.

Let us add that European history, of which hatred of the Jews and the genocide it spawned are essential components, makes people much more attentive to anti-Semitism than to the anti-Arab racism that is more easily tolerated in its different guises – Islamophobia, 'the clash of civilizations', anti-Islamism, and so on. We should also bear in mind the sense of guilt arising from the fact that

---

2   *Le Monde*, 2 December 2006. The Israel–Lebanon War of the summer 2006 did not increase the number of anti-Semitic incidents in France. In 2007 the number dropped by 32.5 per cent, and the year after by 1.2 per cent. See reports by the Commission nationale consultative des droits de l'homme. In 2008, the drop observed during the last three years stopped. See Commission Nationale Consultative des Droits de l'Homme, *La Lutte contre le racisme, l'antisémitisme et la xénophobie. Année 2008*, La Documentation française, 2009.

3   In 1938, the Nazi government organized an immense pogrom that took place during the night of 9–10 November. This *Kristallnacht* or Night of Crystal was ostensibly a response to the assassination, by a Jew, of a German diplomat stationed in Paris.

France acknowledged the Vichy regime's share of the responsibility for the deportation of French Jews only very late in the day. The upshot has been a rush to penance, accelerated by the recent resurgence of anti-Semitism in renewed forms. Rather than calm the situation, all this helps breed a species of fear among many Jews that has also been fuelled by Jewish community leaders and the Jewish press, Israel's plea for emigration from France to Israel, and the alarmist tendencies of certain intellectuals. Finally, politicians' and the mass media's reckless reactions to incidents that are anti-Semitic or are construed as such, together with the emotional excesses to which they give themselves up for fear of being themselves charged with anti-Semitism, have heightened Jewish apprehensions. This throws all the parties involved off-balance; they are put under pressure and feel obliged to react as quickly as possible. The resulting vicious circle engenders hysteria of a kind that ultimately trivializes anti-Semitism and clouds our perception of the real problems.

The sheer volume of information that pours into newspaper, radio, and television editorial offices naturally creates a desire for still more. The general public, in its turn, is immersed in a flood of images and texts. Violence is not only perceived in the image of it given to the world, but is also experienced, as it were, along the veins. Thus it invades households and people's imaginations as events dictate. It has ceased to be something out of the ordinary. The violence characteristic of the Israeli–Palestinian conflict in the Middle East has also been personalized. Everyone can take sides with one camp or the other, projecting its cause onto his or her own history and experience. This is often done in an utterly illogical, undiscerning manner that makes one party victims deserving compassion and the other victimizers who must be condemned, or the other way around. Hatred, today, is the stuff dreams are made of; it can even be converted into a demand for the right to hate, which is parallel to another, the right to victimization, or a claim to pain as a passport. Some may then be tempted to make a spectacle of hate or victimization in order, precisely, to attract the attention of the media, which, albeit in a different way, also transforms them into spectacles.

There are, to be sure, gradations in the scale of 'values' brought to bear on hatred. Because Arabophobia gets less attention from the media (or from society in general), Michaël Tronchon, alias Phinéas, did not content himself, in August 2004, with wounding an Arab by hacking away at him with an axe; he also desecrated a Jewish cemetery, taking his symbols from both Nazi-style anti-Semitism and anti-Arab hatred. Phinéas was a self-appointed victimizer. One month earlier, in July 2004, Marie Leblanc pretended that she had been the target of an anti-Semitic attack in a suburban train in greater Paris, adorning all the symbols of victimization. Tronchon and Leblanc, in different registers but at roughly the same time, replayed scenes that they had watched on television or that have now become part of the collective unconscious, scenes in which victim and victimizer, that eternal couple, face off in their respective roles. In its mythomania, Marie Leblanc's imaginary anti-Semitism resembled the version orchestrated by Phinéas. These two cases are twin symptoms of something working away, far below the surface, at a society that lacks a sense of identity and has run short on imagination. Rather incompatible slogans were again superposed in August 2004, when a Moroccan Jew set fire to the Jewish social centre in Rue Popincourt in Paris: 'France for the French', which is, as a rule, an anti-Arab catch phrase, appeared with 'Long live the Islams [*sic*]' and the inevitable swastikas.

The sometimes excessive panic that overcomes Jews today when they are confronted with anti-Semitism draws some of its intensity from the excesses of the obligation to remember. In French society, many can see only the 'external' signs of the anti-Semitism that led to the annihilation of the Jews; others are rediscovering, horrified, what anti-Semitism actually was. The recent manifestations of anti-Jewish hatred were for a long time unfailingly mentioned only in order to be imputed to Muslim Arabs, so heavily did the Israeli–Palestinian conflict weigh on events in France. Yet, curiously, those who desecrate the cemeteries or simulate anti-Semitic attacks do not come from these circles. They are Europeans, which makes their acts even harder to explain.

Until recently, the watchword was the obligation to remember. Today, it would seem that the 'obligation to be vigilant' in the face of signs of anti-Semitism is in the ascendant. The first of these two phrases was, naturally, brandished by victims of the genocide and their descendants, a majority of whom were Ashkenazim; the second seems to find most, albeit not all, of its proponents among Jews from North Africa. Because the North African Jews never subjected their exile to a real labour of memory, it has not had sufficient recognition as the founding experience of a group that has faced ordeals of its own. These Jews, after going through a period in which they shared, out of a sense of solidarity and as proxies, their Ashkenazi brothers' obligation to remember, have now abandoned their silence in order to assume, fully and sometimes furiously, a pressing 'obligation to be vigilant'.

The great majority of books on anti-Semitism published in France since the second Intifada have been produced by Sephardic exiles or their descendants. All these writers imagine that they have avoided the trap into which the so-called 'old stock' Jews or the Ashkenazim who immigrated to France in the inter-war period are supposed to have fallen: the latter are criticized, perhaps wrongly, for having been insufficiently vigilant in the face of danger. This activism in response to the anti-Jewish hostility that has cropped up recently in France has only one objective, in itself honourable: to forestall a repetition of what the Jews experienced during the war. It remains, however, that such activism generally takes anarchical forms; moreover, while it results from fear, it causes real fear in its turn. Today, such activism has become counterproductive, escaping the control of its initiators. They probably did not foresee such excesses or anticipate how easily this fear, when grafted onto profound traumas such as genocide or exile, could become explosive.

Although only a minority maintains this militant vigilance in its extreme forms, its effects may unfortunately turn against Jews as a whole, further widening the gulf between France and its Jewish citizens. French Jews would then be tempted to cultivate, in reaction, self-defensive attitudes, the first and most spontaneous of which is withdrawal into one's own group and cultural parochialism. While the annual rate of emigration from France to Israel is 3,000 at most, the idea that the Jews are only provisionally in France is spreading in certain strata of the country's Jewish population. It is understandable that the resurrection of an anti-Semitism that was supposed to be a thing of the past has bred disenchantment and anger. But it is not always easy to understand the fierce obstinacy with which some Jews track down anti-Semitism in every word, every gesture, and every criticism of Israeli policy. Such intimidation targets the press, political leaders, and intellectuals in equal measure.

Moreover, the focus on the anti-Semitism that the Israeli–Palestinian conflict has spawned amongst immigrant groups distracts attention from the resurgence, among certain non-Muslim strata of French society, of an anti-Semitism which, taking its justification from the Middle Eastern conflict, does not hesitate to wield arguments drawn from the classic arsenal of this recurrent scourge. The fact of the matter is that the conflict between Palestinians and Israelis has lifted the taboo on anti-Semitism. The memory of the Holocaust no longer suffices to shield Jews against it. The taboo has disappeared for another reason as well: in certain circles, Jews, conflated with Israelis, are no longer protected because they no longer enjoy the status of victim that the Holocaust had conferred on them. The new victim is, now, the Palestinian, identified, in Christian circles that have taken up the Palestinian cause, with a suffering Jesus.

In the race to attain the status of victim, the roles are interchangeable, shifting with the course of events. The July 2006 invasion of Lebanon momentarily assigned the Arabs and, specifically, the Palestinians the victim's role, casting the Israelis as executioners of a civilian population at a time when Hezbollah had emerged as a resistance movement and the saviour of the

Lebanese people. The fickleness of public opinion and the Manichean perception of the roles involved confirm that the concept of victimhood is perversely easy to appropriate.

With the end of this war, it will no doubt be instructive to see the turn that the reception of the Holocaust takes both among non-Jews and in the Jewish world, especially Israel, which, emerging diminished from this campaign, finds itself pinned by its accusers in a posture of absolute aggressor that deserves, in its turn, to be rather more finely shaded. At all events, a few months after the end of a conflict that cost more than 1000 Lebanese their lives, wrought substantial material damage, and caused several thousand more people suffering (to say nothing of the Palestinian victims, whose numbers continued to grow in the same period), there would seem to have been no clear resumption of anti-Semitism and no direct manifestations of anti-Jewish hostility among French Muslim Arabs. It is, of course, hard for a historian to analyze events as they happen. No historian, however, could fail to be amazed by the silence in which this subject has been swaddled since the second, 2006 Lebanese war. Without abandoning the caution that is mandatory here, one can fairly ask whether – in what was, moreover, a pre-election period in which recent events in the Middle East profoundly affected public opinion – it has not simply become discomfiting and decidedly counterproductive to brandish the banner of anti-Semitism in an attempt to protect the Israeli state, which is now too deeply discredited to justify such a strategy.

What is more, despite the fears of anti-Semitism that have been haunting French Jews for the past few years and the strident publicity that Jewish institutions and their representatives have given the subject, it is obvious that the Israeli authorities' plans for massive emigration of French Jews to Israel have failed. This failure has most assuredly served as an incitement to curb the instrumentalization previously pursued without restraint. The French policy of struggling against an outbreak of anti-Semitism has doubtless borne its fruits, but does not by itself suffice to explain why, during the war in Lebanon and thereafter, Jewish institutions' publicity campaigns around anti-Semitism ground to a sudden and virtually complete halt (until the late November 2006 attempt to lynch a Jewish fan of the Tel Aviv soccer team at a match with a French team in Paris). At all events, this throws up a question: is there now an inherent fragility to Jewish identity that makes Jews extremely sensitive to any attack on Israel and to all incidents or forms of abuse related to the general climate of violence that surrounds us today (a climate of which anti-Semitism forms a part)? Or is it this sensitivity which makes it possible to exploit anti-Semitism to political ends rather than resolutely struggle to wipe it out?

Another example is significant here. In January 2006, a young Sephardic Jew by the name of Ilan Halimi was tortured and then murdered by a criminal band known as the 'Gang of Barbarians', some of whose members already had police records. Initially, this tragedy was treated as a human interest story. However, on the evening on which the CRIF, an umbrella organization to which most French Jewish institutions belong, held its annual banquet, which was attended, as usual, by politicians of all stripes, the word 'anti-Semitism' was uttered in connection with Halimi's murder. The repeated evocation of anti-Semitism as a possible motive for the murder immediately heightened tensions. The CRIF, which had previously maintained a low profile on the matter, followed the general trend. In short order, the police and investigating magistrates began treating anti-Semitism as an aggravating circumstance in the Halimi case and made that known, although the pre-trial investigation was far from over. The press jumped on the story. Anti-Semitism, which had seemed to be on the wane in this period, was suddenly and hastily put back on the agenda. The Jewish community's emotions were at a peak. As a matter of fact, it is very probable that Halimi, although he had a modest white-collar job, was kidnapped because he was a Jew and thus rich in his kidnappers' estimation. It is, furthermore, by no means impossible that because he was a Jew, they thought the Jewish community would come together to pay the ransom they had asked for. The murderer and his accomplices were found guilty and sentenced in 2009. The court confirmed the anti-Semitic character of the crime. The State, under pressure from the Jewish community, called for an appeal to consider whether some of the accomplices should receive harsher sentences.

Notwithstanding the uncertainties surrounding his murder, the Jewish community was swiftly overcome by a rare panic. French Jewry more or less felt that death was knocking at its door. Of course, the crime was shocking to Jews and non-Jews alike, for it was, unfortunately, emblematic of the violence that exists for a host of reasons in developed societies today. Shortly after Halimi's murder, a Frenchman who was not Jewish lost his life in similar circumstances: he was tortured to death for a derisory sum. Only a bit later, an Arab was shot to death in Oullins, in circumstances that were troubling, to say the least, with suspicion of racist motives. The murder of the young Halimi sparked a demonstration; most of the participants were Jews, and the event was very emotional. Conversations turned on the anguished question, 'Should we leave for Israel before we, too, are faced with the worst?' This virtually immediate resurgence of an ancient set of fears, brought on by a murder which was, to be sure, inhuman, but hardly confronted Jews as a group with a real threat of death, is altogether representative of the state of mind in which Jewry found itself and continues to find itself.

Furthermore, because the young murder victim was from a Jewish family from North Africa, French Sephardic Jews made him into a symbol. Already tempted, in the past few years, to paint an excessively sombre picture of the history of their ancestors in the Muslim world, these Jews had, like their Ashkenazi brothers, paid their tribute to anti-Semitism with Halimi's death; they, too, now had the right to enrol in the legion of victims. It was not long before Ilan Halimi ranked as a martyr in the strict sense of the term: 'For I maintain that Ilan died "*Al Kiddush Hashem*",[4] as a martyr for our religion', wrote the liberal rabbi Gabriel Farhi.[5] More tellingly, a rabbi who preferred to remain anonymous established a direct correlation between Ilan's case and the Holocaust victims':

> The noblest definition of *kiddush Hashem* is the one where, like certain *tsadikim*,[6] one chooses to die in order to 'sanctify the Name of God'. But the *Gemarah*[7] mentions several instances in which people are said to have died *al kiddush Hashem* not at all because they chose to, but because, in the gaze of those who were torturing them, who were mistreating them, what was expressed was the hatred that these people felt for all of *am Israel*.[8] That is why, whenever someone is murdered because he is Jewish, one uses the expression 'he died *al kiddush Hashem*'. The Jews who were killed during the Shoah were not all religious, of course. Nevertheless, when we recite the famous *El male rahamim*,[9] we always say, 'who were killed and burned *al kiddush Hashem*'. If we apply this to Ilan's case, even if we say that all those people were lost souls, were mentally unstable, even if we say that they attacked both Jews and non-Jews, even if this, even if that ... we know very well that they mistreated that boy as fiercely as they did because he was Jewish. It's in that sense that he died *al kiddush Hashem*.[10]

All this only goes to show the vulnerability of a Jewish community which is haunted by the memory of the suffering of the Holocaust. That suffering is endlessly revived, presented in all its different modes, and directly or indirectly reactivated by any and every anti-Semitic act, real or imagined.

---

4   In an act of 'sanctification of the Name [of God]'.
5   See www.col.fr/article-907.html.
6   Just men (Hebrew).
7   The Talmud.
8   The Jewish people (Hebrew).
9   On this prayer, see above, ch. 2, 40, n. 26.
10   Interview conducted by Catherine Garson for *Actualité juive hebdo*, 6 March 2006, www.actuj.net.

The book by Simon Wiesenthal, *Every Day Remembrance Day: A Chronicle of Jewish Martyrdom*, by itself illustrates the way the idea of a Jewish experience based solely on persecutions, massacres, and catastrophes can take possession of Jewish minds. Cast in the form of a calendar or almanac, Wiesenthal's book lists Jewish misfortunes day-by-day, month-by-month, beginning with the Middle Ages – and, in the introduction, with antiquity. In that introduction, the author does not pass up the opportunity to point out that the people of Israel is first mentioned in history in a narrative about its 1223 BC destruction by the pharaoh Merneptha. Wiesenthal concludes the introduction by announcing that his book has no conclusion, and could well be enriched with new dates forever, inasmuch as new research is continually turning up further tragedies in the millennial history of the Jews. There we have a conclusion that hardly encourages optimism. Can anyone, after finishing this book, still believe that Jewish history also included a few peaceful spells? Can we help thinking that the future is necessarily uncertain when we take a good look at this past? The reader who attends to this accumulation of tragic dates can only be astounded by the fact that the Jews were also able to create and procreate, pray and live, rejoice and hope. It is not superfluous to point out that Wiesenthal, who himself survived the genocide and gained fame by hunting down Nazi criminals, also founded a Holocaust museum in Los Angeles, the Simon Wiesenthal Center/Museum of Tolerance.

The Holocaust ought to be recognized for what it is, namely, a tragic event of major proportions which, like every other human tragedy, is singular; it is a tragedy that appeals to future generations to survive it in order to perpetuate a responsible Judaism. In no case is it the Holocaust's function to provide the absolute schema or sole grid through which Jews have to perceive their millennial history. It would not be going too far to ask that the various Holocaust museums also pass 4,000 years of imaginative, flourishing Jewish life and culture in review, rather than turning all the spotlights on one decade of atrocious suffering. None of these museums speaks of life. All speak of death and victimization, not civilization. Shadows have something fascinating about them, of course; but fascination may eventually trap us in them.[11] That said, the memory of suffering that stands in for Jewish identity in spheres now secularized or on the way to secularization is not a phenomenon imputable only to the central place that the genocide has gradually taken in Jewish life. The fact is that focus on the Holocaust merely accentuated an already existing tendency, carrying it to an extreme. A place had already been prepared for it, so deeply

---

11   Daniel Jeremy Silver, 'Choose Life', *Judaism* 35, 1986, 465–6.

had the rhetoric of suffering saturated Jewish mentalities in the preceding centuries.

Prolonged echoes of this rhetoric have crossed oceans and continue to be heard today. Thus American-language Jewish literature, which proliferated after the Second World War, took up the twofold theme of Jewish life and Jewish suffering.[12] This holds for Bernard Malamud and Philip Roth, even when, as in *Portnoy's Complaint* (1969), the suffering protagonist derives no pleasure from his suffering. In Malamud, Jews suffer because suffering is part of being Jewish, whereas in Roth, suffering, even if it is Jewish, is repulsive when it does not lead to redemption. Since redemption, however, is impossible in a secularized world, repulsion is all that remains. Saul Bellow, for his part, contends that, in narratives in the Jewish tradition, the world turns out to have a human meaning, the two components of which are suffering and comedy. Yet, today, it is plainly suffering which provides the cement of individual identity. In the American context, in which Jews were not directly affected by the genocide, suffering and its supreme incarnation, the Holocaust, made it possible to substitute a civil religion for a religion that was no longer practised.

This remark holds for France as well. As the years went by, moral identification with Holocaust victims and the heritage of suffering came to shore up the identity of the 'imaginary Jews' whom Alain Finkielkraut, basing his work on his own experience, set out to criticize more than two decades ago. Finkielkraut, let us add, wrote exclusively about his own generation, young Ashkenazim living in the imaginary space of what they believed their parents' East European past to have been.

In France, again, with the decline of traditions – although a familial Judaism continues to exist in France, and even if some young people have gone back to observing Jewish religious practices more strictly – the second and third generation of Jews of North African descent have also ended up taking the same path to an identity, the one that passes by way of the internalization of the history of suffering and its climax, the Shoah, as well as that history's redemptive dimension, Israel. A number of these Jews have become devoted guardians of the memory of the Holocaust, in the hope that their vigilance will be enough to prevent the worst from ever happening again. In this way, these Jews, who were scorned by their Ashkenazi co-religionists when they first arrived (the Ashkenazim called the newcomers *shvartse*, 'blacks'), have gradually become

---

12 Mark Cohen, 'The "Suffering Joker" in Jewish Fiction', *Midstream*, 30:7, 1989, 53–7; David Hirsch, 'Jewish Identity and Jewish Suffering in Bellow, Malamud and Philip Roth', *Saul Bellow Journal*, 8:2, 1989, 47–58.

part of the native French Jewish community and adopted its system of cultural references.

Arno Mayer maintains that memory 'can be a source of progress or regression'. 'What is more', he adds, 'memory privileges orthodoxy and consensus at the expense of freedom of thought and criticism'.[13] It must be said that this is what the passage from memory to the dogma of memory has bred over the past few years. It is a dogma which cramps Judaism, trapping it in the iron cage of endlessly remembered pain. Thus it is that the Holocaust – now transformed into the 'Shoah', an isolated phenomenon that has been rigidified, Judaized, and particularized to an extreme – runs the danger, paradoxically, of becoming abstract and opaque for non-Jews.

This paradox stands alongside another: 'Shoah' has become a kind of common noun. In France, people have begun to use the word, indiscriminately, to designate facts or events that bear no comparison with the reality of this genocide, the principal (albeit not the only) victims of which were Jews. This is a response to the reification that the Jews themselves have brought about, a reaction to their claim to exclusive use of the term that takes the form of free and unlimited utilization of it. To cite only a few recent examples, Colette Mainguy in *La Juive*, compares the world of the family to a machine for liquidating human beings.[14] François Emmanuel, in *Question humaine*, conflates the personnel management methods used in industry with the methods employed by those who carried out the Holocaust; his book is full of references to the trucks used as gas chambers in Kulmhof and Chelmno, to the Final Solution, and collaboration with the Nazis.[15] Still more recently, and still worse, were that possible, Brigitte Bardot, in her last book, *Pourquoi?*, labels intensive pig-breeding farms 'concentration camps', uses the word 'holocaust' to describe the practice of abandoning animals in the summer, calls the extermination of seals 'genocide', and nicknames the president of the French Hunters' Association 'Himmler'.[16] It would be easy to multiply examples. Every real or imagined act of violence and every trauma seemingly calls, today, for use of the terminology of the Jewish genocide, a terminology of the extreme

13 Arno Mayer, 'Les pièges du souvenir', *Esprit*, 193, 1993, 48.
14 Colette Mainguy, *La Juive*, Paris: Stock, 2001.
15 François Emmanuel, *Question humaine*, 2nd edn, Paris: Le Livre de Poche, 2002.
16 Brigitte Bardot, *Pourquoi?*, Paris: Éditions du Rocher, 2006. See Jérôme Garcin's essay on this book in *Le Nouvel Observateur*, 19 October 2006, 118.

in which the extreme in question is ultimately trivialized, and disappears from view. The obligation to remember is sidetracked as a result of the heavy emotional charge it carries; the objectives of the guardians of this memory or those who pass it on are thus hopelessly frustrated. Is it the excessive insistence on the obligation to remember which, aiming to heighten awareness of the Holocaust, as it in fact did for some time, now elicits just the opposite reaction, numbness?

Trivialization makes it possible to throw off obligations whose profound purpose one has failed to understand. Singularization, taken to an extreme, can produce the same effects. From here, it is but a short step to saying that the Holocaust is a Jewish affair that concerns only Jews.

These manifold dangers permanently threaten the event itself, for lack of adequate education of the kind that would be based less on death and more clearly oriented toward life. Such education would make it possible truly to share memory by identifying with a peer who actually lived before suffering and dying under the thumb of racists and anti-Semites. History is accessible to all. Memory is necessarily less so, because it belongs or seems to belong, first and foremost, to the group that claims it for itself, remaining inaccessible to others until it is has been integrated into a memory that is truly collective. Even history, which alone can ensure memory's survival, struggles to function properly when it fails to connect the living and the dead, so that the Jewish genocide can take on the value of an experience of absolute evil for all. Empathy for the men and women liquidated by the Nazis can begin here. This necessary historicization would free Jews themselves of the onus of the obligation to remember. History would shoulder that task, and one would then have to do no more than to recall what happened. On this liberation depends, in part, the Jews' normalization as well as the normalization of Israel's relations with its neighbours. In the prevailing situation, this can only look like a pipe dream.

Who would remember the expulsion of the Jews from Spain, the greatest trauma of the late Middle Ages, if history were not there to remind us of it? It is not a question, here, of entering into perilous comparisons between events. Everything distinguishes one catastrophe from another: the context, the way it unfolds, the consequences, the nature and extent of the emotion or despair it calls up in contemporaries. One thing, however, is certain: nothing remains of the 'memory' of the 1492 expulsion of the Jews from Spain and no obligation to remember was able to ensure the survival of the memory of it; that was history's task. I am not here thinking of the kind of history written by experts for experts and destined to be transmitted by a group of initiates. And I am obviously not pleading for the interests of one particular guild. I am speaking of History with a capital H, the history of humanity that is written by men and women in all ages and is the ultimate guarantor of humanity's memory. But history is also salutary because it rescues us from the tyranny of memories and its self-appointed high priests, not for lack of respect for those whose memory it is essential to honour, but simply so that this obligation does not lead to neglect of the simple right to justice and recognition.

For the tyranny of memory began to take form very early, and waxed stronger as the years went by. Hannah Arendt's *Eichmann in Jerusalem*, initially published in five instalments in the *New Yorker* in February and March 1963 and subsequently issued in a separate volume, immediately touched off a debate, unprecedented in the Jewish world, about the historical questions thrown up by the Holocaust. Arendt rejected the increasingly popular idea that only those who had witnessed the genocide had the right to talk about it. Their testimony, treated as sacrosanct, was on the way to becoming an insurmountable component of the memory of the event and had already begun to block the historian's path. Arendt herself regarded this as a major danger for historiography and the preservation of the judicial system. In her *New Yorker* articles, and later her book, she condemns the Jewish leadership that had been established in positions of power in the countries devastated by Nazism. She accuses these Jewish leaders of collaborating with the enemy in one form or another, for one reason or another. She criticizes them for their lack of political insight, contending that if the Jews had not been organized, there would of course have been a great deal of chaos and misery, but that the total number of victims would not have been as high as it in fact was. She further suggests that Eichmann embodied the spirit of a period in which evil had become a social norm. He was one of the many German civil servants who carried out their charge with devotion and rigour. Nevertheless, even if Eichmann was merely a subordinate part of a totalitarian system, Arendt does not absolve him of his individual and universal responsibility. Yet, she says, he was not a dyed-in-the-wool anti-Semite urged on by monstrous desires, but, first and foremost, a government official who took an interest in his work and scrupulously performed them. The validity of this analysis is, of course, open to question. But it at least has the merit of debunking the notion of the absolute, anti-Semitic executioner.

Arendt's strong reservations about the attitude that the Jewish leaders exhibited during the genocide as well as her criticism of Israel's desire to see the trial take place on its territory unleashed a tremendous controversy among Jews worldwide. Her line of argument demolished the myths of her opponents, founded on rigid distinctions between good and evil, horror and banality,

Nazism and humaneness, victimizers and victims, those who held power and those who did not, the Nazis, anti-Semites who had acted with unspeakable cruelty, and a helpless Jewish people forced to contend with an enemy on whom it was impossible to wage war. While there was truth to all this, the boundaries that separated these opposed categories were not as sharp as some had believed. In the view of the writer Aaron Zeitlin, Arendt was an agent of the devil: the Nazis, he thought, ought to be described as demons, and their victims as saints. This differentiation, Zeitlin affirmed, should be maintained for the sake of the post-war generation, and anyone who challenged it ought to be damned. Refusing even to name the adversary whose theses he was refuting, Zeitlin had, as it were, excommunicated the philosopher and effaced her name from the Book of Life. Arendt's detractors wished to defend the memory of victims, the preservation of whose honour required that no one subject them to criticism or scholarly analysis. For Gershom Scholem, a well-known professor at the Hebrew University, Arendt had not shown sufficient 'love for Israel'. Yet she succeeded, despite everything, in transforming the Holocaust into a discipline with its own criteria, in bringing it into the realm of critical analysis, like any other subject, even if some of her approaches to it are indeed open to criticism.[17] An academic, Elhanan Yakira, could write as late as 2006 that Arendt's book on the Eichmann trial was a 'moral failure'.[18] Arendt had, nevertheless, put her finger on a process of sacralization that had already been set in motion, a process that carried within it the future pitfalls of the obligation to remember.

After the period of mourning that ran from 1944 to 1954 came the period of repression. It was followed, in its turn, by the period of the return of the repressed, which ultimately opened onto an obsessive phase.[19] In *Vichy: An Ever-Present Past*, Eric Conan and Henry Rousso warn against the possible 'abuses' of memory.[20] We are, today, clearly in the realm of 'excess', an excess related, as we have already had occasion to point out, to new ways of constructing ethnicity and collective identity based on a universal claim to the

17   Hannah Arendt, *Eichmann in Jerusalem: A Report on the Banality of Evil*, London: Penguin Classics, 2006; Richard Cohen, 'Breaking the Code: Hannah Arendt's *Eichmann in Jerusalem* and the Public Polemic: Myth, Memory and Historical Imagination', *Michael*, 13, 1993, 20–85.

18   Elhanan Yakira, 'Hannah Arendt, the Holocaust, and Zionism: A Story of Failure', *Israel Studies*, 11:3, 2006, 31 and 51.

19   Dosse, 'Le territoire de l'historien et la mémoire fragmentée', *Cahiers français*, 303, July–August 2001, 21–23.

20   Eric Conan and Henry Rousso, *Vichy: An Ever-Present Past*, trans. Nathan Bracher: University Press of New England, 1998.

recognition of suffering.[21] To be recognized is to be recognized for suffering or having suffered. Suffering creates rights, and recognition of suffering is a right. It puts those who suffer and the community of sufferers on a pedestal. This leads to a race to suffer in order to exist. It is as if suffering endured were the measure of the right to full citizenship.

To all those who proclaim their suffering in order to obtain certain rights, the developed societies respond by making gestures of repentance. The obligation to remember engenders repentance, which is a debt paid to memory, not an act ensuring a greater sense of responsibility toward the future. It is a will to non-history which animates various groups and converts the suffering of the past into our present and future. Falling to his knees before the monument to the Warsaw ghetto in December 1970, Willy Brandt inaugurated the age of repentance, which found a continuation in the eminently symbolic gestures of Pope John Paul II and also in recurrent memorial celebrations, of which the last to date, in France, was the commemoration of the 60th anniversary of the liberation of the Auschwitz death camp. This accumulation of events issues a call to the citizen, making him a witness to the gradual abdication of history properly speaking as well as its key dates in the face of a memory situated, first and foremost, within a power relation. Thus one memory has the right to greater consideration than another, as does, by the same token, the group claiming that memory as its own. The resulting competition involves complex, variable political stakes and implies organization and institutional investments by the interested parties.

The unbroken circle of repentance generates suffering rather than assuaging it, or revives other suffering that demands to be acknowledged in its turn. It places society within the ancient religious schema of sin and repentance, yet holds out no prospect of redemption. Such redemption would be something like improvement of the concrete situation of the groups involved, whose members are often targets of discrimination of all sorts because of their skin colour, ethnic and religious background, or the way society percieves them. Repentance is accordingly nothing more than a gratuitous act with no political consequences; it provisionally – indeed, ephemerally – binds up wounds. According to a poll conducted by CRAN[22] and TNS-Sofres and published in the French newspaper of reference *Le Monde* on 1 February 2007, 3.8 per cent of those living in France (that is, 1,865,000 people) consider themselves 'black',

---

21   Charles Maier, 'A Surfeit of Memory? Reflections on History, Melancholy and Denial', *History and Memory*, 5:2, 1993, 136–51.
22   The Representative Council of Black Associations.

and, in this population group, more than one out of two persons (56 per cent) 'of voting age' affirms that he or she is a victim of racial discrimination.

In this respect, the case of the Jews, who are not targets of discrimination in our contemporary societies, differs from that of other minorities. Repentance, here, is meant to make symbolic amends for past injustices while serving as a reminder, for those willing to listen, of the duty to defend Israel.

Many of the other groups that demand recognition and repentance take their inspiration more or less consciously, and more or less openly, from the Jewish model. This skews matters from the outset, leading to competition among victims, and to nothing but competition, since no clear social or political exigency seems to be articulated behind the symbolic demand. In this respect, the January 2005 call launched by a group called *Les Indigènes de la République* ('The Natives of the Republic') is emblematic. The call names a series of facts which legitimately show that the once colonized peoples or their descendants in France are victims, yet at no point does it put forward precise demands for changes that might enable them to leave the status of victim behind. If victimhood drapes itself in 'virtue', then repentance is its 'vice'; it is a sort of trap that ultimately threatens to catch those who have set it, as it has caught the Jews themselves, albeit for different reasons.

Of course, the Jewish obligation to remember might well have impressed these outside observers as a well-oiled mechanism, one deemed worthy of imitation because it works better than the others. Yet neither its constituent parts nor the way it was put in place, to say nothing of the perversions to which it is now subject, predisposed it to serve as a paradigm adaptable to the diverse needs for recognition or demands for rights expressed by other groups. What people tend to perceive as a paradigm very often has all the features of a singular case, and what is borrowed from it does not always produce the same results.

Admittedly, Jewish suffering seems to be an unsurpassable model. The fact that it has so long a history and has been enshrined in Jewish memory confers a label of authenticity upon it. Similarly, the central position it commands in the international imagination considerably reinforces it. Finally, the preponderant or even, in the view of some, excessive place it holds in various national contexts offers its potential imitators an image of efficaciousness and success, if the status of victim in which the memory of the Shoah has culminated may be deemed a success. Jewish suffering has in fact created a 'victimization' that is 'autistic' and 'self-indulgent', as Elazar Barkan says in *Guilt of Nations*.[23]

---

23   Elazar Barkan, *Guilt of Nations: Restitution and Negotiating Historical Injustices*, 2nd edn, Baltimore: Johns Hopkins University Press, 2001, xviii. See also Carolyn Dean,

Paradoxically, this memory presents itself as unique, yet it has been endlessly imitated. Such 'victimization' has been able to strike root only in societies which have a thirst for the moral and go to great lengths to do penance in order to recover their innocence, but in which penance does not lead to real redemption.

In Europe, where the successive stages of the Jewish genocide unfolded, the obligation to remember championed by the Jews achieved paradigmatic status very easily, especially in France, where it was conjoined with a claim to a specific identity that put one of the first visible cracks in the wall of Jacobinism, one and indivisible. Other, later demands for recognition of memories of those who had suffered and bore wounds followed in the wake of this one. Thus the 'Collectif Devoirs de mémoires' (Association for the Duties of Memory), created in 2004, set itself the goal of struggling against all forms of discrimination affecting the 'sons and daughters of slavery and colonization'. The Association presented itself as follows: 'We propose to equip ourselves with all the tools needed to diffuse the liberating knowledge that contributes to the construction of individual and collective identities.' This is not very far from the role that is in fact played by the obligation to remember. After the November 2005 riots in the working-class and immigrant suburbs of major French cities, the Association added to its original name, 'Association for the Obligations of Memory', another phrase, 'The Obligation to React' and, with the support of prominent individuals from showbusiness in particular, launched a campaign to get young people living in low-income housing estates to register to vote; by way of the ballot box, it thought, they could make themselves heard in French politics, which superbly ignores them. In this instance, the Association's action, while it is certainly useful and socially responsible, has only a very tenuous connection with the obligation to remember, the terminology it uses aside. Yet the recourse to such rhetoric, even if inappropriate, is revealing. It attests the existence of a species of imagination – French, in this instance – shaped by the experience of the Jewish genocide and guilt at having stood by and let it happen. Indeed, it effectively repeats a pair of slogans popular with many Jews, especially in the younger generation – 'the obligation to remember' and the 'obligation to remain vigilant' – the striking impact of which hardly requires demonstration today.

In the United States, the demand to honour the memory of the Holocaust was, its specificity notwithstanding, put forward at a time when other minority demands were also coming to the fore. It took its place in a global framework in

---

'Recent French Discourses on Stalinism, Nazism and "Exorbitant" Jewish Memory', *History and Memory*, 18:1, 2006, 43–85.

which non-Jews, too, were demanding rights in compensation for endured suffering. The Jews, for their part, called, here as elsewhere, for the defence of Israel. America, symbol of democracy, human rights, and freedom, stood as the antithesis of what the Nazi regime in Europe had been. By this process, America, too, regained its lost innocence, while the Americans recovered their morality by embracing the obligation to remember the victims of the Holocaust – assuming, of course, that this obligation had the further consequence of erasing all the sombre pages of their history, from the slaughter of the Indians to the Vietnam War. The United States Holocaust Memorial Museum, which Congress voted to create in 1980, was inaugurated by Bill Clinton in 1993. Built in Washington and facing toward the White House, it appropriates the memory of the Holocaust and reminds visitors how crucially important the existence of Israel is to making a repetition of it impossible – a reminder engraved in stone and addressed, first and foremost, to America's leaders. This Americanization of the Holocaust, as Régine Robin puts it, assigns it its place in the saga of democracy.[24]

The recognition of violated memories is an indispensable step on the way to elaborating individual and collective identities in our increasingly secularized societies. As far as the Jewish world is concerned, this holds even for traditionalist (albeit not for Orthodox) circles from which, alongside religious practice, identity based on victimization is far from absent. The more our frontiers shift and the further globalization draws us into the unknown, the more memories are reinforced, tending to provide substitutes for what we lack. In the times of relative economic crisis and fluctuation that our Western societies, French society included, are currently going through, we are witnessing, in the metropolitan countries, a rigidification of nationalism; the response of the minorities on the periphery, visible or not, takes the form of identity-based nationalism and withdrawal into imagined communities (based on 'solidarity') under the banner of memory. The memory involved is, of course, a memory of victimhood that it is difficult to hand down to posterity in the same intense form. Here, too, in another way, the memory of the genocide serves as an example for various groups which demand, legitimately, that their own memory of suffering take its place in the French collective memory. It is only right that these memories be taught to young French people in the first years of school, and this may turn out to be a unifying factor for all the components of the nation, which would thus share the joys and misfortunes of their history – become, at last, a common history.

---

24   Robin, *La Mémoire saturée*, 353.

In fact, if distinct 'community loyalties' do now exist, they do not correspond to what the state imagines: they are not 'nations', as it were, within the nation. Today, the minorities, visible or less visible, aspire to form such imagined communities, expressions of their diasporic nationalism, without putting forward territorial or transnational claims. In question here are 'fatherlands' that would replace, often symbolically, those to which one would like to belong. A *beur* (a Frenchman or Frenchwoman of North African Arab descent) is more French than Algerian, Tunisian, or Moroccan. She would be hard put to find her niche in her father's or grandfather's village, the more so as she does even not know Arabic. The same holds for the Jew deeply attached to Israel who contents himself with going on holiday or buying an apartment in the country in case he should need to seek refuge there one day, thus reproducing, at the imaginative level, the painful episodes that earlier generations endured during the war. One can observe the same process, with variants, to be sure, among Blacks in metropolitan France. These 'imagined communities' and nationalisms of a new kind are founded on memories of wounds and suffering.

But there is more to be said: the attention one commands is proportionate to the quantity of suffering evoked. Positions on the political and social chessboard are accordingly measured on a Richter scale of suffering. A war of memories is the inevitable upshot of the competition that results, since there is not enough room for all the victims. Because the memory of the Jewish genocide has taken the lion's share in the extraordinarily limited space that Jacobinism has consented for the expression of diversity, one dimension of this war of memories is rejection of the Other, of which anti-Semitism, anti-Jewish hostility, and its corollaries are the most striking manifestations in critical periods. The excessive emphasis placed on victimhood is inseparable from the competition of the victims. This tendency has come to France from the United States. In America, however, the legitimacy of multiculturalism prevents the most flagrant sort of imbalance from developing. In France, we stand at the very beginning of the process, and this competition threatens, in the long run, to obscure the real political debate, the more so as the universalism that the French Republic has inscribed on its banners is itself an identity forged in order to bring the nation together. This universalism is white, Catholic (albeit secularized in the long run), and male rather then female. Despite the transformations it has undergone, this 'universal' has created, since the French Revolution, an imagined national community which, in its turn and in its own way, is today entering the lists of the competition between memories, while the memories of suffering inevitably find themselves locked in a power struggle with it.

In the hit parade of memories, that of the Jews is also perceived – quite wrongly – as a ticket to success. Those who are far from the centres of power, outsiders such as Muslim Arabs or Blacks, tend to consider the Jews as insiders; indeed, the Jews, too, are inclined to describe themselves as 'sentries of the Republic'. They do not, however, owe the protection and benevolence that they seem to enjoy in the spheres of power to the memory of the genocide or a sense of guilt. Their long experience of Diaspora, the fact that some of them have been established in France for a long time, the French citizenship rights that Jews of Algerian extraction already possessed when they arrived in France, and a series of other factors have contributed to their social success, while facilitating the social integration, as a minority, of the last of them to migrate to France. As for their proximity to the powers-that-be and the places of choice that certain individuals from the Jewish population hold in various walks of society – circumstances that have earned them consideration from the political parties, forever in search of votes – these, too, are factors that cannot fail to remind us, although Jews are now citizens, of a long-standing tradition of Jewish Diasporic life, the royal alliance. It is as if, in the present as well as the past, Jews considered it more prudent to seek the protection of the powerful. Yet this position does not bring only advantages: in the past, it also made Jews privileged targets of the discontent of those who opposed the kings, a situation that, more often than not, culminated in expulsions. As the Jews were the central government's most vulnerable supporters, they were the first to come under attack. Indeed, the resentment of minorities far removed from the centre of power is often directed against them today. It takes different forms: suspicion, aggressiveness, insults, or even outright anti-Semitism. To this are added the repercussions of the Israeli–Palestinian conflict in the West and the identification of the outsiders with the Palestinians and the insiders with the Israelis.

The inequality of the minorities when it comes to remembrance and their unequal rights to the public's compassion were once again illustrated by the events accompanying and following passage of the 4th article of the 23 February 2005 French law which requires school curricula to give recognition to 'the positive role of the French presence abroad, especially in North Africa'. It will be recalled that this bill, rushed into law without eliciting any particular reaction at the time, became controversial a few months later, especially after the November 2005 riots in the suburbs that, as it were, opened the way to certain commemorative claims, without, however, leading to concrete resolution of the problems that caused these riots.

The 23 February 2005 law should have mobilized Muslim Arabs, the direct, living heirs of the French colonial past. Indeed, the text of the law, genuflecting in the direction of the Frenchmen repatriated from North Africa to France, made things quite clear with the words 'especially in North Africa'. Slavery had a longer history. Colonization and decolonization, for their part, are still very recent processes. Yet it was the slaves' descendants who managed to turn the situation to their advantage. The struggle against the discrimination from which the Black population suffers has, to be sure, a history of its own. The fact remains, however, that, in conformity with the scheme of the Jewish obligation to remember, it was among Blacks that the mobilization against the new law proved most effective, thanks especially to the guidance of French citizens from France's overseas departments and territories, who are more familiar with the way the country's political system works. And it was no accident that the creation of the CRAN, the Representative Council of Black Associations, an organization the very name of which imitates that of the Representative Council of Jewish Institutions of France (CRIF), was announced in this context, in November 2005.

For their part, French Arabs and Muslims, who have less experience with this type of strategy and are, moreover, insistently reminded that they are of the Islamic faith, with all the negative connotations that this has carried since 11 September, have been unable to shake off the religious image that clings to them; it prevents them from organizing at the political level. Indeed, on the authority of the state, they have been locked in to the French Council of the Muslim Religion. Furthermore, the memory of colonization and decolonization, which is a greater embarrassment, politically speaking, than that of slavery, has lagged behind in the race between memories. In this precise instance, it unmistakably lost out to the memory of slavery, which even enjoyed brief support from the Jews. This Jewish backing for the Black cause is nothing new; in the 1950s and 1960s, it will be recalled, Jews were deeply involved in the Black movement in the United States (Jewish–Black relations degenerated thereafter). In contemporary France, it was the barbaric murder of Ilan Halimi by a Black who was also a Muslim that checked the vague desires for an alliance; as we have seen, the Halimi murder became a community issue because it was supposed to have been exclusively motivated by anti-Semitism.

In the years to come, as the visible minorities draw closer to the centres of power, this competition of the victims could become fiercer still, with all parties manoeuvring to conquer a more favourable position on the narrow socio-economic ladder of a hierarchical, immobile society that resists penetration by any new force whatsoever. In this competition, commemorative claims will continue to matter for a long time to come, at least to the elites of these minorities. Yet it is by no means certain that such claims are the ones that count most for the large majority of these groups, who have to contend on a daily basis with forms of discrimination that are more mundane, yet quite real, and are having a great deal of trouble carving out a decent niche for themselves. Will the youngest members of these groups not be rather more inclined to succumb to the appeals of religion, which are more concrete, rather than opting to support demands that are, after all, symbolic and abstract? The writer Ahmed Djouder, for his part, seems, in his superb account *Désintégration*, to be hoping for an abrupt turn, and a positive one, among the French: 'France, considered as a moral person, has to save its honour, which it can do by acknowledging its failures and forgetfulness and correcting them. How? By changing the way it looks at us. By turning a positive, tender gaze on us. That's all. You shall see, France; the result will be heaven.'[25] Yet this positive gaze has to be provided with the conditions it needs to come into existence.

In any case, it is clear that we are not there yet. The course of the war of memories, the proliferation of outbursts of generosity rooted solely in compassion and materialized in commemorative events, and, finally, the competition for votes, put a heavy onus on the future. The parties do not hesitate to cater to community loyalties as circumstances demand, while failing to make the effort required to produce a global evaluation of the situation. How is a nation that so stubbornly resists assuming its diversity to be brought to behave, tomorrow, as a pluralistic, free, egalitarian nation reinvigorated by the energy of a multiplicity accepted at last for what it is? That would be one possible way of moving beyond the competition between victims.

On 29 January 2001, the French National Assembly passed a law recognizing the 1915 Armenian genocide. On 21 May of the same year, France officially recognized, with the Taubira law, the fact that the slave trade and slavery had constituted crimes against humanity. And, on 12 October 2006, a law punishing denial of the Armenian genocide, approved by only 129 members of the National Assembly who were present and took part in the vote[26] – a very small minority of the French parliament – took its place among a set of commemorative laws, peculiar to France, that aim to legislate the way history should be written and restrict intellectual freedom. Undeniably, these legislative measures draw attention to historical injustices, encouraging people to become aware of them and give them the place they deserve in education and research. To what extent, however, do they contribute to creating a 'multiplicity' accepted by the nation at its various levels? Pierre Nora writes about

---

25   Ahmed Djouder, *Désintégration*, Paris: Stock, 2006, 156–7.
26   The bill passed by a vote of 106 for and 19 against.

such laws: 'Behind the noble intentions that inspire them – which are only veils, as a rule, for vote-getting demagoguery and political cowardice – the philosophy of the whole, which spontaneously answers to the spirit of the times, tends to criminalize the past in general. We would do well to ask what that implies and where it is taking us'.[27] Would it not be healthier, or, at any rate, more constructive, to begin by rewriting the muddled pages of our history without falling back on this accumulation of laws – the list will doubtless continue to grow – that tend to replace historians, in the broadest sense of the word, not just the narrow guild of professionals, with lawmakers and judges? A society divided up into 'accusers' and 'criminals', which sees no other way out, can only interfere with the democratic process and prevent it from projecting itself into the future. It will, if it proceeds along these lines, eventually take the path of self-hatred.

These are, then, laws which obscure our urgent need for history while flattering memory, which is more malleable and utilitarian. Utilitarian, to begin with, for base political reasons. Who does not know that the law passed by the lower chamber of the French parliament on 12 October 2006 sought to flatter 500,000 French voters of Armenian extraction (but are they that naive?), while erecting a barrier, a legal barrier this time, to Muslim Turkey's entry into the European Union? An amendment to the 13 July 1990 Gayssot Law, designed to repress all racist, anti-Semitic, and xenophobic remarks and punish denial of crimes against humanity, would have been sufficient, the more so as the French National Assembly had already recognized the Armenian genocide in January 2001 and it can hardly be said that deniers of this genocide are legion in France. To press Turkey to acknowledge the Armenian genocide is one thing; it is quite another to pass laws bearing on its denial in a country such as France, which did not initiate this genocide and on whose territory it did not occur. France has taken advantage of the Armenian cause, as the European powers did in the late nineteenth and early twentieth century, in order to pursue its own interests. On 19 January 2007, Hrant Dink, editor-in-chief of *Agos*, an Armenian weekly in Turkey, was shot down by a Turkish nationalist. Dink had struggled for a rapprochement between Turks and Armenians, even while condemning the treatment that the Young Turk regime had inflicted on his people. Turkish nationalists had dragged him before the courts on a number of occasions for calling the massacres committed in the Ottoman Empire a genocide; yet Dink was opposed to the French law penalizing denial of the Armenian genocide that

---

27   Pierre Nora, 'Malaise dans l'identité historique', *Le Débat*, 141, 2006, 48–9.

was approved by the lower chamber of the French parliament on 12 October 2006.

Thus the West's penchant for cataloguing its own and others' 'sins' in an endless quest for innocence was once again confirmed. It is, to be sure, a selective penchant; the memories of Jews, Blacks, Armenians, Maghrebis, Muslims, and the colonized are not all treated equally. The discrimination that the majority brings to bear in acknowledging the various minorities' memories of suffering, indeed, its ranking of them, is not unrelated to the exacerbation of the competition between the victims.

The Right to Forget

In this book, I have attempted to reconstruct the long history of suffering in the Jewish world, tracing it back as far as its scriptural foundations. My aim has been to understand how suffering and the successive representations and instrumentalizations of suffering shaped the history of a people and a religion or, even more, the idea that this people and the followers of this religion formed of their history. In focusing on the Jewish history of suffering, I believe that I have examined a case which is exemplary in two ways. It is exemplary in that it illustrates, in a form that finds no parallel elsewhere, the destiny of the first monotheism, of the religion and people that claimed it as their own. It is also exemplary in that the Jewish paradigm has become, for many other groups, fundamental, and even a model to imitate.

I have brought this Jewish history of suffering to a close with a consideration of its most recent transmutations, dating from the aftermath of the genocide down to our own day, a period in which suffering functions as a secular religion. In Israel, it has allowed the Jews to renew their ties to their Diasporic past, initially rejected by a Zionist ideology aspiring to construct a new state and, in the process, invent a 'new Jew'. It has also allowed those who had ceased to practice the Jewish religion to renew their ties to Judaism as such. Since redemption had been achieved with the birth of the state of Israel, it is easy to understand how that state very quickly crystallized and, as it were, incarnated in itself the hope which the Jews needed to bind up the wounds of their tragic experience. Yet this hope, always in a precarious balance, fluctuating with the course of the wars between the Israelis and the Arab countries and the vicissitudes of the Israeli–Palestinian conflict, has never managed to banish the anxiety perpetually haunting the Jews, the 'triumphalism of suffering' that leaves them self-absorbed and, often, estranged from the universal concerns that were long theirs. Indeed, this hope is itself a source of anxiety – the anxiety shared by all those Jews who fear the worst for Israel.

I have also considered the theologies of the genocide formulated in Orthodox and ultra-Orthodox circles, theologies different in every respect from the approaches taken by secular Jews. I have come to appreciate, as a result, the need for religion and identity that this new secular religion aspired to fulfil. It was not until the 1970s that the liquidation of the Jews became a

'Holocaust', which later gave rise to the 'Holocaust mania' that Jacob Neusner was among the first to point out. In the same period, the event was ideologized and exploited to political ends by Israel, which was eager to legitimate its new borders after the Six Day War and, especially, after the Likud came to power in 1977. However, neither genocide nor Holocaust were, at this time, terms used exclusively to designate what had happened to Jews. 'Shoah' was such a term, and no doubt leaves the Jews in abysmal solitude, by distinguishing their tragedy from other, merely human misfortunes. This exclusivity creates a gulf between them and the rest of the world, that is, from what had for centuries been the fatherland of Diasporic Jews. Henri Meschonnic recently wrote: 'The word "Shoah", with its essentializing capital S, contains and maintains the accomplishment of the theologico-political, the Final Solution for the "people who murdered God" and thereby became the true chosen people. It would be healthier for the language if, some day, this word were nothing more than the title of a film'.[1] I do not know, for my part, if it is the word itself which is disturbing, or, rather, the closure that it attests and helps reinforce. 'Shoah' is a word that says: these Jews died or suffered so that Judaism could live – almost the way it did in the past, in the epoch of great fidelity to God. I say 'almost', for what kind of Judaism do we have to deal with today?

Partisans of the idea that the Holocaust is unique tend to deny that other genocides should be called genocides. Thus Shimon Peres, then Israeli Foreign Minister, declared to the *Turkish Daily News* on 10 April 2001, while on an official visit to Turkey, that 'the Armenians were the victims of a tragedy, but not a genocide'. The Israeli Ambassador to Armenia, Rivka Cohen, later stated, on 8 February 2002, that 'any and all comparisons between the tragedy suffered by the Armenian people and the Holocaust [were] inadmissible', as if the one might eclipse the other. This debate about the uniqueness of the Holocaust emerged in the United States in the late 1990s, at a time when multiculturalism was on the rise. In France, it has quite simply never taken place: the idea that the Holocaust is unique is regarded as an incontrovertible truth by Jewish institutions, the mass media, and the broad public, especially the Jewish public.[2] Recent political developments seem to have prompted Jewish institutions to take a more open stance toward the Armenian genocide. It is to be hoped that this change in attitude is not merely a tribute paid to the 'clash of civilizations', but, rather, augurs a genuine transition to a more mature phase in which the

---

1   Henri Meschonnic, 'Pour en finir avec le mot "Shoah"', *Le Monde*, 20 February 2005.

2   See Alan Rosenbaum, ed., *Is the Holocaust Unique? Perspectives on Comparative Genocide*, Boulder CO: Westview Press, 2000.

dogma of the uniqueness of the Shoah will yield to recognition of the specificity of each genocide. For what people has the right to claim that its suffering is unique, with the implication that that suffering is in some way morally superior? The French case, perhaps, poses the question more acutely than others. Until quite recently, did taking the full measure of the Jewish genocide and acknowledging that France was partly to blame for it not help the French avoid writing certain other dark pages of their history, having to do with slavery and, in particular, colonialism and decolonialization, subjects that are still delicate and politically explosive in French society?

The Holocaust has not only established itself as a new secular religion, alongside the Judaism of the written and oral Law; in the process of acquiring this status, it has made it possible to put victimhood in general on a pedestal, endowing it with an added measure of 'prestige'. Is the survival of Judaism forever to depend on anti-Semitism, which alone can sustain this sense of victimhood? In either case, we would be confronted with a bloodless, futureless Judaism, standing over and against the Judaism of the traditions and practice. Many contemporary Jews are haunted by this fear. Is there no room for another kind of Judaism? For as long as the sole alternative to a Judaism of faith and observance is a Judaism based on victimhood and suffering, there is every reason to fear that the latter will soon have breathed its last, for lack of a viable future.

Yet if the Jews' new secular religion has led them to shut their eyes to the universal, the way in which Jewish suffering and the memory of it have come to hold the place they currently do can, their irreducible specificity notwithstanding, perhaps help us to anticipate the lines along which demands for commemoration of their past put forward by various other groups in France today will probably develop. It is no accident that the Jews' obligation to remember serves these other groups as a model. Indeed, the exaltation of victimhood is a general tendency that reduces the universalism of the Enlightenment to a 'universalism of suffering'.[3] It is active at all social levels and informs all the demands for commemoration – legitimate or not, it may be added. And all of us are caught up in these relations, which divide humanity into victims and victimizers.

This constantly evolving victimhood daily casts us as voyeurs of the Other's suffering. We cast off our own suffering by watching that of the Other. This voyeurism is sustained by the commemorative spectacles that freeze events and transform them into a form of entertainment. Some have even spoken of

---

3   Carolyn Dean, *The Fragility of Empathy after the Holocaust*, 13.

'pornography' in this connection. Thus Alvin Rosenfeld, a leading Holocaust scholar, expresses his fear that the genocide will be transformed into 'pornography' as a direct consequence of the popularization of its memory. However obnoxious some may find the metaphor, it refers, here, to the commercialization of the event, which comes down to the betrayal of its historical memory.[4] What is alarming is not merely this commercialization, doubtless inevitable in a market economy, but the fact that victims fascinate us when they are in the position of victims. This is a situation that could well become self-perpetuating. We like victims.

Victimhood relegates the reality of the event to the background. Yet nothing is more transitory than the status of victim. Victims can so easily change sides! Since empathy is not stable, but varies as a function of the news and images to which people are exposed, it is frequently observed that the Israelis and, with them, the Jews as well, have ceased to be victims for public opinion and have become, instead, victimizers as a result of the conflicts currently raging in the Middle East. Links are forged between events without discernment. Since emotion takes precedence over thought, we may some day be confronted with pure and simple *rejection* of the Holocaust. That is why it is urgent that we abandon the spectacle of memory in order to find our way back to the memory of history, which is not liable to these fluctuations. Its relative stability endows the event with real permanence and stands as a rampart against the deviations to which every memory that takes the form of a spectacle is subject.

The laws mandating the commemorations that France so loves keep these memories burning bright. They are at the heart of the commemorative policies cultivated by a state intent on ensuring a minimum of national cohesion with their help. Yet, after the violated memories have been acknowledged, everything remains to be done, beginning with the work of integrating them into the collective national memory, which is something that can be forged by history alone. The demand that past suffering be acknowledged is in fact, for a good many groups, a demand to be recognized as an integral part of the nation. For that, however, a politics of compassion no longer suffices. Incorporating these memories into history calls for rewriting national history itself. It should be added, the pressure groups in question do not always want such a rewriting of history; for them, memory is 'an emotional–political issue, something that helps found their identity'.[5] For history rationalizes memory, provides it with

---

4 Dean, *Fragility of Empathy*, 24–6.
5 'La mémoire est une chose, l'histoire en est une autre', interview with Jean-Pierre Azéma, *Tohu Bohu*, Spring 2006, 8–9.

a framework, protects it from deviations, and makes it part of humanity's common heritage. There exists no memory that cannot become history, however tragic or unspeakable the event underlying it.

The Jewish experience cannot be reduced to anti-Semitic persecution; the Black experience cannot be reduced to slavery and racism.[6] Thus narrowing the horizon to victimhood comes down to negating the self as a collective entity, if only by virtue of the negativity that grounds such identity. Victimhood is not part of any group's genetic code: it is always a question of a latent possibility that certain circumstances can actualize.

These circumstances are not themselves insurmountable: there is no reason that they should automatically and definitely burden the victims' future, unless they are treated as things to be played on and exploited to various political or commercial ends. What people can boast that suffering has not entered into its historical make-up? Happy people have no history, the saying goes. Today, in order to be a people or 'community' – indeed, in order, quite simply, to be – one must first have suffered. To construct an identity, an individual or collective history, a past of suffering is indispensable. It is the sole means of setting oneself apart from the mass of those whom one deems not to have suffered or, simply, not to have suffered as much. In a society at pains to proclaim the right to happiness, this claim to misfortune is an indispensable component of individual identity and also of the identity of the group to which one belongs by virtue of this very claim. Oriented toward the past, this affliction is above all else a projection, in most cases: a projection, onto the present, of past suffering that was indeed real yesterday, but is less real or real in a different way today. Moreover, this focus on yesterday's suffering helps to divert the public and especially politicians' attention from today's injustices, thus turning against the very people who promote it – to say nothing of the fact that those who currently count as 'fortunate' have also gone through their catastrophes, famines, and natural, political, or social disasters. Doubtless it is often multiple, convergent acts of day-to-day discrimination which provide certain groups with confirmation that they continue to be excluded from the society of the 'fortunate'. Social reality has a great deal to do with this past suffering, the memory of which people hold aloft, tracing the state of present-day suffering back to it. Of course, for Jews, as, indeed, for Armenians, who have been waiting since 1915 for Turkey to acknowledge the Armenian genocide, the question takes a different form, inasmuch as these two groups are not

---

6   Frédéric Worms, 'Au-delà de la concurrence des victimes', *Esprit*, 322, 2006, 187–93.

the objects of any form of discrimination today. Yet the basic schema involved remains virtually the same, as evinced by the play given to the dangers besetting the Israeli state and the resurgence of anti-Semitism.

While historicizing painful memories and redressing the injustices of the present offer one way out, it is by no means certain that they will suffice to check the expansion of the contemporary religion of suffering for as long as constructing identities holds the central place that it does in our individualistic worlds, whose denizens are so firmly bent on recovering a lost innocence and remaining in a sort of extended childhood from which they can solicit assistance and relief. Suffering is king and continues to be the major temptation of the century of happiness. If that century plunges us into anonymity, suffering sets us apart. For that reason alone, it still has a bright future ahead of it, for better or for worse, with a risk of banalization exactly proportional to its ideologization. The danger against which we should be on our guard is increasing confusion in the ranking of different experiences of suffering: we risk dwelling on some of the less relevant experiences, while treating others, which are real, as secondary. In question here, of course, are not current instances of physical suffering, which we still prefer to veil, but emblematic experiences of suffering that ground demands for rights legitimated by suffering. Nicolas Weill talks about 'Holocaust fatigue' in an attempt to explain the general indifference to the resurgence of anti-Semitism in France between 2000 and 2002.[7] This is not the place to discuss how real or extensive that indifference and resurgence were, but it is plain that the 'fatigue' that Weill denounces also threatens to overcome other memories of suffering that are regularly flaunted in the public arena.

The long-term history of Jewish suffering reveals how deeply it was felt and how often it was called upon over the centuries to cement the unity of the group and its attachment to Judaism. It also reveals, however, that this privileged relationship to suffering was strictly regulated in order to keep it from compromising the love due to an omnipresent God or from replacing the relationship with Him. This explains the rabbis' explicit reservations about martyrdom. Jews were not to let themselves be distracted from the performance of their religious duties, the proof of their fidelity to God. To perform them, they had to stay alive. Of course, the temptation to accede to a better world through martyrdom was not banished for all that, and it continued to exert its fascination down through the ages. But the suffering in question here

---

7   Nicolas Weill, *La République et les Antisémites*, Paris: Grasset, 2004, 88.

opened out onto a promise, the hope of redemption and the mercy of a benevolent God. It forged ties: a history of suffering drawn from the past contained the
promise of a happy future, in this world or the next. Similarly, the ritualization
of the remembrance of past disasters palliated their emotional impact and
assigned them a place in the daily experience of prayer, thus investing being-
Jewish with meaning. This ritualization created an indissoluble bond between a
past of suffering, a present of expectation, and a future of hope.

The historiography of suffering that emerged in the nineteenth century
served, for its part, to forge a collective identity at a time when Jews' community ties were slackening. Indeed, it helped found and structure a new imagined
and imaginary community using fragments borrowed from this past of
suffering. It sought to head off the threat of assimilation looming over modern
individual Jewish identity, then just coming into being.

This Jewish quest for identity, which, in its secularized version, goes back
to the nineteenth century, finds a strange extension in the quest that our
contemporaries have been pursuing for over three decades now. In the nineteenth and twentieth centuries in Europe and, especially, France, Jews looked
for redemption to the new citizenship then being offered them; they hoped to
gain a great deal by it. After the rupture represented by the Second World War,
these expectations could no longer carry the same 'messianic' dimension.
Suffering, today, no longer engenders hope. Its sole end is the expectation of
further suffering, and its main horizon is the threat of anti-Semitism. This
suffering does at least create identity and a sense of collective belonging –
which, however, founded as they are on the Other's hostility to the Jew or the
Israeli, are an identity and a sense of collective belonging created by ricochet. It
is not impossible that this is a transitory phase. But if it should endure, we
might eventually see a proliferation of extreme forms of behaviour: a return to
Orthodoxy on the one hand and assimilation on the other.

In fact, the obligation to remember is of no help when it comes to
projecting oneself into the future; it means, rather, confinement to the past.
Are those who tirelessly watch over memory and make it an obligation
prepared to relax their grip so as to authorize forgetting, which is not abolition
of the event, but merely a withdrawal from memory, now entrusted to history,
just as, yesterday, the 'text' was charged with recalling, at regularly spaced
intervals, the disasters of the past? These ritualized narratives served as places
where memory was conserved, even while freeing the consciousness of the Jews
from the onus of the event and the obligation to experience it anew without
end. It is forgetting of this sort that I have in mind here, and it is historical
narrative, the secular substitute for the religious text, that has the capacity to

initiate this salutary transition. Jorge Semprun attaches indisputable value to forgetting, adding: 'At the collective level, it is also obvious that there exist periods of transition in which forgetting proves to be necessary, on condition that what is involved is silence, not a will to falsify or rewrite History'.[8]

How, once one has jettisoned this victim's memory, is one to approach one's identity, to construct it differently, in such a way as once again to become the active agent of one's history, not merely History's victim? It is hard to meet this challenge, with which all those who bear these memories that they so vociferously proclaim to be theirs are confronted: the memory of the Holocaust, but also that of slavery, colonization, and the Armenian, Rwandan, and other genocides. Is it or is it not possible to break free of the ideology of the victim and to shun the politics of the obligation to remember, the perverse effects of which also engender forgetting, but forgetting of another kind—the blotting out of the reasons for the event, as well as its meaning and import—not the salutary forgetting which makes it possible to look to the future, armed with what one remembers? Therein reside the virtues of the labour of memory. The Jews accomplished that labour throughout their history, until the genocide was transformed into an *obligation* to remember. Answering, during a chat, a question about the necessary obligation to remember, Boris Cyrulnik replied: 'There is no obligation to remember; there is, however, an obligation to make something, a project, of one's memory.'[9]

It is, to be sure, impossible to make light of the injunction that Primo Levi, who was himself deported, addresses to us:

> Meditate that this came about:
>   I commend these words to you.
> Carve them in your hearts,
>   At home, in the street,
> Going to bed, rising:
>   Repeat them to your children.[10]

This is a terrible exhortation; it imposes itself like a religious obligation on the most secularized among us, based as it is on a fundamental biblical text that is part of the daily Jewish liturgy known as the *Shema*, a veritable profession of

---

8   Jorge Semprun and Alain Finkielkraut, 'Comment transmettre l'inimaginable', *L'Express*, 19 January 1995.
9   Boris Cyrulnik, 'Auschwitz: Le cri de la mémoire', *Le Monde*, 25 January 2005.
10   Primo Levi, *If This Is a Man*, trans. Stuart Wolf, London: The Bodley Head, 1960, 1. See also the interview with Jean-Pierre Azéma, 'La mémoire est une chose', 2006.

faith that is recited two or even three times a day by every practising Jew and is pronounced one last time by every good Jew before he or she dies.[11]

May we, however, not consider that the obligation to remember to which Levi here appeals is not just a Jewish obligation, and that the memory which is its object is not just a Jewish memory? Might it not be, in the first place, a demand addressed to everyone to transmit to everyone what men and women had to endure as human beings, and not just as Jews, so that our singular memories become intertwined in our common history as men and women?

Can we forget, we who are not genocide survivors, that the Bible as well as the liturgy enjoin us to remember not only the dead, but, first and foremost, the 'words of the Law'?

It is true that *zakhor*, 'remember', is an injunction as old as the Jewish people itself. In the Pentateuch, it appears in four distinct contexts. But nowhere does *zakhor* call us to an obligation to remember that is based only on the memory of death and suffering. *Zakhor* is, first of all, an exhortation to remember the exodus from the house of servitude[12] and what God did to Pharaoh and all Egypt for the sake of his people and its liberation.[13] It is thus a memory of deliverance, to begin with. *Zakhor* is, next, an injunction to remember that the Sabbath day is holy;[14] it is a memory of creation and freedom, an exhortation to observe the Sabbath in the concrete sense. *Zakhor* is also a call to remember the leprosy that God inflicted on Myriam, Moses' sister.[15] It is the memory of a punishment, without a doubt, but also the memory of an act of forgiveness – since Myriam was forgiven for denigrating her brother and was healed – and thus a warning against denigrating others as well. Finally, it is a reminder of the measures to be taken when one is confronted with a case of leprosy, and accordingly, once again, an exhortation to follow the Law.

---

11   Compare Levi's verse with this text from Dt 6:4–9 'Hear, O Israel: The LORD our God is one LORD: And thou shalt love the LORD thy God with all thine heart, and with all thy soul, and with all thy might. And these words, which I command thee this day, shall be in thine heart: And thou shalt teach them diligently unto thy children, and shalt talk of them when thou sittest in thine house, and when thou walkest by the way, and when thou liest down, and when thou risest up. And thou shalt bind them for a sign upon thine hand, and they shall be as frontlets between thine eyes. And thou shalt write them upon the posts of thy house, and on thy gates.'

12   Ex 13:3.

13   Dt 7:18.

14   Ex 19:4 (the fourth commandment).

15   Dt 24:9.

Once and only once does the biblical *zakhor* clearly apply to a negative collective event: a memory of the attack that Amalek unleashed on the Hebrew people just after it had emerged from Egypt, exhausted and enfeebled.[16] The fact remains that, with God's help, the Hebrews defeated Amalek,[17] and the memory of Amalek himself was destined to be effaced 'beneath the heavens'.

A memory of past danger, awareness of present and future danger? Certainly; but also the constructive memory of a liberated people that will be able to overcome this danger *and even the memory of it*. This warning applies to us, a procession of the faithless, as well.

---

16   Dt 25:17.
17   See Ex 17:8–13.

Bibliography

Aiken, Lisa, *Why Me, God? A Jewish Guide for Coping with Suffering*. Northvale NJ: Jason Aronson, 1996.

Amato, A. Joseph, with David Monge, *Victims and Values*. London: Greenwood Press, 1990.

Amishai-Maisels, Ziva, '"Faith, Ethics and the Holocaust": Christological Symbolism of the Holocaust', *Holocaust and Genocide Studies*, 3:4, 1988, 457–481.

Anderson, Benedict, *Imagined Communities: Reflections on the Origin and Spread of Nationalism*. London: Verso, 1991.

Antelme, Robert, *The Human Race*, trans. Jeffrey Haight and Annie Mahler. Marlboro VT: Marlboro Press, 1992.

Apostolidès, Jean-Marie, *Héroïsme et victimisation. Une histoire de la sensibilité*. Paris: Exils, 2003.

Arendt, Hannah, *Eichmann in Jerusalem: A Report on the Banality of Evil*. London: Penguin Classics, 2006.

Aron, Raymond, *De Gaulle, Israel and the Jews*, trans. John Sturrock. New York: Praeger, 1969.

Aronson, Shlomo, 'The New Historians and the Purpose of the Shoah', *Ha'aretz* (supplement), 24 June 1994 [in Hebrew].

Attias, Jean-Christophe, *Isaac Abravanel, la mémoire et l'espérance*. Paris: Éditions du Cerf, 1992.

——, 'Comment nous ne sommes plus juifs', *Esprit*, February 2005, 17–26.

——, and Benbassa, Esther, *Israel, the Impossible Land*, trans. Susan Emanuel. Stanford CA: Stanford University Press, 2003.

Augé, Marc, *Les Formes de l'oubli*. Paris: Payot-Rivages, 1998.

Auron, Yair, 'The Holocaust and the Israeli Teacher', *Holocaust and Genocide Studies*, 8:2, 1994, 225–257.

——, *The Banality Of Denial: Israel and the Armenian Genocide*. New Brunswick NJ: Transaction Publishers, 2003.

——, 'Auschwitz: le cri de la mémoire'. Discussion with Boris Cyrulnik, *Le Monde*, 25 Jan. 2005.

Banner, Gillian, *Holocaust Literature: Schulz, Levi, Spiegelmann and the Memory of the Offence*. London: Vallentine Mitchell, 2000.

Barkan, Elazar, *Guilt of Nations: Restitution and Negotiating Historical Injustices*. New York: W. W. Norton, 2000.

Baron, Salo W., 'Ghetto and Emancipation: Shall We Revise the Traditional View?', *The Menorah Journal*, 14:6, 1928, 515–526.

——, 'The Jewish Factor in Medieval Civilization', *American Academy for Jewish Research Proceedings*, 12, 1942, 1–48.

——, *Essays and Addresses: History and Jewish Historians*. Philadelphia: Jewish Publication Society, 1964.

Bartov, Omer, 'Intellectuals on Auschwitz: Memory, History and Truth', *History and Memory*, 5:1, 1993, 89–129.

——, *Murder in our Midst: The Holocaust, Industrial Killing, and Representation*. Oxford: Oxford University Press, 1996.

——, *Mirrors of Destruction: War, Genocide, and Modern Identity*. Oxford: Oxford University Press, 2000.

Bauer, Yehuda, 'On the Place of the Holocaust in History. In Honour of Franklin H. Littell', *Holocaust and Genocide Studies*, 2:2, 1987, 209–220.

——, *Rethinking the Holocaust*. New Haven: Yale University Press, 2000.

Baumann, Zygmunt, *Modernity and the Holocaust*. Ithaca NY: Cornell University Press, 2001.

Benbassa, Esther, *The Jews of France. A History from Antiquity to the Present*, trans. M. B. DeBevoise. 2nd edn. Princeton: Princeton University Press, 1999.

——, *La République face à ses minorités. Les Juifs hier, les musulmans aujourd'hui*. Paris: Mille et Une Nuits, 2004.

——, 'Les brouillages sémantiques de Gaza', *Le Figaro*, 29 August 2005.

Benbassa, Esther, and Jean-Christophe Attias, *The Jews and their Future. A Conversation on Jewish Identities*, trans. Patrick Camiller. London: Zed Books, 2004.

Ben Israel, Menasseh, *The Hope of Israel*, trans. Moses Wall, eds. Henry Méchoulan and Gérard Nahon. Oxford: Oxford University Press, 1987.

Berenbaum, Michael, 'The Nativization of the Holocaust', *Judaism*, 35:4, 1986, 447–57.

——, and Abraham J. Peck, eds., *The Holocaust and History: The Known, the Unknown, the Disputed, and the Reexamined*. Bloomington: Indiana University Press, 1998.

Berger, Alan L., *Crisis and Covenant: The Holocaust in American Jewish Fiction*. Albany: State University of New York Press, 1985.

Berkovits, Eliezer, *God, Man and History: A Jewish Interpretation*. New York: Jonathan Davis, 1959.

——, *Faith after the Holocaust*. New York: Ktav, 1973.

——, *With God in Hell: Judaism in the Ghettos and Deathcamps*. New York: Sanhedrin Press, 1979.

Bernfeld, Shimon, *The Book of Tears: Catastrophes, Persecutions and Exterminations*. Berlin: Eshkol, 1923–6, 3 vols. [in Hebrew].

Bernstein, Michael André, *Foregone Conclusions: Against Apocalyptic History*. Berkeley: University of California Press, 1994.

——, 'Victims-in-Waiting: Backshadowing and the Representation of European Jewry', *New Literary History*, 29:4, 1998, pp. 625–51.

Betsalel, Ruth, 'Religion and Martyrology Among the Converted', in *Holy War and*

Martyrology in the History of Israel and the Peoples. Jerusalem: Israeli Historical Society, 1968, 93–105 [in Hebrew].

Biale, David, *Power and Powerlessness in Jewish History.* New York: Schocken Books 1986.

——, 'Power, Passivity and the Legacy of the Holocaust', *Tikkun*, 2:1, 1987, 68–73.

Bilu, Yoram and Eliezer Witztum, 'War-Related Loss and Suffering in Israeli Society: An Historical Perspective', *Israel Studies*, 5:2, 2000, 1–31.

Blanchard, Pascal, and Nicolas Bancel, eds, *Culture post-coloniale 1961–2006. Traces et mémoires coloniales en France.* Paris: Autrement, 2006.

Blanchard, Pascal, Nicolas Bancel, and Sandrine Lemaire, eds., *La Fracture coloniale.* Paris: La Découverte, 2005.

Bodian, Myriam, *Dying in the Law of Moses. Crypto-Jewish Martyrdom in the Iberian World.* Bloomington and Indianapolis: Indiana University Press, 2007.

Boltanski, Luc, *La Souffrance à distance. Morale humanitaire, médias et politique*, Paris: Folio-Essais, 2007.

Bowker, John, *Problems of Suffering in Religions of the World.* Cambridge: Cambridge University Press, 1970.

Boyarin, Daniel, *Dying for God: Martyrdom and the Making of Christianity and Judaism.* Stanford CA: Stanford University Press, 1999.

Brayard, Florent, ed., *Le Génocide des Juifs entre procès et histoire 1943–2000.* Paris: Éditions Complexe/IHTP-CNRS, 2000.

Brodwin, Stanley, 'History and Martyrological Tragedy: The Jewish Experience in Sholem Asch and André Schwarz-Bart', *Twentieth Century Literature*, 40:1, 1994, 72–91.

Brog, Mooli, 'Victims and Victors: Holocaust and Military Commemoration in Israeli Collective Memory', *Israel Studies*, 8:3, 2003, 65–122.

Bruchfeld, Stéphane and Paul A. Levine, *'Tell ye your children...': A Book about the Holocaust in Europe, 1933–1945.* Stockholm: Regeringskansliet, 1986.

Bruckner, Pascal, *La Tyrannie de la pénitence. Essai sur le masochisme occidental.* Paris: Grasset, 2006.

Buergenthal, Thomas, 'Progressive Judaism beyond the Shoah', *European Judaism*, 33:2, 2000, 139–144.

Bulka, Rabbi Reuven P., 'Different Paths, Common Thrust: The "Shoalogy" of Berkovits and Frankl', in Bernhard H. Rosenberg and Fred Heuman, eds., *Theological and Halakhic Reflections on the Holocaust.* Hoboken NJ: Ktav/Rabbinical Council of America, 1992, 165–87.

Cahiers français, 303, 2001, special issue: *La Mémoire, entre histoire et politique.* Ed. Yves Léonard.

Cain, Seymour, 'The Question and the Answers After Auschwitz', *Judaism*, 20:3, 263–78.

Calimani Sullam, Anna-Vera, 'A Name for Extermination', *Modern Language Review*, 94, 1999, 978–99.

Cameron, Esther, 'Post-Holocaust Poetry of Paul Celan', *Tikkun*, 2:1, 1987, 38–43.

Capsali, Élie, *Elijah's Little Order*, Meir Benayahou et al., Jerusalem: Institut Ben Zvi, 1977, 2 vols. [in Hebrew].

——, *Chronique de l'Expulsion*, trans. S. Sultan Bohbot. Cerf, Paris, 1994.

Carlebach, Elisheva, et al., eds., *Jewish History and Jewish Memory: Essays in Honor of Hayim Yerushalmi*. Hanover NH: Brandeis University Press, 1998.

Carmy, Shalom, 'Tell Them I've Had a Good Enough Life', *The Torah u-Madda Journal*, 8, 1998–9, 56–96.

——, ed., *Jewish Perspectives on the Experience of Suffering*. Northvale NJ: Jason Aronson, 1999.

Chaumont, Jean-Michel, *La Concurrence des victimes*. Paris: La Découverte, 1997.

Chazan, Robert, 'The Hebrew First-Crusade Chronicles', *Revue des études juives*, 133:1–2, 1974, 235–54.

——, 'The First Crusade as Reflected in the Earliest Hebrew Narrative', *Viator*, 29, 1998, 25–38.

Chéroux, Clément, ed., *Mémoire des camps. Photographies des camps de concentration et d'extermination nazis (1922–1999)*. N.p., Marval, 2001.

Cohen, Jeremy, 'The Hebrew Crusade Chronicles in their Christian Cultural Context', in Alfred Heverkamp, ed., *Juden und Christen zur Zeit der Kreuzzüge*. Sigmaringen: Jan Thorbecke, 1999, pp. 17–34.

Cohen, Mark, 'The "Suffering Joker" in Jewish Fiction', *Midstream*, 30:7, 1984, 53–7.

Cohen, Raya, 'Le débat historiographique en Israël autour de la Shoah. Le cas du leadership juif'. www.ihtp.cnrs.fr/publications/bulletin72/raya_cohen. htlm.

Cohen, Richard I., 'Breaking the Code: Hannah Arendt's "Eichmann in Jerusalem" and the Public Polemic. Myth, Memory and Historical Imagination', *Michael*, 13, 1993, 20–85.

Cohn, Robert L., 'Biblical Responses to Catastrophe', *Judaism*, 35:3, 1986, 263–76.

Cohn-Sherbok, Dan, 'God and the Holocaust', in Dan Cohn-Sherbok, ed., *Theodicy*, Lewiston NY: Edwin Mellen, 75–96.

Cohon, Baruch, ed., *Jewish Existence in an Open Society*. Los Angeles: Jewish Centers Association, 1970.

Cole, Tim, *Images of the Holocaust: The Myth of the 'Shoah Business'*. London: Duckworth, 1999.

Colloque des intellectuels juifs. Mémoire et Histoire, Jean Halpérin and Georges Lévitte, eds, Paris: Denoël, 1986.

Comité pour la mémoire de l'esclavage, Mémoires de la traite négrière, de l'esclavage et de leurs abolitions. Paris: La Découverte, 2005.

Conan, Eric and Henry Rousso, *Vichy: An Ever-Present Past*, trans. Nathan Bracher. Lebanon NH: University Press of New England, 1998.

Controverses, 2, 2006, special issue: *La Politique des mémoires en France*.

Dadrian, Vahakn N., 'Genocide as a Problem of National and International Law: The World War I Armenian Case and its Contemporary Legal Ramifications', *Yale University Journal of International Law*, 14:2, 1989.

Dan, Yossef, 'Le problème de la sanctification du Nom de Dieu dans la pensée du mouvement piétiste en Ashkénaze', in *Holy War and Martyrology in the*

History of Israel and the Peoples. Jerusalem: Société historique israélienne, 1968, 121–9 [in Hebrew].

Dean, Carolyn J., *The Fragility of Empathy after the Holocaust.* Ithaca NY: Cornell University Press, 2004.

——, 'Recent French Discourses on Stalinism, Nazism and "Exorbitant" Jewish Memory', *History and Memory*, 18:1, 2006, 43–85.

DeKoven Ezrahi, Sidra, *By Words Alone: The Holocaust in Literature.* Chicago: University of Chicago Press, 1980.

——, 'Agnon Before and After', *Prooftexts*, 2:1, 1982, 78–94.

——, 'Representing Auschwitz', *History and Memory*, 7:2, 1996, 121–53.

Eckardt, Alice L., 'Post-Holocaust Theology: A Journey out of the Kingdom of Night', *Holocaust and Genocide Studies*, 1:2, 1986, 229–40.

Einbinder, Susan L., *Beautiful Death: Jewish Poetry and Martyrdom in Medieval France.* Princeton: Princeton University Press, 2002.

El Kenz, David, ed., *Le Massacre, objet d'histoire.* Paris: Gallimard, 2005.

Elkana, Yehuda, 'In Praise of Forgetting', *Ha'aretz*, 2 March 1988 [in Hebrew].

Engel, David, 'Crisis and Lachrymosity: On Salo Baron, Neobaronianism, and the Study of Modern European Jewish History', *Jewish History*, 20:3–4, 2006, 243–64.

Erner, Guillaume, *La Sociéte des victimes.* Paris: La Découverte, 2006.

Ernst, Sophie, 'D'abord enseigner l'histoire ou "devoir ou mémoire"?' *Le Monde*, 25 January 2005.

Esprit, August–September 2000, special issue: *Les historiens et le travail de mémoire.*

——, February 2006, special issue: *Guerres de mémoire à la française.*

——, December 2006, special issue: *Pour comprendre la pensée postcoloniale.*

Fackenheim, Emil, *The Human Condition after Auschwitz: A Jewish Testimony a Generation After.* Syracuse NY: Syracuse University Press, 1971.

——, *God's Presence in History: Jewish Affirmations and Philosophical Reflections.* Northvale NJ: Aronson, 1997.

Fassin, Didier, 'La souffrance du monde. Considérations anthropologiques sur les politiques contemporaines de la compassion', *L'Évolution psychiatrique*, 67:4, 2002, 676–89.

Fellous, Sonia, 'L'iconographie du livre de Job dans les traditions juive et chrétienne', *Les Cahiers du Judaïsme*, 16, 2004, 39–56.

Ferro, Marc, ed., *Le Livre noir du colonialisme.* Paris: Robert Laffont, 2003.

Feuer, S. Lewis, 'The Reasoning of Holocaust Theology', *Judaism*, 35:2, 1986, 198–210.

Ferenczi, Thomas, ed., *Devoir de mémoire, Droit à l'oubli.* Brussels: Complexe, 2002.

Finkelstein, Louis, 'The Ten Martyrs', in Israel Davidson, ed., *Essays and Studies in Memory of Linda R. Miller*, New York: Jewish Theological Seminary of America, 1938, 29–55.

Finkelstein, Norman G., *The Holocaust Industry: Reflections on the Exploitation of Jewish Suffering.* London: Verso, 2001.

Finkielkraut, Alain, *The Imaginary Jew*, trans. Kevin O'Neill and David Suchoff, Lincon NE: University of Nebraska Press, 2nd edn, 1997.

——, 'Les Juifs face à la religion de l'humanité', *Le Débat*, 131, 2004, 13–19.

Fischel, H. A., 'Martyr and Prophet', *Jewish Quarterly Review*, 37:3, 1947, 265–80; 37:4, 1947, 363–86.

Friedlander, Saul, ed., *Probing the Limits of Representation: Nazism and the 'Final Solution'*. Cambridge MA: Harvard University Press, 1992.

Friedman, Harry G., '*Kiddush Haschem* and *Hillul Haschem*'. *Hebrew Union College Annual*, 1904, 193–214.

Garber, Zev, 'The Ninety-Three *Beit-Ya'akov* Martyrs', *Shofar*, 12:1, 69–92.

Gibbs, Robert and Wolfson, Elliot R., *Suffering Religion*. London: Routledge, 2002.

Glazer, Nathan, *American Judaism*. Chicago: Chicago University Press, 1957.

Goetsch, Paul, 'Der Holocaust in der englischen und amerikanischen Lyrik', in Franz Link, ed., *Jewish Life and Suffering, as Mirrored in English and American Literature*. Paderborn: Ferdinand Schoningh, 1987, 165–189.

Goldberg, David Theo and Michael Krausz, *Jewish Identity*. Philadelphia: Temple University Press, 1993.

Goodblatt, David, 'Suicide in the Sanctuary: Traditions on Priestly Martyrdom'. *Journal of Jewish Studies*, 46:1–2, 1995, 10–29.

Graetz, Heinrich, *Geschichte der Juden von den ältesten Zeiten bis auf die Gegenwart: aus den Quellen neu bearbeitet*. Leipzig: O. Leiner, 1853–76, 10 volumes in 11 books.

——, *Popular History of the Jews*, trans. A. B. Rhine. With an additional volume on recent events, by Max Raisin. Ed. Alexander Harkavy, New York: Hebrew Publishing Company, 1919.

Graetz, Heinrich, *History of the Jews*, trans. B. Löwy, Philadelphia: The Jewish Publication Society of America, 1956, 6 vols.

Greenberg, Gershon, '"Faith, Ethics and the Holocaust": Orthodox Theological Responses to Kristallnacht. Chayyim Ozer Grodensky ("Achiezer") and Elchonon Wassermann', *Holocaust and Genocide Studies*, 3:4, 1988, 431–41.

Greene, Yoshua M. and Shiva Kumar, eds., *Witness: Voices from the Holocaust*. New York: The Free Press, 2000.

Grynberg, Henryk, 'Appropriating the Holocaust', *Commentary*, 74:5, 1982, 54–7.

Holy War and Martyrology in the History of Israel and the Peoples. Jerusalem: Société historique israélienne, 1968 [in Hebrew].

Haar, Moshe, 'Israël after Auschwitz: Four Questions about Remembering the Holocaust', in Julius Simon, ed., *History, Religion, and Meaning: American Reflections on the Holocaust and Israel*. Westport CT: Greenwood Press, 2000, 63–70.

Habermann, Abraham Meir, *Catastrophes in Germany and Northern France: Memoirs by Contemporaries of the Crusades, with a Selection from their Liturgical Poems*. Jerusalem: Mosad Ha-Rav Kook, 706/1946 [in Hebrew].

Ha-Cohen, Joseph, *Les Chroniques juives. La Vallée des larmes. Chronique des souffrances d'Israël depuis sa dispersion jusqu'à nos jours*, trans. Julien Sée. Paris: UISF, 1980 [1881], facsimile [Centre d'études Don Isaac Abravanel].

Ha-Cohen, Joseph, *Sefer 'Emeq Ha-Bakha' (The Vale of Tears), with the Chronicle of the Anonymous Corrector,* ed. Karin Almbladh. Uppsala: Uppsala University, 1981.

Halbwachs, Maurice, *The Social Frameworks of Memory,* in Lewis A. Coser, ed., *Maurice Halbwachs on Collective Memory.* Chicago: University of Chicago Press, 1992.

——, *On Collective Memory.* Chicago: University of Chicago Press, 1992.

Halkin, Abraham, 'On the History of Massacres in the Almohadic Period', in *The Joshua Starr Memorial Volume: Studies in History and Philology.* New York. Conference on Jewish Relations, 1953, 101–10 [in Hebrew].

Hammer, Reuven, 'Two Approaches to the Problem of Suffering', *Judaism,* 35:3, 1986, 301–5.

Hannover, Nathan, *Abyss of Despair: The Famous 17th Century Chronicle Depicting Jewish Life in Russia and Poland During the Chmielnicki Massacres of 1648–1649,* trans. Abraham J. Mesch, New Brunswick NJ: Transaction Books, 1983.

Hayes, Peter, ed., *Lessons and Legacies: The Meaning of the Holocaust in a Changing World.* Evanston IL: Northwestern University Press, 1991.

Hebblethwaite, Brian, *Evil, Suffering and Religion,* 2nd edn. London: SPCK, 2000.

Hilberg, Raul, *The Politics of Memory: The Journey of a Holocaust Historian.* Chicago: Ivan R. Dee, 1996.

——, *The Destruction of the European Jews,* 3rd edn. New Haven: Yale University Press, 2003.

Hirsch, David H., 'Jewish Identity and Jewish Suffering in Bellow, Malamud and Philip Roth', *Saul Bellow Journal,* 8:2, 1989, 47–58.

Hornstein, Shelley, Laura Levitt, and Laurence J. Silberstein, eds, *Impossible Images: Contemporary Art after the Holocaust.* New York: New York University Press, 2003.

Ibn Verga, Salomon, *The Sceptre of Judah,* ed. Ezriel Shohat. Jerusalem: Mosad Bialik, 1946 or 1947 [in Hebrew].

Kaenel von, Jean-Marie, ed., *Souffrances.* Paris: Autrement, 1994.

Kaplan, Lawrence, 'Suffering and Joy in the Thought of Hermann Cohen', *Modern Judaism,* 21:1, 2001, 15–22.

Kassir, Samir, *Considérations sur le malheur arabe.* Arles: Actes Sud, 2004.

Katz, Steven T., ed., *The Impact of the Holocaust on Jewish Theology.* New York: New York University Press, 2005.

Katznelson, Ira, *When Affirmative Action Was White: An Untold History of Racial Inequality in Twentieth-Century America.* New York: W. W. Norton, 2005.

Khalidi, Rashid, *Palestinian Identity: The Construction of Modern National Consciousness.* New York: Columbia University Press, 1997.

Klausner, Joseph, 'The Question of all Questions and Answers', in Yehuda Burla, ed., *On Home: Literary Anthology by the Writers of the Land of Israel for their Brothers who Remain in Europe.* Tel Aviv: Agudat Hasofrim Haivriim Be-Eretz Israel, 1945 or 1946, 7–30 [in Hebrew].

'La mémoire est une chose, l'histoire en est une autre'. Interview with Jean-Pierre Azéma, *Tohu Bohu*, 2006, 8–9.

Lang, Berel, *The Future of the Holocaust: Between History and Memory*. Ithaca NY: Cornell University Press, 1999.

——, *Post-Holocaust: Interpretation, Misinterpretation, and the Claims of History*. Bloomington: Indiana University Press, 2005.

Langer, Lawrence L., *Admitting the Holocaust*. Oxford: Oxford University Press, 1995.

——, 'Entre Histoire et Mémoire: A la recherche d'une méthode', in Jean-Clément Martin, ed., *La Guerre civile entre Histoire et Mémoire*. Nantes: Ouest-Éditions, 1995, 39–47.

——, 'The Alarmed Vision: Social Suffering and Holocaust Atrocity', *Daedalus*, 125:1, 1996, 47–60.

Lanzmann, Claude, 'Holocauste, représentation impossible', *Le Monde*, 3 March 1994.

——, *Shoah*. Paris: Gallimard, 1997.

Le Goff, Jacques, *Histoire et mémoire*. Paris: Gallimard, 1988.

Leaman, Olivier, *Evil and Suffering in Jewish Philosophy*. Cambridge: Cambridge University Press, 1995.

Lefeuvre, Daniel, *Pour en finir avec la repentance coloniale*. Paris: Flammarion, 2006.

Leibowitz, Yeshaiah, 'Epreuve et crainte de Dieu dans le livre de Job', trans. Judith Kogel. *Les Cahiers du Judaïsme*, 16, 2004, 21–7.

Levi, Primo, *If This Is a Man*, trans. Stuart Wolf. London: Bodley Head, 1960.

Levy, Daniel and Natan Sznaider, *Erinnerung im globalen Zeitalter: Der Holocaust*. Frankfurt, Suhrkamp, 2001.

——, 'Memory Unbound. The Holocaust and the Formation of Cosmopolitan Memory', *European Journal of Social Theory*, 5:1, 2002, 87–106.

Levy, Isaac Jack, *And the World Stood Silent: Sephardic Poetry of the Holocaust*. Urbana: University of Illinois Press, 1989.

Linafelt, Tod, *Surviving Lamentations: Catastrophe, Lament, and Protest in the Afterlife of a Biblical Book*. Chicago: University of Chicago Press, 2000.

Linenthal, Edward T., *Preserving Memory: The Struggle to Create America's Holocaust Museum*. New York: Penguin, 1995.

Link, Franz, ed., *Jewish Life and Suffering as Mirrored in Jewish and American Literature*. Paderborn: Ferdinand Schoningh, 1987.

Lipstadt, Deborah E., 'The Holocaust: Symbol and Myth in American Jewish Life', *Forum*, 40, 1980–1, 73–88.

Litvak, Meir, and Esther Webman, 'Perceptions of the Holocaust in Palestinian Public Discourse', *Israel Studies*, 8:3, 2003, 123–40.

Loeb, Isidore, 'Joseph Haccohen et les Chroniqueurs juifs', *Revue des Études juives*, 16, 1888, 32–40.

Loewenstein, Rudolph, *Psychanalyse de l'antisémitisme*, 2nd edn, Paris: PUF, 2001.

Löwy, Michaël, *Redemption and Utopia: Jewish Liberal Thought in Central Europe. A Study in Cultural Affinity*, trans. Hope Heaney. Stanford: Stanford University Press, 1992.

Maechler, Stefan, 'Wilkomirski the Victim', *History and Memory*, 13:2, 2001, 59–95.

Magazine Littéraire, 438, 2005, special issue: *La Littérature et les camps.*

Maier, Charles, 'A Surfeit of Memory? Reflections on History, Melancholy and Denial', *History and Memory*, 5:2, 1993, 136–51.

Maimonides, Moses, *Epistles of Maimonides: Crisis and Leadership*, trans. Abraham Halkin. Philadelphia: Jewish Publication Society, 1993.

Manière de voir, 76, 2004, special issue: *Les Génocides dans l'histoire.*

Manuel, Franck E., *The Broken Staff: Judaism through Christian Eyes.* Cambridge MA: Harvard University Press, 1992.

Marcus, Ivan G., 'From Politics to Martyrdom: Shifting Paradigms in the Hebrew Narratives of 1096 Crusade Riots', *Prooftexts*, 2:1, 1982, 40–52.

Masalha, Nur, ed., *Catastrophe Remembered: Palestine, Israel and the Internal Refugees. Essays in Memory of Edward W. Said (1935–2003)*. New York: Zed Books, 2005.

Maybaum, Ignaz, *The Face of God after Auschwitz.* Amsterdam: Polak and Van Gennep, 1965.

Mayer, Arno J., *The 'Final Solution' in History.* New York: Pantheon, 1988.

——, 'Les pièges du souvenir', *Esprit*, 193, 1993, 45–59.

Médiévales, 27, 1994, special issue: *Du bon usage de la souffrance.*

Meschonnic, Henri, 'Pour en finir avec le mot 'Shoah'', *Le Monde*, 20 February 2005.

Mesnard, Philippe, ed., *Consciences de la Shoah. Critique des discours et des représentations.* Paris: Kimé, 2000.

Millen, Rochelle L., ' "Like Pebbles on the Seashore": J. B. Soloveitchik on Suffering', *Modern Judaism*, 4:2, 2004, 150–64.

Miller, Judith, *One by One: Facing the Holocaust.* New York: Touchstone, 1990.

Mintz, Alan, *Hurban: Responses to the Catastrophe in Hebrew Literature.* Syracuse: Syracuse University Press, 1996.

——, *Popular Culture and the Shaping of Holocaust Memory.* Seattle: University of Washington Press, 2001.

Moses, Rafael, ed., *Persistent Shadows of the Holocaust.* Madison WI: International Universities Press, 1993.

Myers, David N., 'Between Diaspora and Zion: History, Memory and the Jerusalem Scholars', in David N. Myers and David B. Ruderman, eds., *The Jewish Past Revisited: Reflections on Modern Jewish Historians.* New Haven: Yale University Press, 1998, 88–103.

——, ' "*Mehabevin et ha-tsarot*": Crusade Memories and Modern Jewish Martyrologies', *Jewish History*, 13:2, 1999, 88–103.

Nachman, Rabbi, *Garden of the Souls: Rebbe Nachman on Suffering*, trans. Avraham Greenbaum. Jerusalem: Breslov Research Institute, 1990.

Nagy, Piroska, *Le Don des larmes au Moyen Age.* Paris: Albin Michel, 2000.

Neubauer, Adolph, 'Le Memorbuch de Mayence. Essai sur la littérature des complaintes', *Revue des études juives*, 4, 1882, 1–30.

—— and Maurice Stern, *Hebräische Berichte über die Judenverfolgungen während der Kreuzzüge*. Berlin: L. Simion, 1892. For a contemporary reprint in English, see *Adolf Neubauer, Mediaeval Jewish Chronicles and Chronological Notes*. Amsterdam: Philo Press, 1970, 2 vols.

Neuman, Abraham A., 'Shebet Yehuda and Sixteenth Century Historiography', in *Louis Ginzberg Jubilee Volume on the Occasion of his Seventieth Birthday*, English Section. New York: American Academy for Jewish Research, 1945, 253–73.

——, 'Abraham Zacuto Historiographer', in *Harry Austryn Wolfson: Jubilee Volume on the Occasion of his Seventy-fifth Birthday*, vol. 2, English Section. Jerusalem: American Academy for Jewish Research, 1965, 597–629.

Neusner, Jacob, 'Stranger at Home: Myths in American Judaism', *Forum*, 39, 1980, 31–38.

——, *Stranger at Home: 'The Holocaust', Zionism and American Judaism*. Chicago: University of Chicago Press, 1981.

——, *Formative Judaism. Religious, Historical, and Literary Studies*, Sixth Series. Atlanta GA: Scholars Press, 1989.

——, ed., *Faith Renewed: The Judaic Affirmation Beyond the Holocaust*, vol. 1: *Judaism Transcends Catastrophe: God, Torah, and Israel Beyond the Holocaust*. Macon GA: Mercer University Press, 1994, 1–17.

Nora, Pierre, 'Mémoire et identité juives dans la France contemporaine. Les grands déterminants', *Le Débat*, 131, 2004, 20–34.

——, 'Malaise dans l'identité historique', *Le Débat*, 141, 2006, 48–52.

Nordmann, Sophie, 'Hermann Cohen et la question du sionisme', *Études Germaniques*, 59:2, 2004, 327–42.

Novick, Peter, *The Holocaust in American Life*. Boston, Houghton Mifflin, 1999.

Ofer, Dalia, 'Tormented Memories', *Israel Studies*, 9:3, 2004, 137–56.

Ophir, Adi, 'On Sanctifying the Holocaust: An Anti-Theological Treatise', *Tikkun*, 2:1, 1987, 61–6.

Pagis, Dan, 'Dirges on the Persecutions of 1391 in Spain', *Tarbiz*, 37:4, 1968, 355–73 [in Hebrew].

Paoli, Paul-François, *Nous ne sommes pas coupables. Assez de repentances!* Paris: La Table Ronde, 2006.

Papazian, Pierre, 'A "Unique Uniqueness"', *Midstream*, 30:4, 1984, 14–18.

Pappe, Ilan, 'The Ethics of the Historian', *Ha'aretz*, 24 June 1994 [in Hebrew].

Pardès, 9–10, 1989, special issue: *Penser Auschwitz*, ed. Shmuel Trigano.

Penkower, Monty Noam, 'Job and Suffering Humanity', *Jewish Spectator*, 58:2, 1993, 24–9.

Perriaux, Sophie and Daniel Steuer, 'Zionism, the Shoah and the Foundations of Israeli Identity', in Ritchie Robertson and Edward Timms, eds, *Theodore Herzl and the Origins of Zionism*. Edinburgh: Edinburgh University Press, 1997, 135–47.

Pétré-Grenouilleau, Olivier, *Traites négrières*. Paris: Gallimard, 2006.

Plotkin, S. Frederick, *Judaism and Tragic Theology*. New York: Schocken Books, 1973.

Ravitzky, Aviezer, *Messianism, Zionism and Jewish Religious Radicalism*, trans. Michael Swirsky and Jonathan Chipman. Chicago: University of Chicago Press, 1996.

Reinach, Théodore, *Histoire des Israélites depuis la ruine de leur indépendance nationale jusqu'à nos jours*, 3rd edn, Paris: Hachette, 1903.

Ricoeur, Paul, *Memory, History, Forgetting*, trans. K. Blamey and D. Pellauer, Chicago: University of Chicago Press, 2004.

Robin, Régine, *La Mémoire saturée*. Paris: Stock, 2003.

Rosenbaum, Alan S., ed., *Is the Holocaust Unique? Perspectives on Comparative Genocide*. Boulder CO: Westview Press, 2000.

Rosenbaum, Irving J., *The Holocaust and Halakhah*. New York: Ktav, 1976.

Rosenfeld, D. Gavriel, 'The Politics of Uniqueness: Reflections on the Recent Polemical Turn in Holocaust and Genocide Scholarship', *Holocaust and Genocide Studies*, 13:1, 1999, 28–61.

Roskies, David G., 'The Holocaust According to the Literary Critics', *Prooftexts*, 1:2, 1981, 209–16.

——, *Against the Apocalypse: Responses to Catastrophe in Modern Jewish Culture*. Cambridge MA: Harvard University Press, 1984.

——, *The Literature of Destruction: Jewish Responses to Catastrophe*. Philadelphia Jewish Publication Society, 1988.

Roth, Cecil, 'The Religion of the Marranos', *Jewish Quarterly Review*, 22:1, 1931, 1–33.

——, 'The Most Persecuted People?', *The Menorah Journal*, 20:2, 1932, 136–47.

——, 'European Jewry in the Dark Ages: A Revised Picture', *Hebrew Union College Annual, Seventy-fifth Anniversary Publication, 1875–1950*, 23/2, 1950–51, pp. 151–169.

Rothschild, Yaakov, ed., *The Sanctification of the Name of God through the Centuries*. Jerusalem: Misrad ha hinuh ve ha tarbut, ha mahlaka le tarbut toranit, bet ha-sfarim ha leumi ve ha universitai, 1968–9 [in Hebrew].

Rousso, Henry, *The Vichy Syndrome: History and Memory in France since 1944*, trans. Arthur Goldhammer. Cambridge MA: Harvard University Press, 1994.

——, *The Haunting Past: History, Memory, and Justice in Contemporary France*, trans. Ralph Schoolcraft. Philadelphia: University of Pennsylvania Press, 2002.

Rubenstein, Richard L., 'In Response to Professor Ophir', *Tikkun*, 2:1, 1987, 66–7.

Said, Edward W. and David Barsamian, *Culture and Resistance: Conversations with Edward Said*. Cambridge MA: South End Press, 2003.

Salfeld, Siegmund, *Das Martyrologium des Nürnberger Memorbuches*. Berlin: L. Simion, 1898.

Sand, Shlomo, *Le XXe siècle à l'écran*, trans. Yaël Shneerson and Michel Bilis. Paris: Fayard, 2002.

Sarot, Marcel, 'Auschwitz, Morality and the Suffering of God', *Modern Theology*, 7:2, 1991, 135–52.

Schechter, Ronald, *Obstinate Hebrew: Representations of Jews in France, 1715–1815*. Berkeley: University of California Press, 2003.

Schindler, Pesach, *Hasidic Responses to the Holocaust in the Light of Hasidic Thought*. Hoboken NJ: Ktav, 1990.

Schorsch, Ismar, 'On the History of the Political Judgment of the Jews', *Leo Baeck Memorial Lecture*, 20, 1976, 3–23.

——, 'The Holocaust and Jewish Survival', *Midstream*, 27:1, 1981, 38–42.

——, 'The Lachrymose Conception of Jewish History', in Ismar Schorsch, ed., *From Text to Context: The Turn to History in Modern Judaism*. Hanover NH: Brandeis University Press, 1994, 376–88.

Schwartz, Matthew B., 'The Meaning of Suffering: A Talmudic Response to Theodicy', *Judaism*, 32:4, 1983, 444–451.

Schweid, Eliezer, *The Jewish Experience of Time: Philosophical Dimensions of the Jewish Holy Days*, trans. Hadary Amnon. Northvale NJ: Jason Aronson, 2000.

Schweizer, Harold, ed., *History and Memory: Suffering and Art*. Lewisburg PA: Bucknell University, 1998.

Segev, Tom, *The Seventh Million: The Israelis and the Holocaust*, trans. Haim Watzman. New York: Henry Holt, 2000.

Seidman, Naomi, 'Elie Wiesel and the Scandal of Jewish Rage', *Jewish Social Studies*, 3:1, 1996, 1–19.

Semprun, Jorge, and Alain Finkielkraut, 'Comment transmettre l'inimaginable', *L'Express*, 19 Jan. 1995.

Shepkarn, S., 'From after Death to Afterlife: Martyrdom and its Recompense', *AJS Review*, 24:1, 1999, 1–44.

Shohat, Azriel, 'The Sanctification of the Name of God in the Thought of Those Expelled from Spain and in the Safed Kabbalists', in *Holy War and Martyrology in the History of Israel and the Peoples*. Jerusalem: Israel Historical Society, 1968, 131–45 [in Hebrew].

Sicher, Efraim, ed., *Breaking Crystal: Writing and Memory after Auschwitz*. Urbana University of Illinois Press, 1998.

——, 'The Future of the Past: Countermemory and Postmemory in Contemporary American Post-Holocaust Narratives', *History and Memory*, 12:2, 2001, 56–91.

Silver, Daniel Jeremy, 'Choose Life', *Judaism*, 35:4, 1986, 458–66.

Soloveitchik, Haym, '*Halakhah*, Hermeneutics, and Martyrdom in Medieval Ashkenaz', *The Jewish Quarterly Review*, 94:1, 2004, 77–108; 94:2, 2004, 278–99.

Steckel, Charles W., 'God and the Holocaust', *Judaism*, 20:3, 1971, 279–85.

Tcherikower, Elias, 'Jewish Martyrology and Jewish Historiography', in *Yivo Annual of Jewish Social Science*. New York: Yiddish Scientific Institute, 1946, vol. 1, 9–23.

Terray, Emmanuel, *Face aux abus de mémoire*. Arles: Actes Sud, 2006.

Todorov, Tzvetan, 'The Abuses of Memory', *Common Knowledge*, 5, 1996, 6–26.

——, *Les Abus de la mémoire*. Paris: Arléa, 1995.

——, *Mémoire du mal, tentation du bien*. Paris: Robert Laffont, 2000.

Tohu Bohu, 10, 2006, special issue: *Le Temps des Mémoires*.

Totten, Samuel et al., eds., *Century of Genocide: Eyewitness Accounts and Critical Views*. New York: Garland Publishing, 1997.

Trautmann-Waller, Céline, *Philologie allemande et tradition juive. Le parcours intellectuel de Leopold Zunz*. Paris: Cerf, 1998.

Traverso, Enzo, *L'Histoire déchirée. Essai sur Auschwitz et les intellectuels*. Paris: Cerf, 1997.

——, *Le passé, mode d'emploi. Histoire, mémoire, politique*. Paris: La Fabrique, 2005.

Trepp, Leo, 'Toward a 'Slihah' on the Holocaust', *Judaism*, 35:3, 1986, 344–50.

Urbach, Éphraïm E., *Les Sages d'Israël. Conceptions et croyances des maîtres du Talmud*, trans. Marie-José Jolivet. Paris: Cerf, 1996.

Usque, Samuel, *Consolação as tribulações de Israel*. Lisbon: Calouste Gulbenkian Foundation, 1989 (1553 Ferrare edition), 2 vols.

——, *Consolation for the Tribulations of Israel*, trans. Martin A. Cohen. Philadelphia: Jewish Publication Society of America, 1965.

Van Bekkum, Wout, 'O Seville! Ah Castile! Spanish–Hebrew Dirges from the Fifteenth Century', in Nicholas de Lange, ed., *Hebrew Scholarship and the Medieval World*. Cambridge: Cambridge University Press, 2001, 156–70.

Vergely, Bertrand, *La Souffrance. Recherche du sens perdu*. Paris: Gallimard, 1977.

Vergès, Françoise, *La Mémoire enchaînée. Questions sur l'esclavage*. Paris: Albin Michel, 2006.

Vidal, Dominique, *Le Mal-être juif. Entre repli, assimilation et manipulations*. Paris: Agone, 2003.

——, and Karim Bourtel, *Le Mal-être arabe. Enfants de la colonisation*. Paris: Agone, 2005.

Wahrmann, Nahum, *Sources on the History of the 1648–1649 Massacres: Prayers and Liturgy for 20 Sivan*. Jerusalem, Bamberger and Vahrman, 709/1949 [in Hebrew].

Walser Smith, Helmut, *The Holocaust and Other Genocides: History, Representation, Ethics*. Nashville: Vanderbilt University Press, 2002.

Webber, Jonathan, 'Jewish Identities in the Holocaust: Martyrdom as a Representative Category', *Polin: Studies in Polish Jewry*, 13, 2000, 128–46.

Weil, Patrick, 'Politique de la mémoire. L'interdit et la commémoration', *Esprit*, February 2007, 124–43.

Weill, Nicolas, *La République et les Antisémites*. Paris: Grasset, 2004.

Weinberger, Theodore, '*Tish'ah B'av* and the Interpretation of Suffering', in Dan Cohn-Sherbok, ed., *Theodicy*. Lewiston NY: Edwin Mellen, 1997, 51–63.

Weintraub, Aviva, 'Some Hasidic Responses to Suffering', *Nitzanim*, 3, 1984–5, 98–105.

Wickersham, Erlis Glass, 'Women as Agents of Suffering and Redemption in the Poetry of Nelly Sachs', in Esther Fuchs, ed., *Women and the Holocaust: Narrative and Representation*. New York: University Press of America, 1999, 63–87.

Wiesel, Eli, 'The Joy of Thought', *Jewish Quarterly Review*, 94:1, 2004, 23–6.

——, *Night*. New York: Hill and Wang, 2006.

Wieseltier, Leon, *Kaddish*. New York: Alfred A. Knopf, 1998.

Wiesenthal, Simon, *Every Day Remembrance Day: A Chronicle of Jewish Martyrdom*. New York: Henry Holt, 1986.

Wieviorka, Annette, *The Era of the Witness*, trans. J. Stark, Ithaca NY: Cornell University Press, 2006.

——, *Déportation et genocide. Entre la mémoire et l'oubli*. Paris: Hachette Littérature, 2003.

Wolf, Joan B., 'Anne Frank is Dead, Long Live Anne: The Six-Day War and the Holocaust in French Public Discourse', *History and Memory*, 11:1, 1999, 104–40.

——, *Harnessing the Holocaust: The Politics of Memory in France*. Stanford CA: Stanford University Press, 2004.

Woocher, Jonathan S., '"Jewish Survivalism" as Communal Ideology: An Empirical Assessment', *Journal of Jewish Communal Service*, 57:4, 1981, 291–303.

Worms, Frédéric, 'Au-delà de la concurrence des victimes', *Esprit*, 322, February 2006, 187–93.

Wyschogrod, Michael, 'Faith and the Holocaust: Review Essay of Emile Fackenheim's *God Presence in History*', *Judaism*, 20:3, 1971, 286–94.

Yakira, Elhanan, 'Hannah Arendt, the Holocaust, and Zionism: A Story of Failure', *Israel Studies*, 2:3, 2006, 31–61.

Yehoshua, A. B., 'From Myth to History', *AJS Review*, 28:1, 2004, 205–11.

Yerushalmi, Yosef Hayim, 'Un champ à Anathoth: vers une histoire de l'espoir juif', in *Colloque des intellectuels juifs. Mémoire et Histoire*, eds, Jean Halpérin and Georges Lévitte. Paris: Denoël, 1986, 91–107.

——, *A Jewish Classic in the Portuguese Language*. Lisbon: Calouste Gulbenkian Foundation, 1989.

——, *Zakhor: Jewish History and Jewish Memory*. Seattle: University of Washington Press, 1996.

Young, James E., 'After the Holocaust: National Attitudes to Jews. The Texture of Memory: Holocaust Memorials and Meaning', *Holocaust and Genocide Studies*, 4:1, 1989, 63–76.

——, *The Texture of Memory*. New Haven: Yale University Press, 1993.

——, 'When a Day Remembers: A Performative History of Yom ha-Shoah', *History and Memory*, 2:2, 1990, 54–75.

——, *At Memory's Edge*. New Haven: Yale University Press, 2000.

Yuter, Alan J., *The Holocaust in Hebrew Literature: From Genocide to Rebirth*. Port Washington: Associated Faculty Press, 1983.

Yuval, Israel Jacob, *Two Nations in your Womb: Perceptions of Jews and Christians in Late Antiquity and the Middle Ages*, trans. Barbara Harshav and Jonathan Shipman. Berkeley: California University Press, 2006.

Zertal, Idith, 'The Poisoned Heart', *Tikkun*, 2:1, 1987, 79–83.

——, 'From the People's Hall to the Wailing Wall: A Study in Memory, Fear, and War', *Representations*, 69, 2000, 96–126.

——, *Israel's Holocaust and the Politics of Nationhood*, trans. Idith Zertal, Cambridge: Cambridge University Press, 2005.

Zuckermann, Moshe, 'The Curse of Forgetting: Israel and the Holocaust', *Telos*, 78, 1988–9, 43–54.

——, *The Shoah in the Padded Cell: The 'Shoah' in the Israeli Press during the Gulf War*. Tel Aviv, privately printed, 1993 [in Hebrew].

Zunz, Leopold, *Die synagogale Poesie des Mittelalters*. Berlin: J. Springer, 1855–7, 2 vols.

——, *Der Ritus des synagogalen Gottesdienstes*. Berlin, Louis Lamm, 1919.

——, *Literaturgeschichte der synagogalen Poesie*. Berlin: L. Gerschel, 1865.

——, *The Sufferings of the Jews during the Middle Ages*, trans. A. Löwy, ed. Alexandre Kohut. New York: Bloch Publishing Company, 1907.

Zweig, Ronald W., 'Politics of Commemoration', *Jewish Social Studies*, 49:2, 1987, 155–66.

Index